Evidence for Christianity in Roman Southern Pannonia (Northern Croatia)

A catalogue of finds and sites

Branka Migotti

BAR International Series 684
1997

Published in 2016 by
BAR Publishing, Oxford

BAR International Series 684

Evidence for Christianity in Roman Southern Pannonia (Northern Croatia)

ISBN 978 0 86054 870 6

© B Migotti and the Publisher 1997

Volume Editor: Rajka Makjanić

BAR Publishing is the trading name of British Archaeological Reports (Oxford) Ltd.
British Archaeological Reports was first incorporated in 1974 to publish the BAR
Series, International and British. In 1992 Hadrian Books Ltd became part of the BAR
group. This volume was originally published by Archaeopress in conjunction with
British Archaeological Reports (Oxford) Ltd / Hadrian Books Ltd, the Series principal
publisher, in 1997. This present volume is published by BAR Publishing, 2016.

Printed in England

BAR
PUBLISHING

BAR titles are available from:

BAR Publishing
122 Banbury Rd, Oxford, OX2 7BP, UK
EMAIL   info@barpublishing.com
PHONE   +44 (0)1865 310431
FAX   +44 (0)1865 316916
www.barpublishing.com

In memory of my father

Contents

Foreword

In the autumn of 1994 the 13th International Congress of early Christian Archaeology was organized in Croatia, its hosts being the towns Poreč, Split and Solin, all three situated along the Adriatic coast. The Archaeological Museum in Zagreb considered it well worth incorporating the Croatian capital into the programme of this most important scientific meeting by mounting an exhibition about the beginnings of Christianity in the continental regions of Croatia. The phenomenon of early Christianity in northern Croatia (the Roman provinces of *Pannonia Savia* and *Pannonia Secunda*) had until then been insufficiently researched and unjustifiably ignored; the original idea was modestly to show what little there was in the continental part of the country in comparison with the abundance of Christian remains in its coastal regions. I was entrusted with gathering the material for the exhibition. Having, however, some reservations about the commonly accepted conception of northern Croatia as something in the nature of an archaeological 'early Christian desert', I turned the collecting of the known scanty material into a search through museum collections and depots, as well as through archaeological literature, for new, or rather, neglected and inadequately appreciated items. The task appeared to be a rewarding one, resulting in quite a considerable expansion of the exhibition material: instead of some 30 expected, or rather, planned objects, more than 200 items found their place in the exhibition. Not all of them were indisputable early Christian artefacts in terms of symbolism, but were given or at least envisaged a Christian significance based on context, on analogies from elsewhere or on some general characteristics of the period and ambiance to which they belonged.

Since 1994 no new excavations of early Christian sites have taken place that would significantly alter the then drawn contours of the given period in northern Croatia; yet a variety of reasons urged me to reconsider, rewrite and expose in a more coherent manner the early Christian material I dealt with in 1994. First, my results then were very much limited both by working to the demands of the exhibition time limit and by virtual postwar conditions in Croatia, which rendered access to the material in the museums of the war-stricken areas very difficult or even impossible. Second, to be better understood and possibly used for further scientific research this material needed to be analysed according to criteria other than those valid for an exhibition catalogue. Last, I was eager to correct some mistakes or misconceptions in the evaluation of the material made initially due to haste or to inadequate data at my disposal. My insight into the material, as well as my knowledge of it, more profound now than it was in 1994, has, it is hoped, enabled me to achieve this.

Acknowledgements

First I would like to express my gratitude to Ante Rendić-Miočević, Director of the Archaeological Museum in Zagreb, who in 1994 entrusted me with the material for the exhibition on the theme of early Christianity in continental Croatia, kindling thus my lasting interest in it. However, my research would never have been carried out but for the help of many colleagues from the museums throughout northern Croatia; I am therefore extremely grateful and much obliged to all those who either supplied me with information and practical assistance considering location, description and evaluation of items, or else commented and discussed with me various theoretical issues. They are too many to be all mentioned here, but their names are listed in the catalogue of the exhibition 'From the Invincible Sun to the Sun of Justice' (Zagreb 1994). Yet I feel obliged to single out three of them, whose expert advice and help was most invaluable: Mrs. Zdenka Dukat, Dr. Nenad Cambi and Dr. Željko Demo. Finally, to Dr. Rajka Makjanić and Dr. David Davison go my sincerest thanks for correcting my English and for other varied academic, editorial and friendly help and support; without both of them this book would have never been published.

B. M.   Zagreb, October 1997

Introduction

1. Aspects of the political geography of Pannonia in the times of nascent Christianity

Note

This study is limited to only the Croatian portion of the Roman province of Pannonia; although somewhat artificial, such an approach is apparently inevitable given the nature and scope of the material evidence available and presented here. Early Christianity in Hungary (northern Pannonia) has been thoroughly studied by Dr. Dora Gáspár and the results were scheduled for publication even before this study (Dora Gáspár pers. comm.) The presentation of the material from the easternmost section of southern Roman Pannonia also lies within the competence of scholars from another country (Yugoslavia).

Until the end of the third century, present-day northern Croatia encompassed the southern parts of the Roman provinces of Upper and Lower Pannonia (*Pannonia Superior* and *Inferior*). Through Diocletian's administrative division imposed in 297, Pannonia was formed into four provinces: *Prima, Valeria, Savia* and *Secunda*; northern Croatia encompassed the southern parts of these provinces, i.e. *Pannonia Savia* and all but the easternmost portion of *Pannonia Secunda*. This area bordered with *Noricum* (Slovenia) on the west, with *Pannonia Prima* and *Valeria* (Hungary) on the north and with *Dalmatia* (central Croatia and Bosnia and Herzegovina) on the south. (Map 1)

Southern Pannonia was covered by a network of roads in both north-south and east-west directions. The two most important traffic lines ran along the valleys of the Sava (Siscia - Sirmium) and Drava (*Poetovio - Mursa*) rivers; they established important overland connections (while the rivers were also partly navigable) between the western and eastern parts of the Roman Empire. This in return made southern *Pannonia* an outstanding crossroads point. Of particular importance in terms of early Christianity was the route of the *Itinerarium Hierosolymitanum* (*Burdigalense*), which streched along the Drava and carried pilgrims from the western parts of the Empire to the holy places in the Near East.

The prime fact from the point of view of political geography and accordingly the ecclesiastical history of *Pannonia* is its

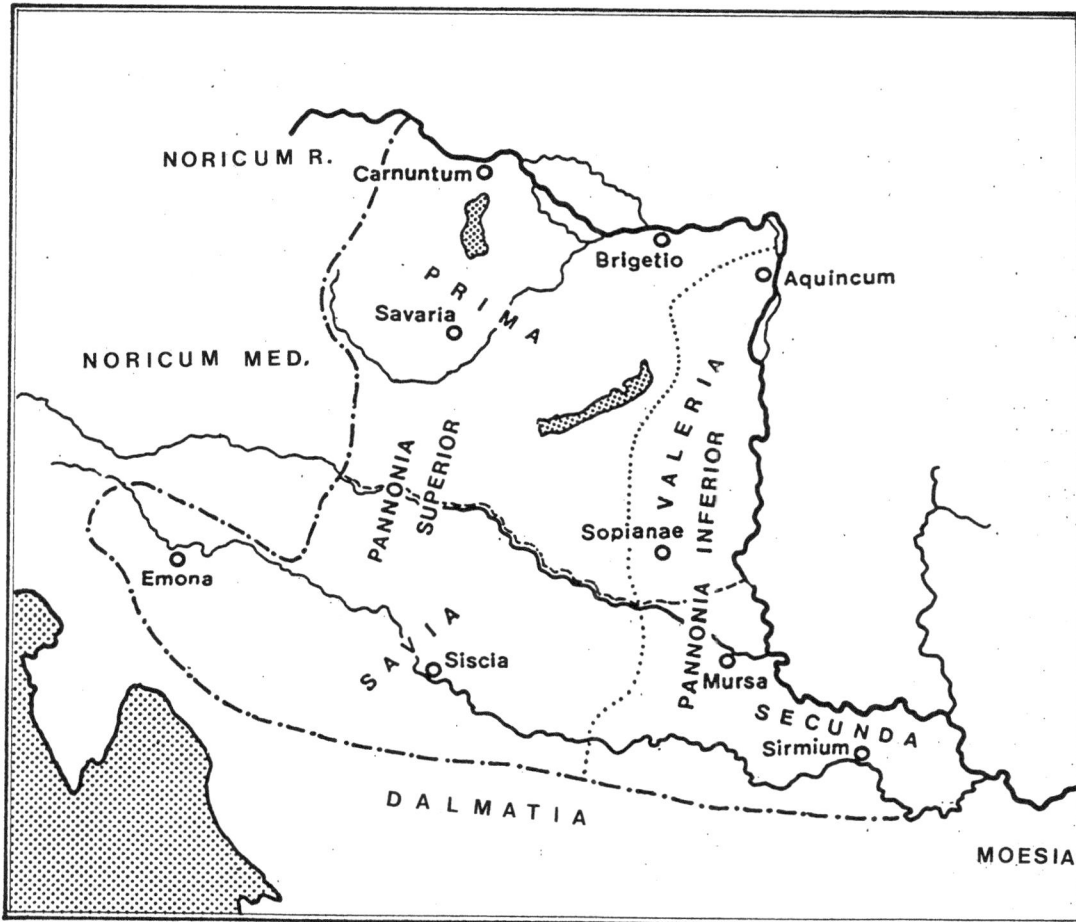

Map 1: *Pannonia in the late Roman period (readjusted after Soproni 1980)*
— . — . —   *Borders of Pannonia*
....   *Borders in the time of Traian*
-----------   *Borders in the time of Diocletian*

1

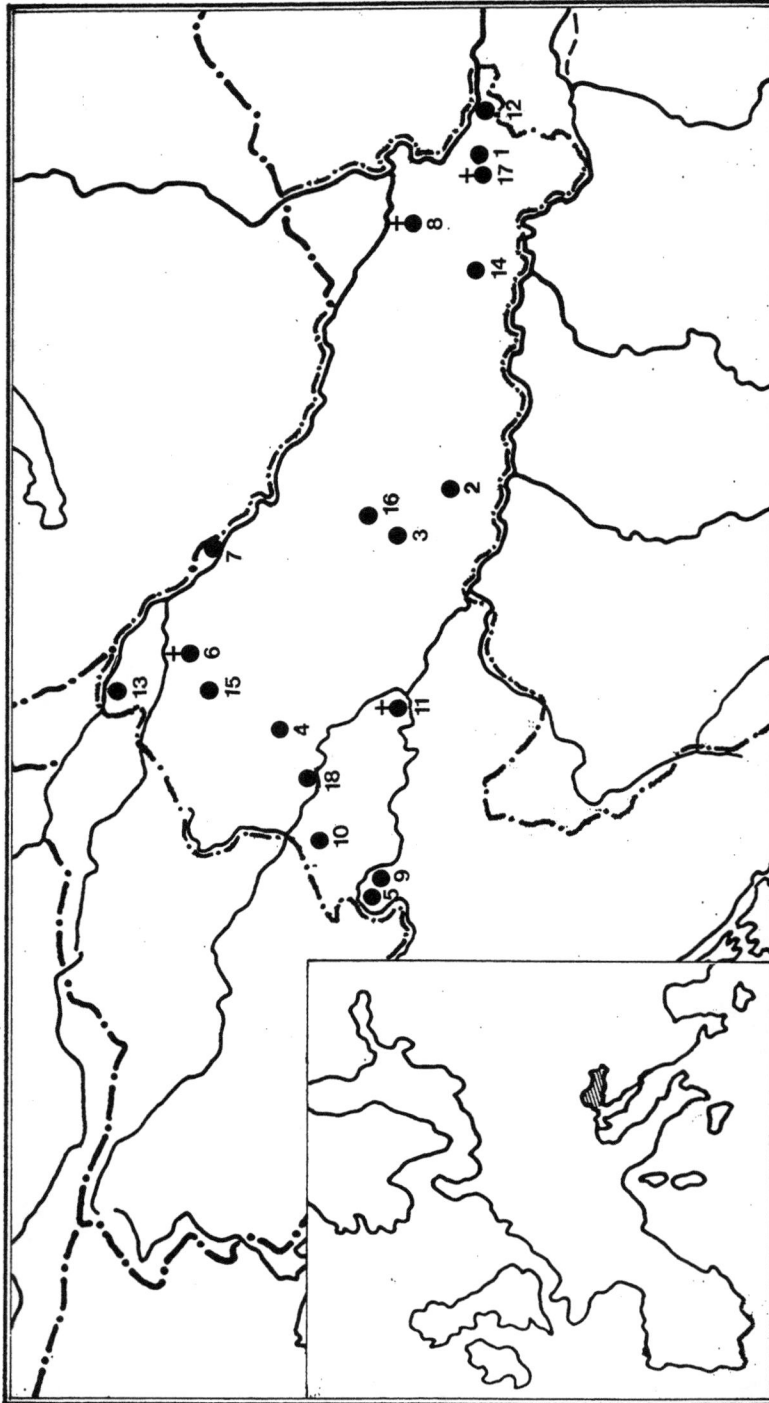

Map 2: Distribution and list of sites
1. Cerić; 2. Čečavac (Rudina); 3. Daruvar; 4. Donja Glavnica (Kuzelin); 5. Kamanje (Vrlovka); 6. Ludbreg; 7. Novačka (Gradina); 8. Osijek; 9. Ozalj; 10. Samobor; 11. Sisak; 12. Sotin; 13. Sveti Martin na Muri; 14. Štrbinci; 15. Varaždinske Toplice; 16. Veliki Bastaji; 17. Vinkovci; 18. Zagreb.

gaining in military and political importance precisely in the late Roman period. Nor was it economically or demographically so backward and deserted towards the end of the 4th century as has been occasionally suggested. Both literary sources and archaeological material fail to support convincingly enough this commonplace of Pannonian Roman archaeology. Admittedly life went on on a more reduced scale than previously, but the province stayed on its feet and within the sphere of Roman, i.e. Byzantine interests until the beginning of the 7th century.

An axiom of early Christian territorial administration - that Roman municipalities (municipii and coloniae) as a rule (although with due exceptions) grew into bishoprics - establishes urban development as one of the most important preconditions for successful Christianization. It is therefore important to bear in mind that southern Pannonia was urbanized and so potentially Christianized before the north of the province. This is only understandable in the light of the fact that from the beginnings of Romanization, southern Pannonia was traffically more important, and that in later times it suffered less from Barbarian inroads than the northern portion of the province. Quite a number of Roman settlements of varying status are recorded in various Roman itineraries (*Tabula Peutingeriana, Itinerarium Antonini, Itinerarium Hierosolymitanum, Ravennati Anonymi*

Cosmographia) and other sources (*Notitia Dignitatum, Claudii Ptolomaei Geographiae*) in the territory of present-day northern Croatia. The majority of minor settlements is, however, only hypothetically identified or located, their status usually remaining a moot question. What I have in mind here are settlements without municipal rights, the backbone of the urbanization of the northern Croatian territory being three Roman colonies, the bishoprics to-be, verified by both literary and epigraphic sources: Siscia (Sisak), Mursa (Osijek) and Cibalae (Vinkovci). To them can be added few settlements with the status of municipium: Iovia (Ludbreg?), Aquae Balissae (Daruvar) and Cornacum (Sotin). A number of other places yielding Christian material remains should also be mentioned in this context; their Roman names are attested, but not so their civil status. Most important among them are Aquae Iasae (Varaždinske Toplice), Incerum (probably around Požega) and Certissa (probably on the site of Štrbinci). (Maps 2 and 3)

Literature
CIL III; Mócsy 1962; Oliva 1962; Barton 1975; Barkóczi 1980; Fitz 1980; Lengyel - Radan 1980; Póczy 1980; Soproni 1980; Soproni 1980a; Soproni 1980b; Thomas E B 1980a; Pavan 1991; Christie 1995; Lippold 1996; Weiler 1996.

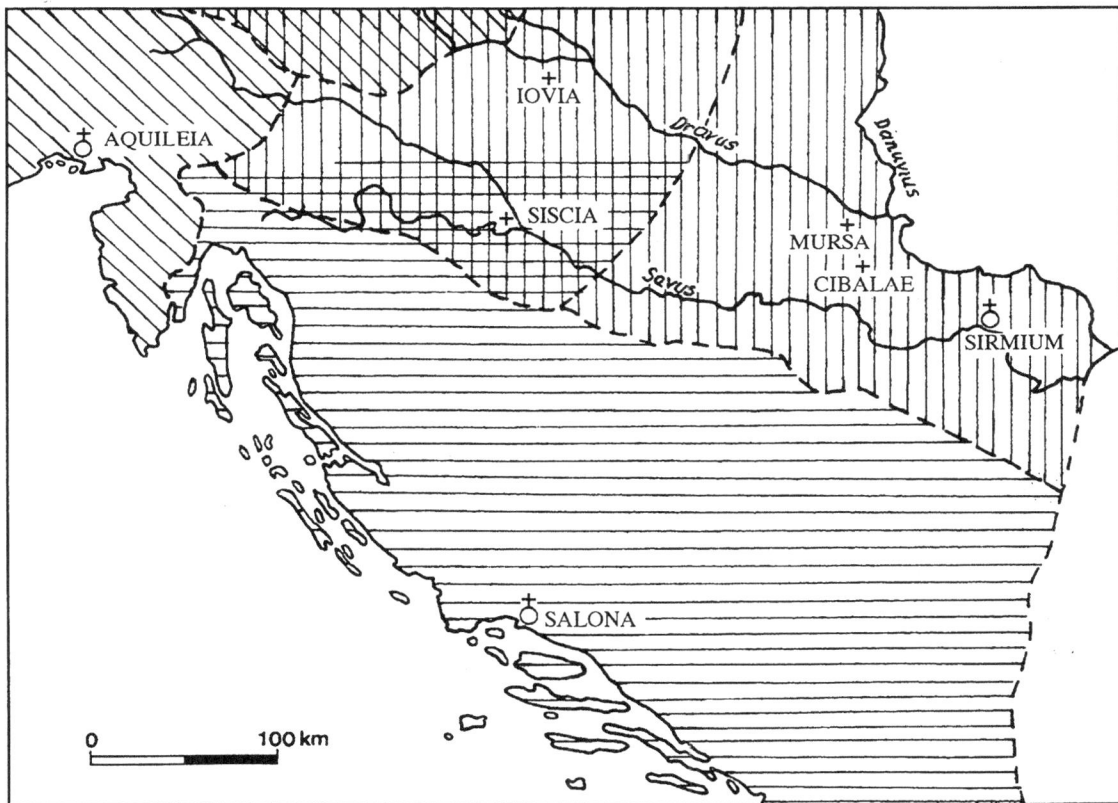

Map 3: *Ecclesiastical jurisdictions of early Christian sees on the territory of northern Croatia (after Jarak 1994).*

☩	Archbishoprics	══════	territory of the see of Salona in the 6th century
+	bishoprics	══════	
---	borders of provinces		
¦¦¦¦¦	territory of the see of Sirmium	＼＼＼＼	sphere of influence of the see of Aquileia
¦¦¦¦¦	at the end of the 4th and in the 5th centuries		

3

2. Aspects of the ecclesiastical history of Pannonia

As an historical occurrence, Christianity emerged in the 1st century and was destined to mark not only religious, but also broad material and political identities of the late Roman and early mediaeval civilizations from as early as the end of the 4th century. Roman Pannonia ranks among provinces which saw organized Christian communities later than some of the more developed and earlier Christianized western and particularly eastern Mediterranean areas of the Roman Empire; yet material remains of Pannonian Christianity should reasonably be expected at least as early as the first half of the 3rd century. This presumption is based not only on the overall historical circumstances, but also on the fact that the first organized Christian community in the whole of Panonnia was attested at Cibalae (Vinkovci) in the middle of the 3rd century, when its bishop Eusebius was recorded as a martyr. A bishopric in the middle of the 3rd century should normally be expected to have been at least a loosely organized community of Christians as early as the beginning of the 3rd century. This would then correspond to the general socio-political and religious circumstances of Pannonia during Severan rule when the province was favoured by the Roman emperors, especially Septimius Severus (193-211), who owed much of his power to the loyalty of the Pannonian legions and cities. In the same period many orientals settled down in Pannonia furthering their predilections for mystery and saviour religions and propagating above all the idea of monotheism. Such ideas were an introduction to, rather than an obstacle in the way of the spreading of Christianity.

With the 3rd century, a series of more or less devastating Barbarian inroads into Pannonia that lasted until the end of its Roman history. These incursions ended on occasion by the settling down of groups of barbarians, whose most conspicuous and influential presence is attested through the Germanic kingdoms - first that of the Ostrogoths (493-539/540), and then the Longobards (548-568). Barbarian peoples usually ended by becoming Christians of mainly Arian appurtenance.

During the reign of the emperor Valerian (253-260) the written history of the Church in southern Pannonia begins. Hagiographic literature (*Passio S. Pollionis*) makes mention of the bishop Eusebius from Cibalae, presumed convincingly to have been martyred in the persecution of 259. Roman Siscia, a bishopric from at least as early as the 3rd century, emerges under the emperor Diocletian (284-305) as a flourishing city and the capital of *Pannonia Savia*. In terms of Christianity, Diocletian is still remembered more for his notorious persecutions than for promoting of building activities or introduction progressive economic and political reforms. More Christians were probably murdered in the Diocletianic persecutions than were recorded in the documents relating to the Croatian part of Pannonia; the single martyr appears to be Pollio, the first lector (*primicerius lectorum*) of the church community of Cibalae. The third martyr (alongside Eusebius and Pollio) from the area in question - Quirinus, bishop of Siscia - is one of the most famous Pannonian martyrs. He is supposed to have been killed in the persecution of the emperor Galerius in 308.

The period of Constantine the Great's rule (306-337) marked the beginning of the history of the Christian civilization, this being true for Pannonia no less than for any other part of the Roman Empire. The Emperor's repeated stays in Pannonia resulted in building activities and the general flourishing of its towns, Siscia (Sisak) and Aquae Iasae (Varaždinske Toplice) figuring prominently among them. Pannonia Savia and Pannonia Secunda remained in the sphere of interests of Constantine's successors and its persons and places are accordingly often mentioned in historical sources, both civil and ecclesiastical. In 351 the armies of the emperor Constantius II and the usurper Magnentius clashed in battle near Mursa (Osijek). In connection with this event, several important details touching on the Christianity of the area were recorded in the documentary sources, above all in Sulpicius Severus. Sulpicius relates that, during the battle. Constantius withdrew to the *basilica martyrum* outside the the town wall, accompanied by Valens, Arian bishop of Mursa. Adherence to Arianism of the eastern parts of southern Pannonia is attested in other sources, as is the Mursan bishop Valens. On the other hand, Sulpicius's description of the mentioned battle is the only source to testify to the existence of a basilica and indirectly to the (local?) martyrs of Mursa.

In addition to the above-named Eusebius, Pollio, Quirinus and Valens, a few more bishops are recorded in the sources, four of them originating from Siscia (Marcus and Constantius in the 4th century and Joannes and Constantinus in the 6th), and one from Iovia (Amantius in the 4th century), hypothetically located on the site of the present-day Croatian town of Ludbreg. Two of the Siscian bishops, Joannes and Constantinus, figure among the participants of the councils of Salona, metropolitan see of *Dalmatia*, convened in 530 and 533, this being most precious information in terms of a reconstruction of the Pannonian metropolitan organization in the given period. As regards historico-ecclesiastical development, the whole of Pannonia stood, from its beginnings, at the crossroads of influences of the churches of Aquileia and Sirmium respectively. While the Aquileian jurisdiction over the Croatian part of southern Pannonia can reasonably be hypothesized for the 4th century, the metropolitan of Sirmium exerted his jurisdiction over at least the eastern part of southern Pannonia in the period from the end of the 4th century until 441 - the year of the surrender of Sirmium to the Huns. After the fall of Sirmium the metropolitan jurisdiction over the area in question was divided between the archbishoprics of Aquileia and Salona. Although the precise contours, either spatial or chronological, of this administrative-ecclesiastical division cannot be established, the participation of Siscian bishops at the Salona councils in 530 and 533 testify to the unquestionable submission of at least *Pannonia Savia* to the metropolitan jurisdiction of Salona in the 6th century. (Map 3)

The hallmark of the religious life of Pannonia in the 4th century was the Arian creed, concentrated mostly in its eastern areas influenced by Sirmium. Adherents of Arianism in the Croatian part of southern Pannonia were mostly centred at Mursa (Osijek), while their presence at Cibalae (Vinkovci) can be hypothesized on the sole basis of its situation at a small distance from Mursa. Contrarily Siscia is supposed to have been something of a stronghold of Christian orthodoxy, touched by the Arian heresy only superficially and temporarily, if at all. Arianism exercised its basically oriental influence not only upon ecclesiastical history, but also upon general socio-political processes of the area. This is reflected in the relationships between the two contemporary ruling pairs of imperial brothers: Constans (337-350) and Constantius II (337-361) on the one hand and Valentinian I (364-375) and Valens (364-378) on the other, antagonized deeply over the question of their religious affiliations. The western rulers Constans and Valentinian were orthodox catholics, while the other two, ruling in the East, adhered to Arianism. The inclusion of, mostly Arian, Germanic allies in the Roman military, let alone their permanent settling down on Pannonian soil, must also have had some impact on the religious affairs of the province. Yet historical sources on this issue are disappointingly meager and hazy, resulting in incongruous interpretations; equally, interpretation based on the material evidence is ultimately not sufficiently secure, let alone being hardly achievable in the first place. We nevertheless posses sufficient data for a general understanding of the foregoing situation, which can be pictured as follows: as an oriental feature Arianism was potentially a conflicting and disjunctive factor for the already antagonized eastern and western halves of the Empire. Arians being predominantly peoples of Germanic stock, the antagonism between them and the Romans was in fact triple: religious, ethnic and cultural. Although the Arian heresy was in name and in law, if not in fact, subdued by the end of the 4th century, there is every reason to believe it lingered on till the end of antiquity. In the light of these circumstances the significant role of the Church as the basic factor for the preservation of the Roman empire and of antique civilisation is particularly defined; the Church organization was the sole force to maintain, for three centuries after the beginning of Barbarian attacks and infiltration, the spiritual and material unity of the Empire on any level. Although meager, this unity was meaningful enough for the incorporation of the heritage of Roman Christianity into the European Middle Ages; it thus secured its civilisational substratum. Concurrently one of the most impressive paradoxes of Roman spiritual and material reality of the later period, that of equating *Romanitas* with *Christianitas*, turns the archaeological research of the late antique/early Christian periods into a particularly stirring task.

Mainly for the foregoing reasons, the approach was adopted in this study of seeking not to establish the difference between Barbarian and Roman Christianity, but to identify Christian remains in general terms. Besides, with large late-Roman mixed cemeteries in southern Pannonia virtually unknown and barbarian artefacts mostly chance and isolated finds, it would amount to an almost impossible task to deal successfully with complicated questions of the processes of Romanization of Barbarians and *vice versa*. Moreover, interrelations and mutual influences of the Romans and Barbarians were reflected in the art and craft production of the period, rendering it in some instances very difficult and indeed impossible to discriminate fashions Roman from Barbarian. If any question within the religious interrelations of the Romans and Barbarians should still deserve special attention, it is obviously a search after the archaeological traces of basically oriental Arian presence in the politically, lingually and culturally western province of Pannonia. The material evidence for exploring this topic is, however, sadly insignificant and the prime task remains to establish the overall extent of Christianization of the population of Pannonia in the Roman period.

Literature

Mócsy 1962; Milojčić 1963; Thompson 1963; Frend 1964; Sutherland - Litt - Carson 1966; Barkóczi - Salamon 1971; Vinski 1971; Mócsy 1974; Vinski 1974; Barton 1975; Tóth 1977; Pinterović 1978; Barkóczi 1980; Salamon - Sós 1980; Thomas E B 1980a; Sutherland - Litt - Carson 1981; Brato` 1986; Sokol 1986; Thomas E B 1987; Schulze-Dörrlamm 1990; Pavan 1991; Šašel 1992; Bierbrauer 1994; Harhoiu 1994; Jarak 1994; Migotti 1994; Wolfram 1994; Christie 1995.

3. History of research into the early Christian period in northern Croatia and objectives of this study

Research into the early Christian history of Pannonia as a whole has a long tradition rich in discoveries. They are mostly based on the abundant documentary material, both literary and epigraphic, on the clergy, martyrs and church communities of Pannonia. It should, however, be borne in mind that the majority of the evidence relates to Sirmium, which presently lies outside Croatian territory and is consequently omitted from this study. Quite considerable numbers of documents concern the Croatian section of southern Pannonia, but only minority relates to northern Pannonia (present-day Hungary). Presumably the silence about north-Pannonian bishops should be ascribed to an accident of history and archaeology; the prevalence of the documentary evidence for the Croatian section of Pannonia still remains surprisingly significant. Three bishoprics there - Cibalae, Mursa and Siscia - are securely documented and the fourth one is hypothetical (but highly probable), providing the identification of the bishopric Iovia with the present-day Croatian town of Ludbreg is correct. Equally as many as eight (nine if Iovia is included) members of the clergy, mostly bishops, are documented. Paradoxically enough, the Hungarian section of Pannonia still appears to be richer in material remains than the Croatian portion of the province. The extremely scanty archaeological material from northern Croatia was somewhat augmented after the research in 1994, but is still disproportionate to the written source material. Illogical as it is historically, this paucity of material remains nevertheless used to be taken as an archaeological fact not to be further questioned or proved. However, questioned it should be, and two tentative reasons can consequently be proposed that resulted in a somewhat distorted conception of the early Christian, or rather, the whole of the Roman period, in northern Croatia. Historians and commentators accompanying Roman armies in their taking over of

Pannonian territory, spoiled Mediterraneans as they were, experienced the area as hostile and repulsive in terms of people, landscape and climate. It appears that this initial negative experience of Pannonia somehow lingered on throughout its ancient and modern history, becoming in time transformed (not generally though) into a somewhat vilified picture of the area as a poor heir to Roman monumental heritage. Such a negative psychological attitude has in Croatia further been fostered by a comparison of Pannonia with the flamboyant classical remains of the Mediterranean section of the country; it was occasionally overlooked by scholars that it was exactly in the late Roman period that *Pannonia* became a most important province politically and in every other aspect. Within the context of the consequently neglected research into classical antiquity in northern Croatia, the early Christian horizon was left, so to say, completely aside. One of the reasons probably lies in the lack of any spectacular chance discovery that would have prompted research into the early Christian period in the course of the 19th century - the period of nascent academic archaeology in Croatia. Had an important initial discovery occurred in Siscia, the site would have probably acquired a label of 'early Christian Salona of Pannonia'. Instead, Siscia is archaeologically neglected. Systematic large-scale archaeological excavations of early Christian sites in northern Croatia have only been conducted at Ludbreg and Varaždinske Toplice. Early Christian finds have often been dealt with in papers on mixed or even exclusively early mediaeval topics. The single study (Vikić-Belančić 1978) to discuss the early Christian finds of northern Croatia was a broad survey that could not encompass either the breadth or the complexity of the period in question. To these limiting factors should be added another, which is in fact a serious deficiency of both Croatian and Hungarian late antique archaeology (3rd to 7th centuries) - the lack of joint research by specialists in classical and early mediaeval archaeology. Consequently a strict division of the horizons of the 1st/4th and 5th/7th centuries leaves early Christian archaeology in a state of limbo.

Faced with such obstacles, the early Christian archaeology of northern Croatia experienced a situation contrary to that in the majority of European countries; a wish to ascertain the Christian background of peoples and societies led there to an engaged pursuit of early Christianity as early as the 18th century. This resulted at times not only in over-interpretation of the material, but in conscious forgeries. Not so in northern Croatia, where the early Christian horizon was set aside to the point of neglect and/or even misinterpretations of some very important finds of the 19th century (see for example nos. III.b.4. and III.c.3.). The result is as could be expected: a distorted conception of the exceptional scarcity of early Christian finds in northern Croatia, hardly sustainable at the recently achieved stage of research. The veracity of such an image can be suspected primarily on the basis of comparisons with northern (Hungarian) Pannonia; while much poorer in sources, it is richer in material remains, particularly architecture, than the Croatian portion of the province. Both these sections were, however, parts of a single natural, historical, geopolitical and cultural unit. A question therefore arises of why should northern Croatia

(southern Pannonia) figure as an early Christian 'archaeological desert', when at the same time surrounded with provinces rich in remains of the early Christian period (northern *Pannonia*/Hungary, *Noricum*/Slovenia and Dalmatia/central and southern *Dalmatia* and Bosna and Herzegovina)? It was such a line of reasoning that prompted me into the initial research in 1994; however incomplete and perfunctory, it justified my expectations, bringing at the same time to light an urge for a thorough investigation of the early Christian period in northern Croatia. Accordingly the present study has primarily been envisaged as a background to such a task, but not only that: it should also be of help to broader academic circles to become acquainted with the present-day understanding of the early Christian period in northern Croatia.

In a word, the primary aim of the study was a reconstruction of the early Christian period in its prevalently material aspects, while spiritual components were not altogether excluded. Their value was limited by the lack of a sound context for many artefacts, but the acquired picture should nevertheless be able to prove the basic unreliability of the conception of southern Pannonia as an area deficient in early Christian remains in comparison with its northern counterpart. To illustrate a continuity of life in 5th and 6th century Pannonia, if at a much reduced level, has also been one of the major objectives of the present work, and one that can most accurately be achieved by research into the early Christian remains: they represent the most conspicuous material evidence of the late antique period, comprising the Roman and Barbarian finds and ascertaining the link between the Roman and early mediaeval civilisations.

Historico-archaeological works on Pannonia in its entirety have as a rule been written by non-Croatian authors, mostly Hungarian. This has resulted in consequences which have impeded the understanding of the archaeology of the Croatian section of Pannonia: sometimes works relating presumably to Pannonia as a whole comprise its northern sections only. At other times studies aiming at territorial completeness very often include quite deficient, incomplete or even distorted data on southern Pannonia. I should like to give here just one example to serve as an illustration: in an otherwise very thorough and systematic reference book on early Christian archaeology, the birth-place of the famous Pannonian martyr Quirinus - Siscia - was by an incorrect combination of two literary sources placed within an archaeological context related to the Hungarian town Szombathely/Roman Savaria (Testini 1958, 316). Misapprehensions like this one can never be altogether excluded but, it is hoped, may be significantly reduced when more accurate and authentic data on early Christianity in northern Croatia are available in foreign languages.

Literature

Brunšmid 1909; Brunšmid 1911; Testini 1958; Mócsy 1962; Salamon - Barkóczi 1971; Pinterović 1978; Vikić-Belančić 1978; Dimitrijević 1979; ARP 1980; Fitz 1980; Thomas E B 1982; Thomas E B 1987; Simoni 1988; Simoni 1989; Jarak 1994; Katalog 1994; Migotti 1994; Tóth 1994; Christie 1995; Gáspár 1995; Koščević - Makjanić 1995; Mawer

1995; Burkowsky 1996; Buzov 1996.

4. Chronology and classification of material

Different opinions have been put forward about both the nature and scope of early Christian archaeology in general and its relation to the conception of late antiquity. Nor is its chronological framework, stretching from the 2nd to the 8th centuries, firmly established. The chronology adopted in this study (3rd to 7th centuries) should be explained in some detail. The fact of the official Christianization of the Roman empire from the rule of the House of Constantine the Great in the course of the 4th century is basically accepted; through Christianity transforming from a faith into an attitude towards the world, all of Roman civilisation officially became Christian. However, the emergence of Christianity as a historical occurrence as well as its first material manifestations fall in the period from the 1st to the 3rd centuries. With this in mind it is no wonder that the researcher into Roman Christianity in a certain province hardly escapes the trap of seeking to establish it as early as possible, even if it be too early. On the other hand some scholars tend to handle the situation by avoiding to connect with Christianity any material earlier than the 4th century; both attitudes, if strictly adhered to, are apparently wrong. The hesitancies result from the early Christian period as characterized (more than any before) by the ambivalent symbolism of works of art which do not display only what the author meant to say, but also what the viewer sees in it. Consequently it should be a mistake to dismiss a putative significance of generic ('neutral') images on 2nd and 3rd century material, especially if the archaeological context is suggestive of a Christian context. It is an accepted fact that the basically insoluble question of Christian symbolism stems from the inherently syncretic and compilatory nature of the early Christian material and spiritual cultures: not a single individual Christian motif, including the cross, was a creation of Christian artistic-symbolical conceptions. To quantify therefore the criteria for Christian evidence and for grading its significance is a most demanding and virtually unattainable task. It is inevitable at times for the researcher into Roman Christianity to try to discover dubious and hidden or else specifically stylized Christian symbols and phrases; they can be traced not only in the earliest period, but also in times when Christianity gained its freedom and became the sole official religion. Accordingly it often remains dubious whether various stylizations came as a result of the artist's particular attitude or maybe of the necessity to camouflage, or were just unconscious debasements of the symbol due to lack of basic understanding of its original significance. The cross itself, originating in prehistoric oriental milieus, stands for both pagan and Christian religious conceptions; it furthermore represents ideas other than strictly religious and can, for instance, represent a cosmic metaphor. This is true not only of the pre-Constantinian period, but also of the very end of Roman civilization. Besides, the cross is occasionally employed as a purely structural or fortuitous feature, deriving from geometrico-technical premises. On the other hand it has often been remarked as an axiom of archaeology (shown in the material evidence and additionally corroborated by literary sources) that the late Roman/early Christian period is deeply imbued by the allegory, the symbol and the metaphor. In a word, it is impossible to establish the firm chronological limits of probable or even possible Christian subject matters, particularly when a reliable archaeological context is missing, such as is most often the case in northern Croatia. With this in mind, I considered it both allowable and worthwhile to include not only indisputably Christian items, but also those potentially so. True, by taking into consideration the latter, a possibility of reaching definite and completely reliable conclusions about the early Christian civilization on the territory in question is somewhat diminished. On the other hand, both the variety and relative abundance of disputable items make possible a broader insight into some aspects of Christianity, which additional investigation might confirm or reject. Within this approach I strove against the over-generous inclusion of too speculative items: those either too remote in time (earlier than the 3rd century) or with too flimsy Christian associations. Inclusion was made only exceptionally and then with a due explanation.

To circumvent a justified suspicion of the Christian material being basically not susceptible enough of the positive qualification of its symbolic meaning, I tried to grade its significance by sorting it into three categories:

I: Indisputable. Items determined by the unmistakably recognized Christian devices or the like archaeological context. By unambiguous indicators are meant the devices (signs, formulae and figural depictions) that are only ever found in Christian contexts.

II: Probable. Items without determining archaeological context or devices, yet associated with symbols which are not definitely Christian, but are very frequently found in Christian surroundings. Also included are objects lacking any devices, but discovered within a very probable Christian context or in tandem with indisputably Christian items. This was based on the fact that a multiple juxtaposition of definitely Christian symbols - for example the chi-rho - with various other 'neutral' motifs like the palm, the dove, the peacock etc., has a bearing on the components of the ambiguous symbolism when these are found in isolation. Although inevitably open to alternative interpretations, their possibly Christian nature always lingers on; when backed by a suggestive context, they may legitimate be considered as probably Christian.

III: Possible. Items dated to the 3rd or exceptionally the 2nd century, but also those from the 4th to 7th centuries, if marked by an ambiguous symbolism. In both instances a determining context is lacking. Over-speculative objects in this category are preferably omitted.

The two last categories are somewhat fluctuating, depending too often on the broad knowledge (which at times confuses

7

rather than clears the insight into a problem) or parallels from elsewhere. Consequently the classification in categories II and III is not always quite clear-cut, which is occasionally true even of the first category. In such instances a question mark has been associated with the classification number.

A word should be also said about the upper chronological limit of the material comprised here, which is connected with the presence of barbarian peoples in Pannonia. From the end of the 4th century the Germanic Barbarians ceased to be satisfied either with the role they had in the Roman military or with the sporadic settling down on Pannonian soil on command of the Roman emperors. Instead, their growing ambitions resulted ultimately in the creation of various Barbarian kingdoms within the borders of the Empire; the kingdoms of the Huns, Goths and Langobards, created in Pannonia in the 5th and the 6th centuries, were still only transient, as was their very presence. The first to settle down permanently and create a mediaeval state to last were the Slavs, i.e. Croats, reaching southern Pannonia together with the Avars in the course of the 7th century. This event can therefore justifiably be considered as a virtual ushering in of the early mediaeval period in present-day northern Croatia. At the same time it determines the upper chronological boundary of the early Christian horizon in the area. Yet another reason for including this full time-span within the framework of Roman Christianity lies in the dependence of the barbarian states on Pannonian soil both on the Catholic Church and the Roman emperor. The Christianized barbarian chieftains and kings recognized the political and moral authorities of the Romans and therefore developed their kingdoms under the auspices of the Roman Church and State.

Literature
Testini 1958; Cumont 1959; Harmatta 1970; Barkóczi - Salamon 1971; Barton 1975; Vágó - Bóna 1976; Quacquarelli 1978; Murray 1981; Salamon - Barkóczi 1982; Post 1984; Reinhard Seeliger 1985; Corby Finney 1987; Thomas E B 1987; Šašel 1992; Šašel 1992a; Jarak 1994; Migotti 1994; Christie 1995; Gáspár 1995; Mawer 1995.

5. Structure and organization of the catalogue

This work comprises the material evidence, while the documentary sources have been adequately dealt with elsewhere (Jarak 1994). All types of material evidence have been included: small finds, structural materials and non-portable items, an approach conditioned by the relatively small amount of the total of the material. Its advantage lies in the fact that only by relying on various kinds of material evidence is it possible to recreate a picture of a period to any level of accuracy. On the other hand, a serious setback to such an achievement concerning south-Pannonian early Christianity is the lack of excavation and consequently of archaeological context for the majority of the evidence.

As a 'compilatory', religion Christianity is firmly rooted in its pagan religious background; its interrelations with various Roman and especially oriental religions were extremely complex and manifold. As an introduction to Christianity

two basically 3rd century religious features have been chosen here: the cult of the Invincible Sun and Christian gnosticism. These themes are not quite an arbitrary choice, but rather one that represents very visually and meaningfully the essential core of the late antique pagan-Christian syncretism. In the section on gnosticism I have presented items dated mostly to the 3rd century and bearing iconographic elements that might reasonably be assessed as gnostico-Christian. It should also be noted that scattered among the Christian material of the 4th century there appear some objects which also display elements suggestive of gnosticism: they are being discussed in the appropriate places in the catalogue. To introduce the cult of the Invincible Sun (*Sol Invictus*) the artefacts were chosen that were presumably, indeed probably, viewed by the Christians as quite acceptable in terms of their religious affinities.

A catalogue was the most convenient way to present the material, particularly small finds. However, a variety of types of objects prevented a catalogue schema from being carried out systematically and consistently: entries in the chapters on urbanism and architecture are different for obvious reasons from those containing small finds; they still share a description of the items or sites and a commentary/discussion on various questions in their regard. Discussion is distributed throughout the catalogue in the form of either introductory text to groups of items or commentary on individual objects or groups of kindred artefacts. The significance of each object as evidence for Christianity is discussed in relation not only to data at disposal, but also to its importance or applicability in the reconstruction of a Christian ambiance. Understandably, special attention is devoted to ambiguous or syncretistic subject matters. Introductory texts are exceptional, as they are inherently based on the general theoretical data available in various other text books and studies. Contrarily, particular prominence has been attached to the commentaries at the end of a single entry or groups of them. They figure in place of final synthetic conclusions, which, at the present stage of insufficient level of investigation and insight into archaeological contexts of the Christian material remains, would be too unreliable and disputed.

The organization of the catalogue is based upon the following overall scheme with further subdivisions:

Cult of the Unconquered Sun (Sol Invictus)

Christian gnosticism

Christianity:

I.	Urbanism and architecture
II.	Structural church members, fittings and decoration
III.	Funerary constructions and furnishings
IV.	Imperial inscriptions
V.	Objects of ornament
VI.	Utilitarian decorated small objects
VII.	Instruments
VIII.	Coins
IX.	Objects of uncertain use

Concluding discussion

The foregoing division is conventional and is therefore arbitrary in several aspects, particularly when it comes to distinguishing between 'decorative' from 'utilitarian'.

Entries in section I (Urbanism and architecture) could not be laid according to a strict catalogue scheme, but were organized as a series of texts in various units, mostly urban, with the stress laid upon urbanistic and architectural features implying Christian associations. Within other sections each catalogue entry contains the following elements:

1. Name with classification mark (I-III); 2. Provenance; 3. Location; 4. Description; 5. Dating; 6. Literature; 7. Commentary.

The whole of the material evidence for Christianity is divided into nine large sections according to their nature (I-IX) with a further subdivision into smaller groups based on types of kindred objects (a, b, c etc). The sequence of items within these units is conditioned by classification, objects of the class I coming first. An exception to this procedure was made when a possibility arose of separating items within a smaller group according to artefact types (for example in the sections II., V.e., VI.c). A similar line was applied for group I (Architecture and urbanism). A complete title of an entry therefore contains (in addition to its name and classification denominator) the division, subdivision and sequential numbers (for example II.2; III.a.1.). Provenance generally includes basic information on the place, method and time of discovery, but quite often some essential data are missing. In the majority of instances location relates to the museums (with accession numbers given if known). Museum titles are given in abbreviations which are explained immediately after the list of the main literature. References are made to items that are either missing or kept in private collections, and as a consequence usually inaccessible. Descriptions are accommodated to the heterogeneity of the material in that they are basically summary, minimising both technical precision and complete archaeologically relevant details; prominence was attached to their Christian significance and symbolism. Understandably, this is true for the ambiguous specimens more than any others. Fabric is always specified, but is mostly not quite accurate, owing to the lack of chemical analyses. Not all dimensions are given, but those sufficient for a rough estimation of the size of the artefact. Datings are derived from the relevant literature and is occasionally corrected according to my own opinion. This is not apparent from the entry rubric of dating, but is, if problematic, usually discussed in the commentary. It should, however, be kept in mind that the lack of contextual evidence for many objects leaves them as virtually undatable save on insecure typological and art-historical grounds. A number of items therefore have an uncertain or too wide a chronology (while question marks are attached only in instances when a doubt is particularly pronounced). It was the purpose here to present a complete literature for each item; this would be too much of a burden for the main literature at the end of the book. On the other hand, the most recent works are always included, with an intention to add data to previous references. There is a fairly ample bibliography at the end of the book with titles in minor languages (e.g. Croatian) accompanied by summaries in English, German, Italian or French. If such works are bilingual, only the title in a major language is given. The references within individual entries are entered in chronological order. Within the commentaries in the catalogue as well as in the concluding discussion, references are made in accordance with the Harvard system, while occasional additional notes are placed within brackets in the text. As mentioned already, entry commentaries with elaborations on the Christian interpretation of items and their significance for south-Pannonian early Christianity substitute for a final synthetic discussion, unattainable at this stage. They relate to either one or more kindred entries.

Each artefact except IV.2. and VI.c.11. is illustrated with a drawing or a photograph, sharing the same designations/captions with entry titles of the objects they relate to (e. g. II.1; III.b.1 etc.). Scales are usually omitted as a consequence of the majority of drawings being taken from existing publications and often augmented in copying. Photography was by Nenad Kobasić of AMZ. Drawings III.b.3.; III c.9.; V.a.6.,7.; V.b.2.,4.; V.d.3.; VI.c.6.,7.; VII.2.; VIII.1.,2. and IX.2. were made by Krešimir Rončević, while the remainder are taken from the relevant literature. Items of the cult of Sol Invictus and Christian gnosticism are abbreviated as S. and G. respectively.

Cult of the Unconquered Sun (Sol Invictus)

Introduction

The emperor Aurelian (270-275) was the first successfully to impose the worship of Sol Invictus as the sole state religion. The basic theological components of this cult were the solar pantheism of essentially monotheistic nature, the victory of good over evil and the conception of life as overcoming death. These notions were very kindred to Christian attitudes; accordingly Christian theologans made use of them in their struggle to eliminate sun-worship as the exclusive religion of the state. The result was the creation of Solar Christology which identifies Christ with the deified sun. The idea is amply documented throughout the patristic literature, where Solar Christology is philosophically explained and placed within the framework of Christian doctrine, with Christ frequently designated as Sol Salutis or Sol Iustitae or Lux Mundi. Tradition has it that Constantine the Great (306-337), a keen adherer of Sol Invictus at the beginning of his rule, ended up as a Christian, whether formal or real (Vogt 1957; Winkelmann 1961; Alföldi M R 1964; Rahner 1964: 104-114; Sutherland - Litt - Carson 1966: 61-64; Halsberghe 1972; Forstner 1982: 95-99; von Heintze 1983). Constantine apparently never would or could differentiate Sol from Christ or separate the two ultimately; no wonder then that during the 3rd and 4th centuries many of both the common believers and clergy accepted the same attitude, as transpires from historical sources (Marbach 1927: 911; Johnson 1982: 67). Constantine's institutionalization of the connection between Sol and Christ was accompanied by the conscious creation of an iconography associating the Sun and the cross. This is traceable as early as the 2nd century, but is typical of the 3rd and 4th centuries (Kühnel 1994: 164-165).

As an illustration of the Solar-Christian syncretism a number of votive and apotropaic lead pendants are singled out, based on a decorative concept composed of a round frame enfolding either a cross or its substitutes. The result is basically solar symbolism, but one with Christian associations, secret during the first three centuries A.D. and overt later on. Objects in question were dated to the second half of the 3rd century on the analogy of moulds for producing of similar or even quite identical items (Schmitz 1993:50). The hypothesis that Christians were capable of attaching a Christian meaning to these pendants is based primarily on the idea of the Solar-Christian syncretism explained above. Yet another argument (corroborated time and again in historical sources from the 2nd and 3rd centuries) in this regard is equally persuasive, that of early texts relating to Christians as permeated with the sign of cross in various aspects of their daily life (Dölger 1958: 5-7). What is to be born in mind here is the lack of an 'orthodox' Christian iconography at that time, so that any shape of the cross would probably do. Furthermore, in the 4th century the chi-rho was accepted as both a Christian symbol and a powerful heavenly sign, and therefore possibly a token of the Sun worship (Sutherland - Litt - Carson 1966: 61). Quite

edifying as regards the mixed Solar-Christian symbolism of the 3rd and 4th centuries are funerary stone reliefs from 6th century Gaul, featuring both Solar and Christian crosses (Salin 1952: 86, Fig. 43; 99, Fig. 102)

S.1. Pendant (I)

Provenance: Sisak (Siscia); dredging of the River Kupa in 1912.
Location: AMZ (6589)
Description: Lead; height 3 cm, circle diam. 1,9 cm. A thin and fragile openwork pendant featuring an equal-armed cross within a circle. A fairly massive rectangular vertically bisected suspension loop is attached to the body. The front bears all over a motif of a palm branch or a herring bone in low-relief. It is flat on the back.
Dating: 2nd half of the 3rd century.
Literature: Katalog: 73, n. 2a.
Commentary: To the encircled cross - the so-called sun-wheel endowed with a cross ('radkreuz') - similar symbolic associations have been attached from prehistory to the Roman and Christian periods. Within the conception of Solar monotheism, the circle stands for both the sun and the cosmos, while the cross is a metaphor for the eternal supreme divine power. The motif then, as a whole, represents the idea of inextinguishable life and happiness achieved through a supreme divine being. For Christianity it has almost the same association, only the supreme being is embodied in the person of Christ and eternity is achieved through his sacrifice and sufferings, i.e. his death and resurrection. The motif in question appears in Christian iconography in the 4th century at the latest and probably even earlier, achieving its greatest popularity during the 5th and 6th centuries (Salin 1959: 109-112; Sági 1968: 394-395; Daniélou 1969: 277; Lowrie 1974: 112; Higgins 1987: 59-63, Fig. 20; Barnea 1977: 242, Fig. 96; Forstner 1982: 19; Watts 1988: 213-214; Schmitz 1993: 59-65; Salona I: Pls. 78-85).

S.2. Pendant (I)

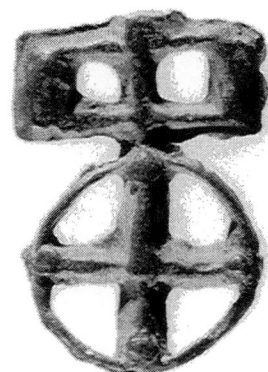

Provenance: Sisak (Siscia); dredging of the River Kupa in 1912.

Location: AMZ (6580)

Description: Lead; height 2,6 cm, circle diam. 2 cm. A thin (although slightly more massive than S.1) openwork pendant in the form of an equal-armed cross in a circle with a fairly large rectangular vertically bisected suspension loop attached to the body. Flat on the back, while the front has slight relief, featuring five pellets: four at the ends of the cross' arms and one at their intersection.

Dating: 2nd half of the 3rd century.

Literature: Katalog: 73, n. 2b.

Commentary: Statements about the iconographic symbolism of S.1. are basically true for this item as well, the difference being only in the pellets. In terms of solar iconography a decoration in the form of pellets accompanying sun and moon is understood as stars. Used in conjunction they are believed to symbolize never-ending existence and eternal life (Salin 1959: 134-135). A Christian intepretation for this item would point to a rudimental form of the so-called gemmed cross (*crux gemmata*); the idea of resurrection is thus added to the basic cosmic symbolism of eternity. This reflexion is readily apparent in the history of cross worship and is also attested in documentary sources. As early as the 4th century and particularly in the 5th and 6th centuries the gem-decorated cross gained more and more in popularity; it represented not Christ's sufferings, but his glorious triumph over death - the Resurrection (Salin 1959: 370-372; Dinkler 1964; Hayes 1972: Figs. 56, 57).

S.3. Pendant (I)

Provenance: Sisak (Siscia); dredging of the River Kupa in 1912.

Location: AMZ (6588)

Description: Lead; circle diam. 2,3 cm. A tiny and fragile openwork pendant in the form of two obliquely intersected lines enfolded within a circle. Damaged at the section where a now missing suspension loop was attached. The front bears all over a motif of a palm branch or a herring bone in low relief, while flat on the back.

Dating: 2nd half of the 3rd century.

Literature: Katalog: 73, n. 2c.

Commentary: The encircled cruciform design bears indisputable solar associations, but the specific type of cross as represented here requires a further elaboration concerning its symbolic meaning: this is usually either denied or at least suspected. The shape in question is often described as a saltire, a cruciform design or simply an 'x' motif. However, more precise iconographic terms exists for it: the *crux decussata* or the St Andrew's cross. Very powerful and complex symbolic meanings attach to this sign, pertaining to pagan, gnostic, Jewish and Christian apotropaic-magical beliefs and true religious subjects at the same time. The saltire is a known Jewish-Christian and Christian-gnostic emblem representing either Christ himself or various christological conceptions; it stands for any other type of cross, as documented in both the literary sources and the archaeological evidence from at least as early as the 3rd century (Garrucci 1873: 58, Tav. 55; Kaufmann 1913: 643; Leclercq 1924: 152; Fig. 34; Lassus 1935: 15, 24, Figs. 16, 24; Nagy 1945: 278; Dölger 1958; Dölger 1959: 17-18; Dölger 1960; Dinkler 1962; Dölger 1967: 12-13, Taf. 116; Daniélou 1969: 290; Benea - Şchiopu - Vlassa 1974; Watts 1988: 210-211). A Christian interpretation of the saltire should obviously depend either on the context or its position within an artefact. As regards position, an intrinsic Christian significance is contained on crosses that bear saltires at the intersections of their arms: a place reserved otherwise for a bust of Christ (Salin 1952: 80, Fig. 35; Gough 1973: 161, Fig. 155; Cambi 1975: 54-55, Fig. 5; Higgins 1987: Figs. 17: 57, 18: 67, 30: C)

S.4. Pendant (I)

Provenance: Sisak (Siscia); dredging of the River Kupa in 1912.

Location: AMZ (6841)

Description: Lead; 2,1 x 1,9 cm. A thin openwork pendant in the shape of a rectangular (almost square) frame enveloping an equal-armed cross with slightly expanded terminals. At the intersection of arms is a solid disc with another equal-armed cross depicted slightly in very low relief. The front bears all over a motif of a palm branch or a herring bone, while the back is flat and the suspension loop missing.

Dating: 2nd half of the 3rd century.

Literature: Katalog: 73, n. 3a.

Commentary: Symbolic references of the encircled cross have already been commented upon (see S.1.-3.). In this instance the symbolism is enriched by a blend of a circle (standing for the heavenly, astral, eternal, divine) with a rectangle (representing the earthly, human, perishable, temporary). The basic symbolism in terms of Solar theology rests upon a fusion of seemingly incompatible elements, united through a divine power on the principle of eternity. To such an understanding a Christian interpretation would add the idea of eternity achieved through resurrection (Eliade 1952: 33-65; Forstner 1982: 60-64; Pillinger 1989: 95).

S.5. Pendant (I)

Provenance: Sisak (Siscia); dredging of the River Kupa in 1912.

Location: AMZ (6854)

Description: Lead; 1,6 x 1,5 cm. A thin openwork pendant in the shape of a rectangular (almost square) frame enfolding a solid equal-armed cross. An 8-pointed star is depicted in very low relief within the solid disc in the middle of the cross. The front of the frame bears a motif of a palm branch or a herring bone, while the disk in the middle of the cross is decorated by parallel strokes, featuring probably a wreath. The back is flat and the suspension loop missing.

Dating: 2nd half of the 3rd century.

Literature: Katalog: 73, n. 3b.

Commentary: The symbolic meaning of the blend of circle and rectangle has been dealt with (see S.4.). In terms of Solar theology the star in itself, and especially within a sun-disc, epitomizes eternity (Salin 1959: 134-135; Forstner 1982: 103). Symbolic associations of the star are manifold in Christian iconography, depending mostly on context. They range from the star of Bethlehem clearing darkness and bringing salvation, through the apostle or the faithful to Christ himself in the guise of Lucifer - the morning star (Leclercq 1924f; Rahner 1964: 107-109; Forstner 1982: 103-106). Yet another Christian symbolic meaning of either a six- or an eight-pointed star can tentatively be inferred from their shapes as designed on the model of monogrammatic devices. The 6-pointed star (iota-chi) is a blend of the initials of Christ's names and the 8-pointed star may be understood as a fusion of the upright and oblique crosses. Both these devices figured as Christian crypto-symbols in the pre-Constantinian period; they gained popularity again during the 5th century and particularly in the 6th. Christian associations attached to them in later times are amply corroborated by the specific position, reserved otherwise for a cross, within the decorative conception on all kinds of monuments (sarcophagi, church furniture and architectural decoration, small decorative artefacts, etc.) and in various media. They can even be said to have replaced the classic chi-rho, itself slightly outmoded by the 5th and 6th centuries (Garrucci 1877: Tav. 225; Garrucci 1879: Tav. 337:3; Kaufmann 1913: 637-647; Nagy 1945: 278; Leoni 1950: 966; Salin 1952: 46, figs. 12 ff.; Sauer J 1958: 1177; Testini 1958: 353-356; Kempt - Reusch 1965: nos. 43, 46 ff.; Forstner 1982: 40-41; Watts 1988: 212-213; Salona I: Pls. 90-92).

S.6. Pendant (I)

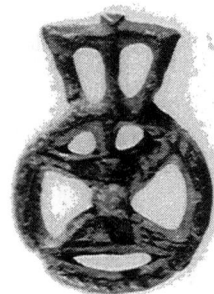

Provenance: Sisak (Siscia); dredging of the River Kupa in 1912.

Location: AMZ (6593)

Description: Lead; height 2,3 cm, circle diam. 1,6 cm. A thin openwork pendant in the shape of a circular frame encompassing a solid orant figure with upraised arms and triangular upper and lower body. It is stylized as an hour-glass and features a bulbous stump (navel?) in its centre. The front of the figure's body is flat as is the back of the whole artefact. The frame bears on the front a motif of a palm branch or a herring bone. A fairly massive vertically bisected trapezoidal suspension loop is attached to the body.

Dating: 2nd half of the 3rd century.

Literature: Katalog: 73, n. 2d.

Commentary: The basic symbolism of the orant is shared by pagan religions (the cult of Sol Invictus included) and Christianity alike. In each case it was viewed both as a representation of a worshipper in prayer and as a metaphor for religious piety (Klauser 1959; Forstner 1982: 316-317). According to documentary sources the orant position was from the beginning an accepted gesture during prayer with Christians. It entered Christian iconography roughly in the 3rd century, figuring also as a crypto-symbol of the cross during the pre-Constantinian period (Klauser 1959: 116; Forstner 1982: 20; Dölger 1964: 13). Of utmost significance is apparently the fact that in Solar iconography the orant represents not only the worshipper, but also the sun-god himself. (Salin 1959: 369, note 1).

S.7. Pendant (I)

Provenance: Sisak (Siscia); dredging of the River Kupa in 1912.

Location: AMZ (6815)

Description: Lead; 3,2 x 3,2 cm. A solid triangular pendant with a crescent lower section and a fairly massive suspension loop. In the middle of the triangular field an equal-armed cross in a circle, apparently a wreath, is rendered. Five bulbous knots are attached to the edges of the lower section of the pendant, with three additional pellets interspersed in the field around the encircled cross. The edges bear all along on the front a motif of a palm branch or a herring bone, while the back of the artefact is flat.

Dating: 2nd half of the 3rd century.

Literature: Katalog: 73, n. 4.

Commentary: In the iconography of this object - featuring the sun (circled cross), the moon (crescent lower section) and the stars (bulbous knots and pellets) - well-rounded and elaborate Solar and Christological theologies are contained. In terms of the former the above-mentioned figures represent the whole of a cosmic-astral divine conception, reinforced by the shape of the object: a triangle with its tip upwords symbolizes the male divine principle - Sol Invictus in this instance - amalgamated with his female counterpart, Luna (the moon), as is typical of the solar cult (Barb 1953: 226, note 145; Halsberghe 1972: 70). This union must have in effect been decisive for the survival of the solar cult as amalgamated with Christianity; at the same time its fiercest oponent - Mithraism, deprived of a female divine counterpart and turned to exclusively male adherents - was destined to die out. Christian associations of the foregoing figures are very akin to the Solar and are unquestionably confirmed in Christian doctrine of the Fathers of the Church, primarily Origen. The incidence of Solar Christology came as a result of the struggle of Christian theologians against the overwhelming popularity of astral mystery religions in the 2nd and 3rd centuries. Solar Christology encompassed eventually the basic ideas and hopes of a variety of saviour religions, creating an astral conception of Christian eschatology. This should have been achieved through the interrelated operating of all the three components: the moon (the Church) transmitting the light of the sun (Christ) to the faithful (the stars). The idea of the whole of the divine-human life-circle and eternity is thereby completed (Rahner 1964: 91-173; Forstner 1982: 95-103).

Christian Gnosticism

Introduction

Gnostic sects on the fringes of 'orthodox' (orthodox from obviously the subsequent and not contemporary point of view) Christianity based their theologies on a number of components: pagan religious mythologies and philosophical reflexions, Jewish and Christian doctrines and magical-apotropaic conceptions and procedures. The last-mentioned are intrinsic to gnosticism and essential for it, yet extremely difficult to disclose and define in precise terms: magic was typical of all antique religious systems, Christianity included. These assumptions, although not accepted by scholars universally and in every detail, relate to both religious theories and iconographies of gnostics. To disclose gnosticism and establish its artistic fashions appears to be as difficult today as it was in the 2nd and 3rd centuries - the period of the flourishing of gnostic sects. In the eyes of the then official Church, gnostics were heretics and enemies to the true faith. It should, however, be borne in mind that many religious writings, among them the Revelation, were labelled heretic prior to becoming canonized in the 3rd century or even later. From the historical point of view, then, should gnosticism with its artistic material evidence be equalled to 'purely' Christian remains. There exists an abundant literature on and a profound general knowledge of numerous gnostic theologies and other theoretical aspects of gnostic teachings. Conversely, discerning gnostic traces in the material evidence is as yet very tenuous, debatable and inconclusive. In art historical and archaeological terms gnostic conceptions are supposed to show in the form of unintelligible writings, as well as in individual signs, characters and motifs or groups of them. It is accordingly fairly easy to hypothesize gnostic iconographic traces, but more often than not quite impossible to explain or prove them beyond doubt. All the more difficult appears to be to try to attribute such material evidence to specific gnostic sects, however familiar and well-documented their theologies might be. The total of the known gnostic material evidence is consequently meagre and inconclusive even in the academic milieus with a more developed Christian archaeology than is the case with northern Croatia (Hopfner 1928; Barb 1953; Testini 1958: 523-524; Barb 1963; Craveri 1969; Daniélou 1969; Grant 1969; Engemann 1975; Corby Finney 1978; Johnson 1982: 43-45; Philipp 1983; Stutzinger 1983; Post 1984; Kákosy 1989).

It was the purpose of this section of the study to present artefacts showing a blend of secure or probable gnostic and Christian associations. To ascribe these to specific gnostic sects was an ultimate objective, but one that at this stage remains mostly disputed and inconclusive.

G.1. Inscribed tablet (I)

Provenance: Vinkovci (Cibalae); excavated during

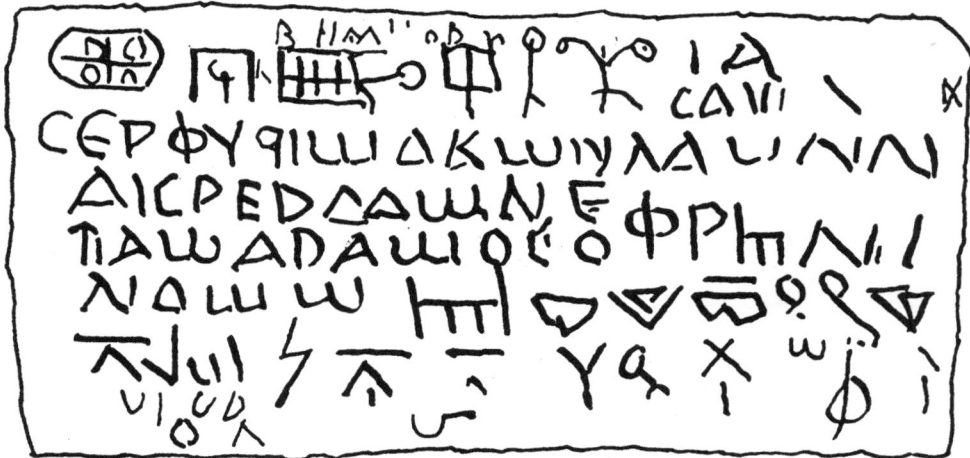

construction work in 1932. It had been rolled (flattened after discovery) and put into the mouth of a skeleton in a grave at some distance from the north cemetery of Cibalae.

Location: GMV (A-904)

Description: Gold; 5,1 x 2,5 cm. A tablet made of a thin gold sheet with an inscription on the front running in six lines. The plate has originally been rolled and folded for use as an amulet. The actual inscription, overlying scanty traces of a previous one, contains two lines (the first and the last) of unintelligible simple and compound signs and characters, some of which terminate in small rings, and four central lines written in Greek letters, yet incomprehensible to view.

Dating: 2nd half of the 3rd century.

Literature: Dimitrijević 1979: 238-239, Taf. 18:1; Migotti 1994: 189-190, n. 7.

Commentary: The inscription has not yet been read, i.e. deciphered and interpreted. A few details concerning both its configuration and the archaeological context can nevertheless hypothetically be related to the gnostic sect of Basilidians. Similar tablets made of precious materials have been found at various places; in the majoritiy of cases they contained names of divinities, among them Yahveh, derived by combinations and permutations of the vowels I, A and O, amounting to a number of variants of the Jewish God's name - Iao, Adonai, Sabaoth, etc. (Leclercq 1924: 154-155; Hopfner 1928: 338; Burger 1966: 110, Fig. 86; Benea - Şchiopu - Vlassa 1974; Fiedler 1992: 170; Lucchesi-Palli 1994: 172-173).

An understanding of the difference between white and black magic appears to be essential for determining this object as gnostic, in contradistinction to ordinary curse plates (*tabellae defixionum*). The latter were sheets made of the sinister metal - lead. They would be hidden at various places, but were most often buried secondarily in graves with skeletons, after being inscribed with names of persons who were to be harmed by an invocation of infernal demons and gods. Alternatively, a benign kind of magic, the so-called white magic, encompasses various supplications (concerning well-being, gain of money or health, love etc.) written as a rule on silver or gold sheets; both the Christian and Jewish God is occasionally involved. Within this framework, gnostic texts should be understood as the most sophisticated form of white magic with a strictly religious background, employed in achieving eternal peace and salvation: by means of such writings composed of secret words or signs the initiated soul assures a return to its heaven after death (Hopfner 1928; Kubinyi 1948; Testini 1958: 149; Barb 1963; Wortman 1968; Vágó - Bóna 1976: 84, 193, Taf. 17:10; Kákosy 1989: 271-273; Bargebuhr 1991: 27; Fiedler 1992: 170; Lucchesi-Palli 1994). The procedures of both black and white magic are related to the dead, but in an essentially different manner. While the white magic amulets were usually buried together with their owners, black magic would not hesitate to disturb skeletons of persons dead for a period of time and to use them as media (Hopfner 1928: 332; Wortmann 1968). Here the circumstances of the magical procedure were specific and at the same time typical of gnostic surroundings: the tablet from Vinkovci was found in the mouth of a deceased person, excluding thus a possibility of it being placed there after burial. This procedure should then be viewed in the light of the basic conception of gnosticism, that gnosis is a capability of learning the mysteries of God, reserved solely for the initiated and intended for their ultimate salvation. The

situation as described here is reminiscent of a quotation in the Revelation of St John (10: 9-10), having John the Evangelist swallowing the Book of the Mysteries of God (Hopfner 1928: 35; Stutzinger 1983: 83), probably as a symbol of mastering its secret messages.

Among secret magical characters and signs typical of gnostic texts, most frequent are those with ring-like terminals, conspicuous also on the artefact from Cibalae (Leclercq 1924: 152, Fig. 34; Leclercq 1924c: 610; Leclercq 1931a: 1289; Wortmann 1968: 103-111; Vikan 1984: 76-78, Figs. 13, 14, 18). A couple of other details of the text appear to suggest Basilidian gnostic associations. First, it is the vowels A, I and O, discernible at several places in the central lines of the inscription, and probably suggestive of the name of the Jewish God. Second, specifically Christian should be two basically cruciform compound signs in the first line. Also to be observed are characters in the form of letters X and Y, and a trident- or omega-like sign, all interspersed within the text. All of them figure at least theorethically as Christian-gnostic crypto-symbols standing for the cross (for the cruciform signs see Ljubić 1876: 60-73; Marucchi 1903, 389; Testini 1958: 357, Fig. 153; for Y: Kaufmann 1917: 303, n. 2; Leclercq 1924c: 610; Kubinyi 1948: 278; Guarducci 1969: 469; Forstner 1982: 38; Mawer 1995: 101, 138; for X: Leclercq 1924: 152, Fig. 34; Leclercq 1931a: 1289; Kubinyi 1948: 278; Hermann 1967: 80; Daniélou 1969: 290; for the trident/omega motif: Cabrol 1924: 5; Reinecke 1927: 166; Lassus 1935: 75-76; Figs. 83, 85; Dannheimer - Kriss-Rettenbeck 1964: 199, Abb. 5:21; Engemann 1975: 27-28; Forstner 1982: 34-36; Buhagiar 1986: 330, Fig. 114 A; Fiedler 1992: 167-168).

G.2. Pendant or appliqué (II)

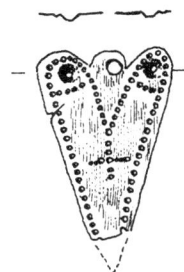

Provenance: Sisak (Siscia); dredging of the River Kupa in 1912. .

Location: AMZ (6554)

Description: Silver; 2,5 x 1,7 cm. Triangular and slightly anthropomorphic pendant of a very thin silver sheet. Left and right upper angles are each marked by a boss, possibly stylized shoulders or breasts, while a similar device in the middle between them is likely to have been pierced for attachment rather than suspension. The edges are bordered with a repoussé beading, employed also for rendering a chain with an equal-armed cross-pendant in the middle of the triangular field - the chest if this be a stylized anthropomorphic figure.

Dating: 3rd-4th centuries.

Literature: Katalog: 89, n. 67.

Commentary: At a first glance this object features a kind of prehistoric anthropomorphism, without obviously revealing either its nature or function. The cross-pendant on the necklace is nevertheless suggestive of the Christian significance of the artefact. It is more than probable that Christians used to wear decorations in the form of the cross even prior to mentions of this habit in 4th century sources (Dölger 1966: 34; Mawer 1995: 82). However, no conclusive or immediate parallels to this object are known to me from any Roman or Christian context; it should be gnostic. Presuming such a context for it, I was further prompted by a suggestion of the worship of the Diva Matrix (the Divine Womb, i.e. the deified uterus) being represented here (Dora Gaspar pers. comm.). Within this framework the closest iconographic parallels can be found in the realm of the Diva Matrix cult, which stem from 17th-16th century B.C. Palestine. They are triangular gold-sheet pendants with the face and sex organs of a mother-goddess clearly indicated (Barb 1953: 197-199, Pl. 29: g-i). There is no denying that the possibility of a meaningful comparison of artefacts out of phase by so many centuries is debatable; it can still reasonably be assumed that the cult of the deified uterus found its way to Christian-gnostic doctrines by way of various oriental mythologies and mystery religions. It would have been met there with the conception of unity of the male and female procreative principles and more specifically with the Virgin-Christ mythology (Barb 1953: 197-199; Stutzinger 1983: 85-89). From this point it was but a step towards the dogma of the Mother of God ('theotókos'). The occasional refutation of an otherwise very convincing hypothesis of the unbroken continuity between the cults of oriental mother-goddesses and that of the Virgin Mary (Barb 1953: 230-232, notes 203, 215) should not be particularly problematical here. In terms of Christianity this artefact should then be interpreted as a metaphor for the dogma of the Motherhood of God, the cross-pendant on the necklace within the triangle (the Virgin's body?) standing for Christ. Its function within Christian-gnostic worship can still only be speculated upon, a private use being most probable on account of its small size.

An indirect parallel is brought to mind through a series of triangular votives, both pagan and Christian (the latter obviously deriving from the former), made of thin gold or silver sheets. These are much larger than the item from Sisak, and therefore probably not of the same function, but are nevertheless strongly reminiscent of the idea of a pagan-Christian religious syncretism, both speculative and iconographic (Thomas E B, 1980a: 187, Pls. 124-125; Spätantike: 551, n. 156; Mawer 1995: 87-89).

G.3. 'Abraxas' gem (I)

Provenance: Sisak (Siscia); dredging of the River Kupa in 1912.

Location: AMZ (7140)
Description: Lead; 1,6 x 1,2 cm. On the upper surface of an oval bezel within the moulded rim depicted in low relief is a fabulous creature featuring a human torso, a cock's head in profile to the left, snake feet, and a whip and shield in the hands. Three Greek letters are arranged around the figure, composing the word Ιαω
Dating: 3rd century.
Literature: Katalog: 74, n. 9.
Commentary: The common term for a broader group of similar gems corresponds to the word abraxas or abrasax, which is quite often inscribed on such artefacts either alone or in tandem with other words, characters or signs (Leclercq 1924; Šeper 1942; Turchi 1949; Philipp 1983; Stutzinger 1983; Post 1984). There is some ambiguity concerning a putative gnostic significance of these artefacts, and a recent tendency is to leave them with only magical-apotropaic associations, suggested by the syncretic (prevalently solar) nature of their typical iconographic configuration (Philipp 1983: 154; Post 1984: 435-438). This view is additionally substantiated by the fabric of these gems, lead being attributed sinister associations in all of antiquity (Hopfner 1928: 326-327). The term abraxas is a derivative of numerical values of the constituent letters adding up to the total of 365. It therefore has no original symbolic meaning and its subsequent theological significance was based on the word Ιαω as the equivalent for one of the names of the Jewish God, which at the same time denotes the highest divine creature in the Basilidian gnostic system. Associated initially with Jahweh solely, the name Ιαω found in time its way to various religious systems (mystery religions in the main) and ultimately to Christianity and Christian-gnostic doctrines; it quite frequently stood for Christ there. The Christian origins of the name Abraxas can be assumed on the basis of its similarity with the apocalyptic letters alfa and omega, known from the Revelation of St John the Evangelist; it is also found in the Apocrypha and other early Christian sources (Šeper 1942: 43-44; Craveri 1969, 478). Consequently, claims for gnostic significance for abraxas gems, on the level of speculation at least, appear to be justifiable. On the level of practical working they certainly belong primarily to the realm of magic.

G.4. Ring (II)

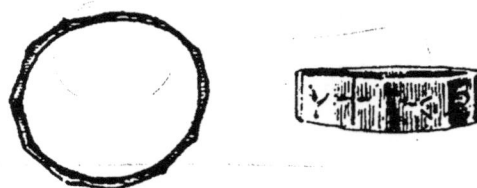

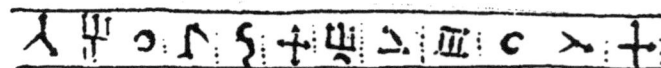

Provenance: Vinkovci (Cibalae); construction works in 1887; grave-find in the area of the Roman cemetery.
Location: AMZ (misplaced).
Description: Silver; diam. 2,2 - 2,4 cm. A polygonal ring containing twelve facets with various characters and signs ingraved in each of them.

Dating: 3rd century/first half of the 4th century.
Literature: Brunšmid 1902: 160, Fig. 90:2; Katalog: 74, n. 8.
Commentary: Rings count among the jewellery destined to express religious and magical-apotropaic feelings pertinent to their very function, and are accordingly often employed in magical-gnostic religious rituals (Marshall 1907: xxiii; Barb 1963: 112-113; Forstner 1982: 397-399; Guiraud 1989: 176). If there is any sense to the inscription as a whole, it has as yet not been found out, but a few details testify to its probable gnostic references: the number twelve is typical of Jewish-Christian and gnostic speculation (Barb 1963: 118; Forstner 1982: 56-58), as is a symbolically arranged system of mystic numerals and characters. Accordingly, quite a significant number of Christian-gnostic sects used frequently to employ recurring secret signs and letters in their writings (Hopfner 1928: 340-343; Leclercq 1931a: 1289; Testini 1958: 523-526; Barb 1963: 118; Craveri 1969: 553; Daniélou 1969: 262; Guarducci 1969). This is only a natural and expected consequence of the basic gnostic principles, gnosis being essentially viewed as a capability of the initiated to learn divine secrets (Hopfner 1928: 367-369; Stutzinger 1983: 83; Bargebuhr 1991: 27). Each of the signs depicted on this ring finds its place within Christian-gnostic systems, either featuring the cross itself (cf. Daniélou 1969: 269) or standing for its various equivalents, for instance Y and omega/trident (see G.1.). The letter C, interpretable also as a Greek S, stands at times for the alfa in the known alfa and omega syntagm, representing possibly the word Soter (Saviour) (Testini 1958: 355). The same could hold good for the Latin letter s, only the number of possible clues is more ample, comprising tentatively *spes, salus, sanctus, servus* etc. (Kaufmann 1917: 39; Guarducci 1969: 475; Higgins 1987: 126; Forstner 1982: 400-402).

G.5. Signet ring (II)

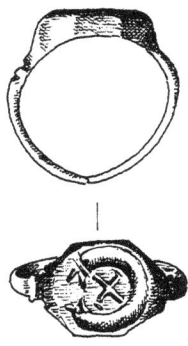

Provenance: Sisak (Siscia); dredging of the River Kupa in 1911.
Location: AMZ (4963)
Description: Bronze; ring diam. 2,2 cm, bezel diam 1,4 cm. A damaged and distorted ribbon hoop expanding at the top towards a massive octagonal bezel. Engraved or rather chiselled on it is a curled snake entwining a serifed saltire (oblique cross potent). It can not be properly discerned whether a snake is depicted devouring its tail, or a snake with two confronting heads should be envisaged. Both variants are well-known in the repertory of antique snake-decorated jewellery, particularly rings and bracelets.
Dating: 3rd/4th centuries.
Literature: Katalog: 88, n. 60.

Commentary: The ring is of 3rd/4th centuries type, attested as a rule in a gemstone variant, and not a signet ring, as here (Marshall 1907: 46, Pl. 7:266; Guiraud 1989: 186, Fig. 22: 3a, b). A Christian significance to the octagonal shapes of bezels has at times been suggested, but equally often rejected (Mawer 1995: 66). Yet ruling it out undeniably would mean overlooking the distinguished symbolism of the number 8 in early Christian doctrine (Forstner 1982: 54-55; Quacquarelli 1978). The depiction proper on the bezel is definitely symbolic and most probably suggestive of gnostic speculation: both its components, the snake and the serifed saltire, are deeply rooted in magic-apotropaic and religious (Jewish, pagan, Christian and gnostic) symbolism (for the saltire generally see. S.3., and the saltire within gnosis G.1.). Highly significant and edifying as regards the role of the saltire in gnostic iconographies is a 5th century Coptic stone relief ornamented scatteredly with saltires, featuring a child-bath. It was ascribed to late antique gnostic surroundings and interpreted as a depiction of a spiritual baptism (Hermann 1967, 80, Taf. 1a). The cult (and iconography) of the snake figures among most animal-worship imbued with manifold symbolic references, which present the snake as the lord of life and death, of good and evil, and of eternity as well. (Salin 1959: 241-244; Forstner 1982: 288-292). Though basically pagan, this cult was in time Christianized, acquiring thereby the associations of eternity, immortality and the power of Christian ruling (Kaufmann 1913: 642-643; Bargebuhr 1991: 44). Most significant in the present context are obviously those Christian-gnostic conceptions of snake-worship that refer primarily to wisdom and knowledge and were consequently apposite to artistic material with gnostic significance (Grant 1969: 324:325). A snake coiled up and biting its tail was the most distinguished metaphor for the virtues of wisdom, gnostic knowledge and watch over some value, either material or spiritual (Salin 1959: 244; Barb 1953: 202). If now to these conceptions the saltire is added representing Christ, the dogma of the Christian Saviour emerges, expressed by means of a gnostic iconographic vocabulary. It is important to note that a few gnostic sects were concentrated on the snake as the envoy of God and that one of them, the Ophites, was even named after the snake (Leclercq 1936).

G.6. Gem (III)

Provenance: Osijek (Mursa); donated to MSO in the second half of the last century.
Location: MSO (1391)
Description: Whitish-rose steatite; 1,7 x 1,2 cm. On the upper surface of the oval bezel engraved in rough and sketchy contours is a figure of naked Hermes with frontal body and head in profile to the right. The god is shown as

leaning with his right arm on a staff with cross-bands; in the empty space below his left arm a sign similar to the Greek letter ψ (psi) is depicted.

Dating: 3rd century.

Literature: Pinterović 1965: 38-39, n. 8, T. 2:8; Katalog: 74, n. 11.

Commentary: A few details suggest some peculiar, rather than classic decorative function to this gem. It is first its rough and imprecise execution, typical on the whole of later classical periods when gems tend to lose their qualification of objects of art for art's sake on behalf of prevailing apotropaic-magical and symbolic qualities (Furtwängler 1900: 363; Šeper 1942: 6). The gem from Osijek, with some of its attributes suggestive of magical-gnostic surroundings, fits happily within this framework, as does the figure of Hermes in the first place. This god was primarily a guide of souls on their journey to the underworld (psychopompos), but not only that: he was also considered to be a protector of witchery and owner of a wand - a most important instrument of divine creatures in magical-gnostic speculation, particularly with the Basilidians and the Naassenes (Leclercq 1925: 518; Hopfner 1928: 303 ff.; Leclercq 1931: 1095-1096; Leclercq 1932: 456; Šeper 1942: 31; Engemann 1975: 28). A number of details on the depiction in question feature a blend of prevalently gnostic and some Christian components: Hermes' staff with cross-bands in the form of saltire looks less like the classic attribute of this god - kerikeion - and more like a cross-sceptre, as appears frequently on coins of mediaeval Christian rulers (Whitting 1973: 37-38, nos. 42, 43). Equally the oblique cross on the sceptre is also reminiscent of specifically gnostic conceptions (see G.1; G.5). The use and significance of the staff was frequently commented upon by Christian writers, who connected it either with Christ himself or his crosslike attributes (Daniélou 1966: 142-143). On the other hand, a gnostic content of the gem is possibly suggested by a sign similar to the Greek letter 'psi' beneath Hermes' left arm, which could have stood for the word psychopompos (Pinterović 1965: 39). Alternately it could have contained some magic symbolism or even figured as a metaphor for the cross (cf. Milojčić 1968: 247; Forstner 1982: 38-39). Whatever the case, it should be borne in mind that secret letters, which this character obviously is, are very typical of gnostic material (Leclercq 1924: 52, Fig. 33; Leclercq 1931a; Barb 1953: 195-196; see also G.4).

Christianity

I Urbanism and architecture

Introduction

It might seem somewhat pretentious to dwell on the topic of urbanism and architecture with the lack of material evidence based on thoroughly-investigated urban structures of the early Christian period in northern Croatia; systematic excavations over years were undertaken only at Varaždinske Toplice and Ludbreg. It is therefore only periodical rescue works or small-scale trial excavation or even mere field survey that have produced information on the topic in question (Iskra Janošić 1984: Demo 1986; 145; Bulat 1989: 5-6). Some urbanistic-architectural structures and features have nevertheless been investigated, while a number of them can be established or hypothesized on grounds of topographic-archaeological data, based on a combination of surface observation of archaeological sites and examination of literary-archival sources.

I.a. Episcopal Sees

I.a.1. Osijek (Mursa) (II) (Fig. 1)

Among Pannonian cities in northern Croatia only Mursa can pride itself on an original historical document attesting the existence of a church building termed *basilica martyrum*. The Roman chronicler Sulpicius Severus relates that during the battle of the armies of the emperor Constantius II and the usurper Magnentius in the vicinity of Mursa in 351, the former, accompanied by Valens - Arian bishop of Mursa, withdrew to the *basilica martyrum* outside the town (Pinterović 1980: 62). It has been hypothesized that the *basilica martyrum* could be identified with the architectural remains outside the southwestern city wall, near also to the proposed site of the amphitheatre (Figs. 1: 1; 2). On the basis of data gathered from 18th century finds and the results of recent rescue excavations, Pinterović (1980) hypothetically identified the martyrial basilica of Mursa as a small circular structure with a rectangular addition. This suggestion convinces only as concerns its location in the area of the southern Roman cemetery. The cemetery had also extended to the inside of the city perimeter, yielding a number of late Roman tombs. A lead sarcophagus was found there with grave finds among which a possibly Christian gemstone was

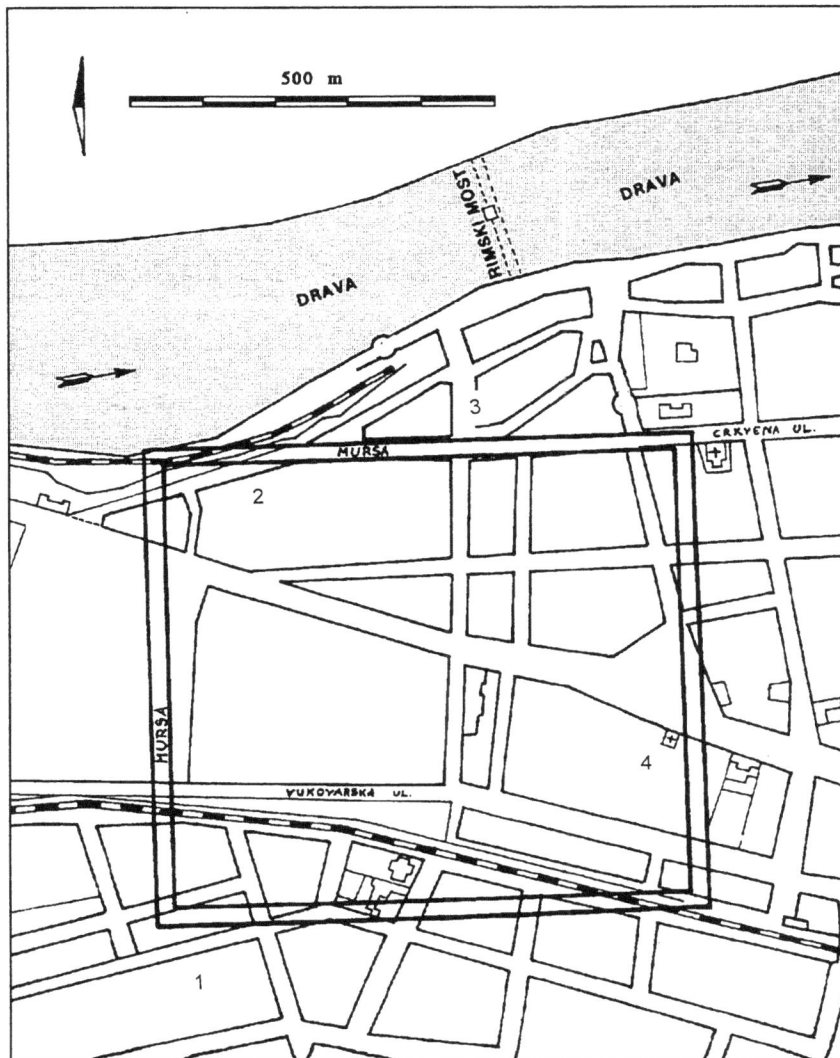

Figure 1: *Plan of Mursa (Osijek) with putative early Christian sites (readjusted after Katalog).*
1. Basilica martyrum(?); 2. Early Christian basilica(?); 3. Early Christian(?) finds; 4. Early Christian(?) finds

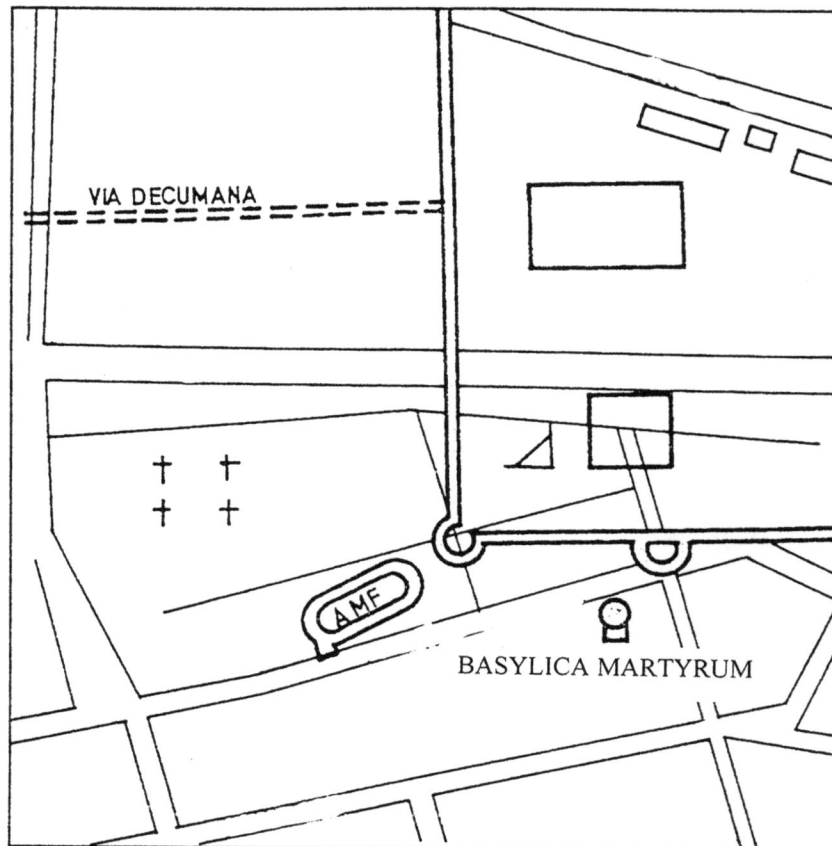

Figure 2: *Plan of the south-western section of Mursa (Osijek) with the hypothetical site of the basilica martyrum (readjusted after Pinterović 1980).*

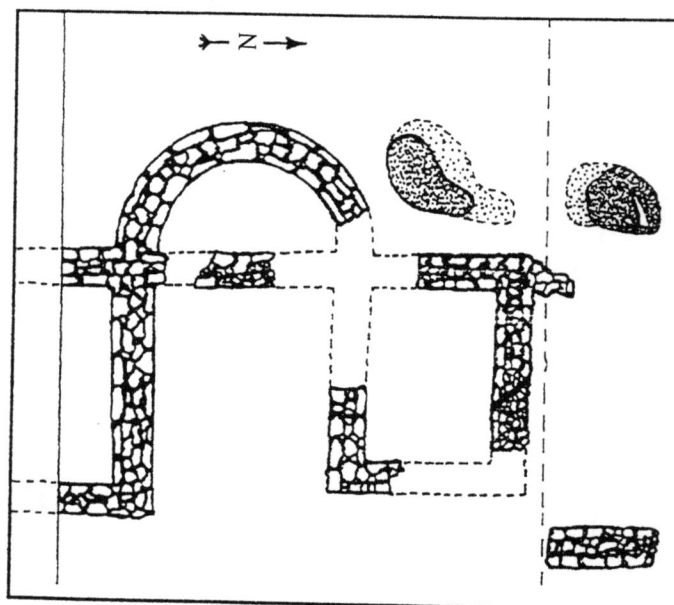

Figure 3: *Plan of the apsed basilical structure at Mursa (Osijek) (see Fig. 1:2) (after Katalog)*

identified (V.e.12.). However, an inconspicuous round structure as hypothesized to be a Christian building would have hardly been named basilica by Sulpicius Severus and would have probably not been considered worthy of housing the Roman emperor either. True, circular buildings were at times termed basilicas in documentary sources, but larger dimensions were as a rule implied in such cases (Krautheimer 1965: 53; Deichmann 1970: 152). A basilical building with a western apse (Figs. 1: 2; 3) was partially excavated in 1971 within the northwestern corner of the town, and was dated to the 4th century (Bulat 1989b: 199). An early Christian brooch (V.a.1.) was found there in 1934. The hypothesis that the building was a Christian church could be additionally, although not conclusively, corroborated by its position on the edge of the town, as is typical of some of the earliest Christian urban structures (Krautheimer 1963: 7; Claude 1969: 89-93). Immediately outside the north town wall (Fig. 1:3) an early Christian dish (VI.d.2.) and a marble receptacle very similar to the one from Sisak (II.4.) were found. A certain grouping of possibly Christian finds can be noted in the south-eastern section of the town (Fig. 1:4). In addition to a marble vessel, very similar to the one from Sisak (II.4.), and a figurine of a lamb (V.g.2.), a fragment of a fresco with the image of a fish in a medallion (as yet unpublished) was discovered there.

I.a.2. Vinkovci (Cibalae) (II) (Fig. 4)

Owing to one exceptional historical document from the 4th century - the hagiographical legend of the lector Pollio (Passio S. Pollionis), martyred in the persecution of Diocletian in 304 - more is known about the spiritual ambience of early Christian Cibalae than the material structures that must have existed there. No traces of them were ever found during quite abundant rescue excavations within the town perimeter. Possible early Christian sites can therefore only be hypothesized on the basis of both small finds and general parameters about the placement of early Christian structures (Fig. 4: 1-5). In the eastern section a powerful Roman horizon was documented mostly by rescue excavations and chance finds (Fig. 4: 1); a fragment of an early Christian funerary inscribed stone (III.c.6.) was excavated there in the 19th century. A little farther west from this place a pottery fragment was also excavated recently with a graffito cross incised (VI.d.4.), and in the vicinity of the mentioned finds, remains of a temple to Liber and Libera were partially investigated several decades ago (Dimitrijević 1979: 219). Curiously enough, the present-day orthodox-Christian church from the 18th century stands on this site, pointing possibly to a very long continuity of the cult place. Now, scattered burials inside Pannonian towns in late

Figure 4: *Plan of Cibalae (Vinkovci) with putative early Christian sites (after Katalog)*
1. Early Christian burial
2. Late Roman (Christian?) architecture
3. Memorial-cemeterial architectural complex (Kamenica)
4. Early Christian burials in the area of the Roman cemetery
5. Site of Meraja

antiquity are as a rule considered to be a result of the general decay of urban life (Mócsy - Szentléleky 1971: 34; Fitz 1980b: 155-156; Christie 1995: 307). Yet another explanation should, however, be considered - that such burials were the nuclei of early Christian cemeteries within town walls, as are otherwise typical of medieval periods (Salin 1952: 35; Testini 1958: 159; Krautheimer 1963: 69; Menis 1976: 401). The next hypothetical early Christian site at Vinkovci (Fig. 4: 2) is situated immediately within the north town wall, where in the vicinity of a collapsed Roman temple, sumptuous columnar architecture (assumed to be a civil basilica or a commercial building) was erected in the 2nd half of the 4th century (Dimitrijević 1979: 219-220; Iskra Janošić 1984: 146). Arguments for a suggested Christian site are two. First, prior to erecting the fourth century building, the Roman temple was broken down and fragments of statues of pagan gods were built into the nearby town wall; a hypothetical Christian building would then have been installed in the former civil building, as was frequently the case with various commercial structures and civil basilicas (Vaes 1989: 300, 303). Second, late Roman burials were found in the vicinity (Iskra Janošić 1984: 146) that might point to the nucleus of an urban cemetery within the walls, as hypothesized for the situation of the site in the centre of the town (see Fig. 4: 1). This suggestion might further be substantiated by the fact that at least a section of the northern cemetery of Cibalae, stretching from the town walls towards the north (Fig. 4: 4), was Christian (see G.1., III.b.3 and III.c.1.). This, then, would correspond to an axiom of early Christian urbanism, that each church within a town is connected with the nearest cemetery outside the walls (Marucchi 1903: 124; Lowrie 1974: 25).

Very important remains of early Christian architecture were found on the site of Kamenica (Fig. 4: 3) about 1,5 km outside the east town wall beside the road to Sirmium. While portable and non-portable finds from this spot will be discussed at some length in sections II and III of the Catalogue, we are here dealing with architectural remains solely. During a cursory and incoplete trial excavation in 1968 two underground grave chambers were uncovered, each containing two graves and hypothetically put together within an above-ground construction in the form of a mausoleum (Dimitrijević 1979: 247-250). This type of grave, considered to be an oriental feature, was widespread in late Roman/early Christian *Pannonia* (Fitz 1980: 172; Tóth 1994: 253). The supposed mausoleum, together with a wealth of architectural fragments and inscriptive funeral stone slabs found on the site during previous field surveys (II.5.6.7.; III.c.7), resulted in a persuasive hypothesis for Kamenica as the spot of the martyr Pollio's death and possibly subsequent worship as saint (Dimitrijević 1979: 248). This hypothesis seems to be reinforced also on grounds of the distance of Kamenica from the town wall, corresponding fairly exactly to the data from the Passio (one Roman mile = 1478, 5 metres). In the 19th century a stone capital was found at Kamenica (II.5.) of a size indicating monumental architecture on the site greater than a mere mausoleum. A basilica should in fact be expected, datable to the 4th or 5th centuries according to these stone remains.

Before the discoveries at Kamenica, the site of Meraja, immediately outside the west town wall (Fig. 4: 5), was often mentioned as the prime early Christian nucleus of Cibalae. A

mediaeval Christian centre with the church of St Elias developed there in the proximity of luxury Roman structures and other contemporary finds. However, the proposal for this place as the most important Christian centre of Cibalae from ancient times has never been confirmed either in the archives or on the ground (Dimitrijević 1979: 264-268).

I.a.3. Sisak (Siscia) (III) (Fig. 5)

Roman Siscia is an example of an archaeological site intolerably neglected in comparison to its importance and representation in documentary sources. There exists a relative abundance of written material on Siscia as a very important south-Pannonian Roman town. The majority of papers are, however, based on documentary sources, small scale rescue excavations and chance/surface finds. Systematic investigations are completely lacking, while rescue excavations have been too few and of limited scope (Katalog 1994: 82-97, 192-193; Koščević - Makjanić 1995; Burkowsky 1996; Buzov 1996). Small finds are accordingly plentiful, contrary to the scanty data on urbanism and architecture. It is nevertheless possible, with the help of previously acquired data and new discoveries, to determine the certain, probable and hypothesized positions of early Christian finds (Fig. 5: 1-6). Two apsed structures were discovered during construction work in the 1950s. One of them, with a northern apse (Fig. 5: 1), was subsequently considred to be the basilica described in the mid 19th century as a 'large church' (Nenadić 1987: 78, Fig. 4). The site, however, remains questionable, as it is still disputed whether the foregoing data refer to the same building, or whether it was early Christian at all. The second of the two mentioned apsed buildings was oriented east-west (Fig. 5:2), which would make a hypothesis of its religious appurtenance slightly more convincing (Nenadić 1987: 78, Fig. 3). The most probable location of an early Christian site within the walls would, however, be at its south-eastern corner, in the vicinity of the present-day parish church of the Holy Cross, erected on the site called 'Stari Sisak' ('Ancient Sisak') (Fig. 5: 3). This was most probably the findspot of the early Christian sarcophagi of Severilla (III.b.1.) and Felicissima (II.b.2.); they were found in their original position rather than brought from elsewhere, as indicated by a pagan sarcophagus excavated long ago at the site. A luxury late Roman dwelling or a commercial building was partially excavated at the northern edge of this section of the Roman town (shadowed on the plan in the Fig. 5: 3). A water cistern, an indispensable element of early Christian architectural complexes, was found in the vicinity in 1954 (Koščević - Makjanić 1995: 8). Curiously enough, this section of the town displays a modification in the orientation of architecture, a disturbance indeed of the regular grid-layout, typical of the remainder of the urban fabric (Faber 1973: 143; Buzov 1996: 56). It thus cannot be excluded that at Siscia, like so many other early Christian cities, the nucleus of the Christian community originated around a formerly private building, transformed subsequently into a so-called house-church (*domus ecclesiae*). The hypothesis is apparently becoming more and more convincing: the current archaeological excavation in front of the present church has revealed remains of a large late Roman structure with stone columns (Zdenko Burkowsky pers. comm.). If, then, a Christian centre at this site was conjectured rightly, a connection with the south-eastern cemetery outside the town wall (Fig. 5: 3, 5) could

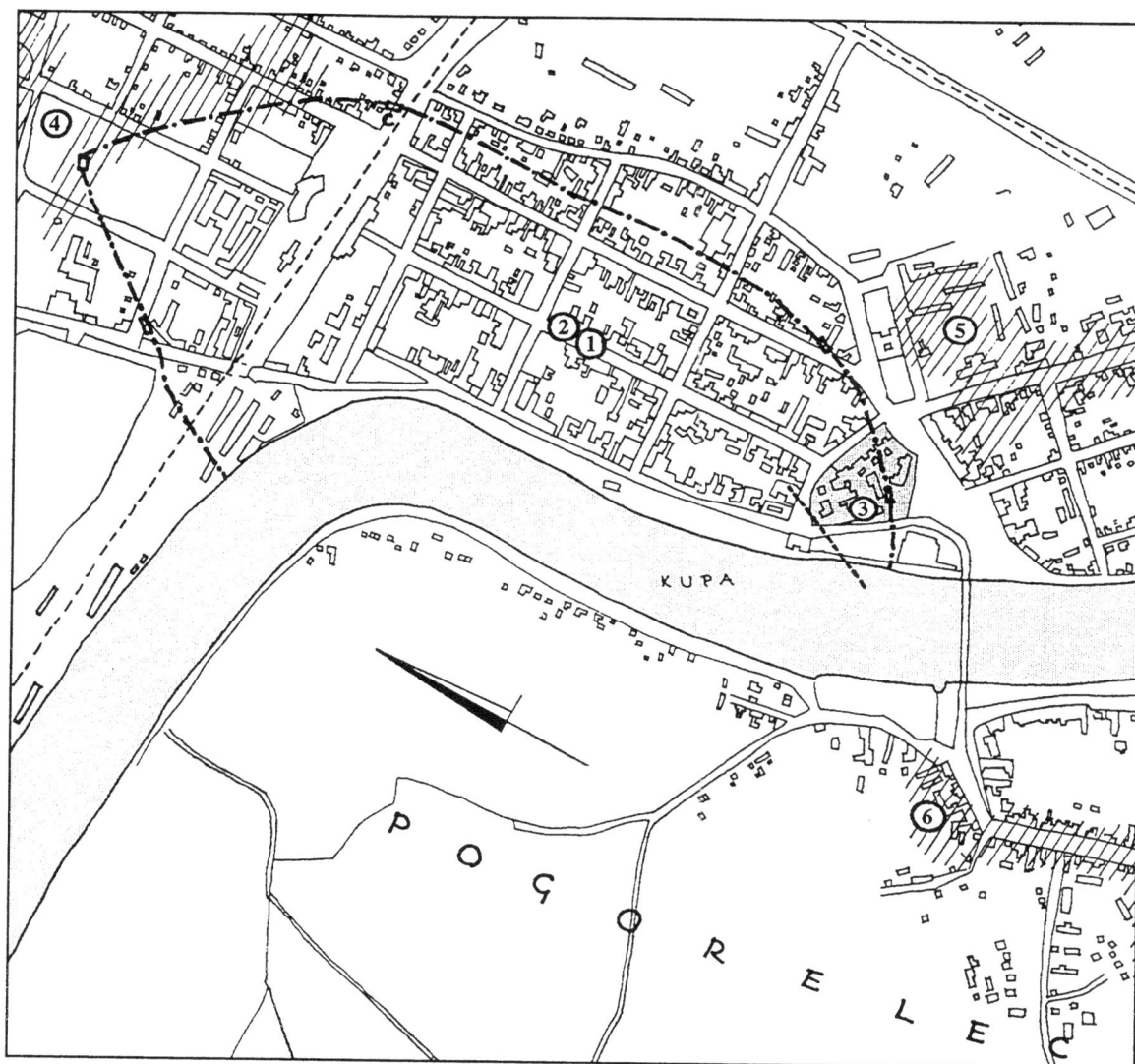

Figure 5: Plan of Siscia (Sisak) with putative early Christian sites (after Katalog)
1. *Early Christian(?) apsed building*
2. *Early Christian(?) apsed building*
3. *Early Christian sarcophagi and Christian(?) architecture.*
4. *Early Christian burials in the area of the northern Roman cemetery*
5. *Early Christian(?) burials in the area of the eastern Roman cemetery*
6. *Early Christian(?) burials in the area of the southern Roman cemetery*

equally be envisaged. In the area of this cemetery an early Christian ring, since lost, (Nenadić 1987: 85) and probably also the brooch V.a.4. were found. The 19th century parish church of the Holy Cross was built there on the site of an earlier one, and was surrounded by a graveyard until half a century ago; a religious continuity to the present day can accordingly be percieved.

The early Christian suburban topography of Siscia is characterized by a merger of pagan and Christian burials as a result of the continuation of Christian cemeteries in the area of their pagan predecessors. In the area of the north-western Roman cemetery (Fig. 5: 4), where a baroque chapel of St Quirinus was demolished during construction work in the 1970s, early Christian graves of various forms had been discovered during the last century (Burkowsky 1996: 78). More recently a metal lamp in the shape of the Lamb of God (VI.b.1.) was unearthed there during construction work. Christian burials were noted in the northern section of the southern cemetery (Fig. 5: 5); yet another late Roman

cemetery was discovered at the site of Pogorelec (Fig. 5: 6) on the right bank of the River Kupa, which yielded fragments of marble tombstone inscriptions, some of which were possibly early Christian (III.c.8. and III.c.9).

I.a.4. Ludbreg (Iovia?) (II) (Figs. 6, 7)

The question mark by the Roman name denotes a hypothetical, yet sufficiently convincing, identification of Ludbreg (Roman Iovia) with the historically-documented early Christian see of Iovia, situated on Pannonian soil between Poetovio and Mursa (Jarak 1994: 175-176; Tóth 1994: 251-252, note 48; Bratož 1996:329).

Rescue excavations carried out in 1968-1979 established the contours and urban layout of the Roman town and confirmed its settlement from the 1st to the 6th centuries (Fig. 6) (Vikić-Belančić 1984; Vikić-Belančić - Gorenc 1984). Had these excavations brought to light indisputable early Christian finds, the hypothesis about the see would be even

Figure 6*: Plan of Iovia (Ludbreg) with the site of thermae and early Christian(?) church (readjusted after Vikić - Gorenc 1984).*

Figure 7*: Plan of the adapted early Christian church(?) at Iovia (Ludbreg) (after Vikić - Gorenc 1984).*

more convincing. No traces of an early Christian cemetery have been found either. Sarcophagi without specific Christian attributes, suggestive though in themselves of a Christian context, were discovered at a cemetery south-east of the town, along the road to Varaždinske Toplice (Aquae Iasae) (Vikić-Belančić - Gorenc 1984: 92). It has been hypothesized, and convincingly, that in the 2nd half of the 4th century the first Christian church in Iovia was installed in the building of the 2nd century baths. This should have been rendered by removing of one of the three apsidal pools at the eastern end of the building and turning that section of the building into a porch (Fig. 7) Thus obtained, the Christian building, if it was one, had a plan in the form of a double apsed and double-naved church with lateral gallery (Vikić-Belančić 1978: 591-592).

Double apsed churches are not exactly a very typical early Christian type, but are not altogether absent either (Moracchini-Mazel 1984; Chevalier 1995: 246-249, Pl. 41). This type could alternatively be understood as a variation on the so-called double or twin churches, widespread in early Christian architecture and symptomatic especially of episcopal centres (Duval 1974: 354-356; Kondić Popović 1977: 104; Piva 1995).

The urban development of Iovia is particularly marked by a curious feature related to the lay out and orientation of architecture in that older buildings were oriented north and south, while late Roman structures followed the east and west direction (Vikić-Belančić 1984: 161). This phenomenon might have been caused by the introduction of Christian elements into the urban lay-out, in which case late-Roman buildings would have superseded the orientation of the baths remodelled into a church, or else would have followed a correspondingly oriented episcopal basilica of Iovia. This building could hypothetically be envisaged at the site of the present-day parish church of the Holy Trinity in the far north-western corner of the town (Fig. 6); in addition to taking an east-west orientation, it overlay a mediaeval church erected directly above the late Roman town walls (Vikić-Belančić 1984: 135).

I.b. Other Roman Towns

I.b.1. Varaždinske Toplice (Aquae Iasae) (I) (Figs. 8, 9)

Although a very important Roman settlement, a town indeed, Aqae Iasae is unattested in historical sources as having had any municipal status. The thermal complex there had a mainly therapeutic and religious character having a capitolium and a nymphaeum and yielding a great number of dedicatory and votive inscriptions to various gods. Under Constantine the Great (306-337) the thermal section of the town was spatially and functionally reorganized; while turning into a most prominent spa centre, its religious function became even more marked than previously (Gorenc - Vikić 1979: 41-42). At the same time the Emperor's monotheistic (possibly Christian) religious affiliations (Vogt 1975; Vinkelmann 1961) could be envisaged in the renovation of the Capitolium: what had originally been a symmetrical building containing three equal-sized shrines dedicated to the Capitoline triad, turned now into a tripartite structure with the temple to Jupiter gaining in prominence (Fig. 8). A number of pagan votive inscriptions were used to pave the concurrently reconstructed forum, pointing to a somewhat nonchalant attitude towards the classical religious culture (Gorenc - Vikić 1979: 42). With Constantine's proverbial religious hesitancies between the worship of Sol Invictus and Christianity in mind, it is particularly significant that the altar with a votive inscription to Sol (Katalog: 72, n. 1) was placed in the forum arcades and remained undamaged. Constantine had an inscription set up (IV.1.) on the occasion of the renovation of the town, previously badly damaged in a fire. Its content is suggestive of the Emperor's mixed religious feelings, wavering between Solar worship and Christianity. During Constantine's remodelling of the thermal complex, the largest building - a north-south orientated rectangular hall - was endowed with a semicircular apse enclosed within the straight rear wall, and was accordingly interpreted by the excavators as a *basilica thermarum* (Fig. 9) (Gorenc - Vikić 1979: 36-37). It is a commonly-held opinion that this building passed into Christian use some time towards the end of the 4th century,

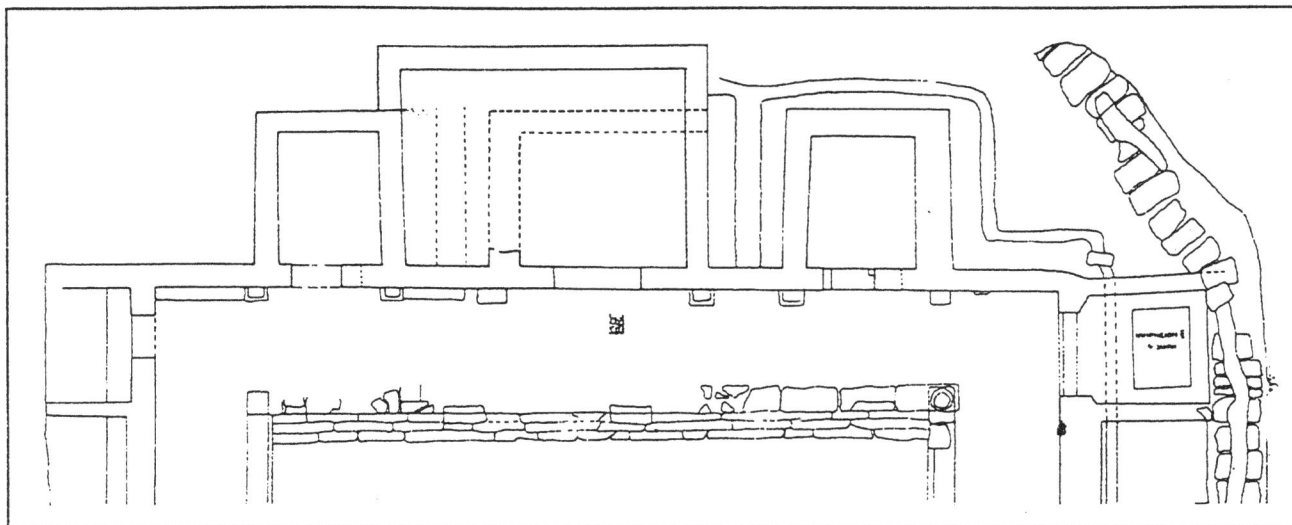

Figure 8: *Plan of the Capitolium temple at Aquae Iasae (Varaždinske Toplice) with phases marked (after Gorenc - Vikić 1979).*

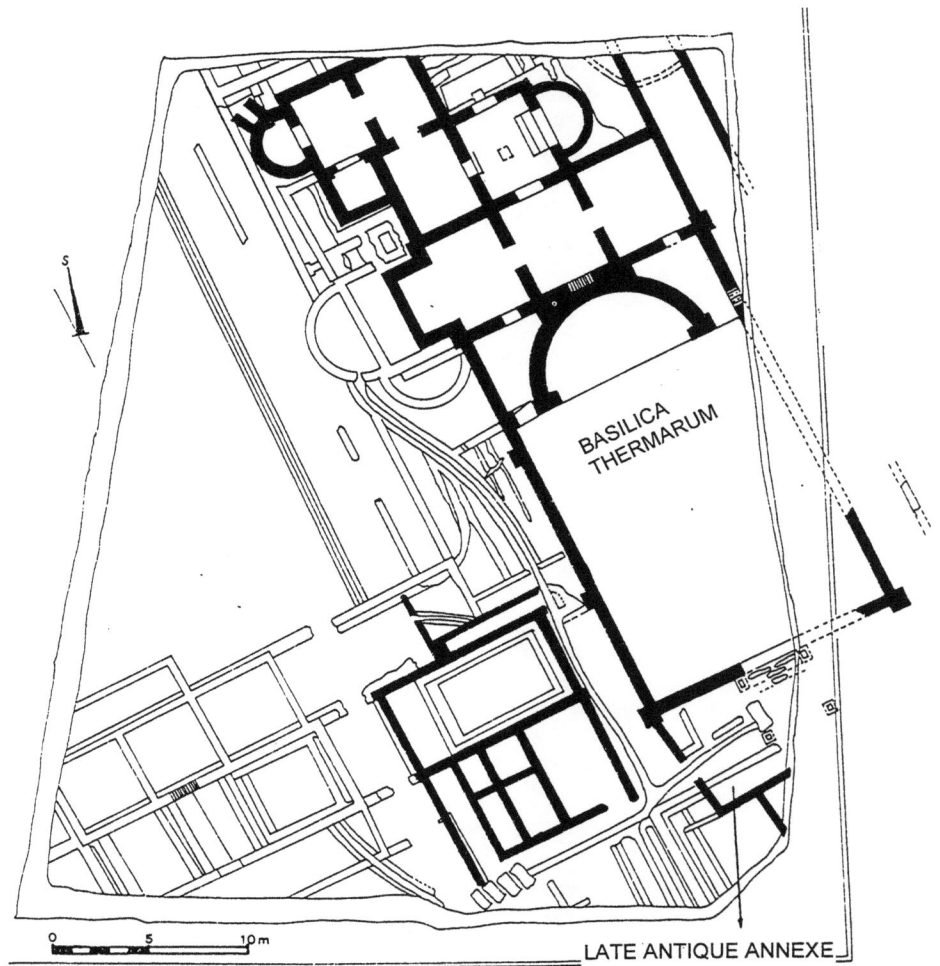

Figure 9: *Plan of the basilica at Aquae Iasae (Varaždinske Toplice) (after Vikić -Belančić 1978).*

and that a narthex-like ancillary room was attached to its southern facade on the same occasion (Gorenc - Vikić 1979: 43; Migotti 1994: 195). It should be noted that among existing structures likely to be converted into places of Christian worship, thermal constructions are apparently frequent (Zellinger 1928; Stommel 1959a; Krautheimer 1963: 8; Vaes 1989: 301). The conversion at Aquae Iasae is further attested by a fragment of a ceiling fresco featuring the head and part of the bust of a bearded saint with an aureole (II.8.), found on the floor in the middle of the main basilical hall. Scanty remains of another fresco are still traceable *in situ* on the interior surface of the northern wall of the hypothesized narthex. A St Andrew's cross painted in red on a background of yellow-greenish nuances (II.9.) is all that remains of the former geometrically-stylized compositional scheme arranged in the form of a network of saltires, representing the fence of paradise. Both these frescos were taken as a singular proof for the Christianization of the building in the 2nd half of the 4th century (Vikić-Belančić 1978: 590). Yet another possibility should, however, be considered, that already with the first Constantinian remodelling of the rectangular bath building into an apsed one its envisaged function was religious. A couple of arguments can be proposed in favour of this suggestion: First, in its plan, the Constantinian *basilica thermarum* resembles very much the type of the so-called hall or box-churches (either provided with interior apses or lacking them altogether), typical of early Christian architecture of various parts of the Empire, including the Alpine-Pannonian region which at that time was strongly influenced by the Church of Aquileia (Duval 1974: 358-360; Krautheimer 1963: 134;

Menis 1976). Addmitedly with the Aquileian type of the box-church a detached clergy bench is more common than the real apse, but it is equally true that liturgical-stylistical conceptions underlying the function of both these versions are akin. There is yet another argument - art-historical, relating to the foregoing frescos - to back the case for a Constantinian church at Aquae Iasae. The one in the narthex is quite plain and completely schematized, fitting thus possibly into the framework of the style of painting as typical of the end of the 4th century (see II.9.). Contrarily, the fresco with the depiction of a saint is a work of much higher quality and skill, and is presumably reminiscent of one of the artistic trends of the Constantian period, defined as the fine or the classical style (see II.8.). In brief, a possibility cannot be excluded of the existence of a Christian church at Varaždinske Toplice as early as the first half of the 4th century and its subsequent renovation and partial reconstruction at the end of the century. At the same time contemporary existence of pagan temples and a Christian church should not be inconceivable, given both the Constantinian period, syncretistic in terms of religion, and the cosmopolitan air of Aquae Iasae.

Systematic investigations of the Roman town of Aquae Iasae carried out over a long time-span (1953-1982) have established its continuing settlement from the 1st century to the end of the 4th. With this in mind, both the scarcity of small finds on the whole and the complete lack of movable Christian artefacts remain unexplained. An artefact with a possible Christian connotation was, however, found in a 3rd century layer in the area of the later narthex and was reconstructed as a belt made of eight individual scrolled bronze letters, put together to form a word *Teofialae*. The object was only mentioned without being properly published (Vikić-Belančić - Gorenc 1970: 132), but the word obviously relates to the name Teofila in the genitive, meaning 'belonging to Teofila'. The name is by no means conclusive Christian evidence; yet theophoric names of this kind are attributable to Christian rather than pagan attitudes (von Harnack 1915: 409-412; Kaufmann 1917: 36; Testini 1958: 370; contrary: Kajanto 1963: 61).

I.c. Upland Settlements with Christian Architecture

I.c.1. Ozalj (II)

Stari grad Ozalj (the Old Town of Ozalj) is a mediaeval castle on a high crag above the right bank of the river Kupa, built on the site of a late Roman castrum. Archaeological research has been going on there fairly regularly from 1991 onwards; during excavations parts of masonry of late Roman walls were found under the foundations and in the immediate vicinity of the romanesque church. A section of a hypocaust system was also discovered in addition to a number of small finds, two of which were Christian in terms of symbolism (V.a.3.; VI.d.5.). With this in mind the excavator rightly judged the late Roman walls as probably belonging to an early Christian building (Čučković 1992; Čučković 1994). As churches were commonly heated in the areas of the severe climate (Barton 1975: 64-65), the heating system should not be an obstacle to the proposition. Yet another possibility

should also be considered as an explanation for the hypocaust system - that a thermal structure was adapted into a church, as was often the case in early Christian building (Zellinger 1928; Stommel 1959a; Krautheimer 1963: 8; Vaes 1989: 301).

Under the foundations of the mediaeval fortifications, slight remains of late Roman walls were hypothetically envisaged, designating possibly the whole complex as a late Roman hillfort settlement with sacred architecture.

I.c.2. Čečavac - Rudina (III) (Fig. 10)

Two churches were unearthed and investigated during the 1980-1987 excavations at the mediaeval hillfort site Rudina above the village of Čečavac. On the eastern section of the plateau a larger (14 x 8 m) romanesque oriented monastery church with three projecting semicircular apses was found; at the western part of the site a smaller romanesque (12th century) aisleless chapel (9.5 x 6 m) with a projecting eastern apse was discovered (Fig. 10). Concomitantly a rather rich Roman layer was established at the site, containing building materials (bricks, tiles, dressed stones, marble), hypocaust remains, funerary stone slabs, glass, coinage etc. (Sokač-Štimac 1984; Sokač-Štimac 1989). An interesting proposal was consequently put forward for the chapel as originally an early Christian building, renovated and reconstructed in the Middle Ages (Klaić 1986: 42). The hypothesis passed virtually unremarked, but is worth reconsidering, the more so as a stone funerary slab (III.b.5.) from the site was recently

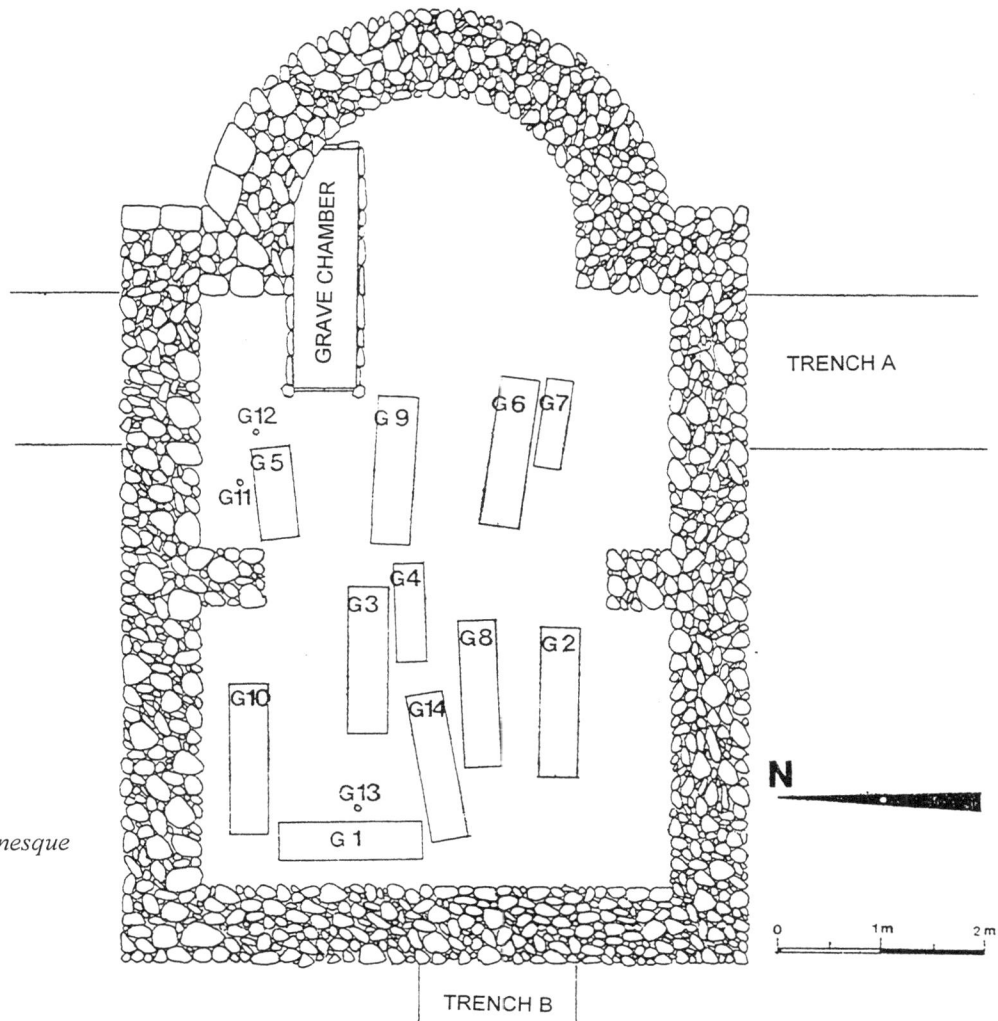

Figure 10: Plan of the Romanesque chapel at Čečavac (Rudina) (after Sokač-Štimac 1984).

recognized as most probably Christian (Migotti 1994: 202). The hypothesized Christian church from Rudina would then be attributable to a common type of early Christian hall architecture, characterized by a single-naved building with either one curved side or else provided with an apse narrower than the nave by exactly the width of the nave's walls (cf. Marucchi 1933, 257 ff.; Krautheimer 1963: 105, Fig. 39, 136, 146, Fig. 60; Chevalier 1995: Pls. 6:1; 8:1,2; 11:3 ff.). Parallels for mediaeval adaptations of early Christian churches in the neighbouring province of *Dalmatia* (Fisković 1995) come to mind in this context.

A coherent picture of the urbanism and architecture cannot obviously be drawn at this stage, with data far too scanty, fragmentary and inconclusive. It should not, however, be right to neglect the topic altogether; both the historical circumstances and documentary sources testify to the presence of early Christian buildings on south-Pannonian soil, at least in towns.

A number of urban and architectural features associated with Christian attitudes can be established in regard to both towns and the country. First, there is a surprising lack of architectural remains (and other early Christian finds for that matter) in the rural areas, especially in villas, typical otherwise of northern Pannonia's 'rural urbanism' (Christie 1995: 304-305). The second concernes the situation in the westernmost section of northern Croatia, which in terms of natural and geographical conditions is closely related with the Alpine area of neighbouring Noricum (modern Slovenia). The entire early Christian landscape there is characterized by a series of upland settlements with prominent sacral architectural complexes (Ciglenečki 1987). The only site so far known in the sub-Alpine area of northern Croatia featuring a very similar configuration is Ozalj; another one - Čečavac (Rudina), possibly akin to them - is located in the hilly area of central northern Croatia. The presence of late-Roman hillfort settlements in southern Pannonia can possibly be related to a historical document having that the emperor Justinian (527-565) bestowed upon the Longobards the fortresses of *Pannonia* (Degmedžić 1979: 98; Šašel 1992: 758; Christie 1995: 309). It is a general assumption that by *Pannonia* the province of *Pannonia Savia* was ment, to which both north-Croatian sites in question - Ozalj and Rudina - belong.

As for towns, a specific urban feature has been observed concerning the restructuring of their lay-outs in terms of modifications in the orientation of the urban fabric. Such features are fairly well documented at Sisak (see I.a.3) and Ludbreg (see I.a.4), and can convincingly be hypothesized as procedures associated with Christian surroundings. Modifications of the kind were further envisaged for the late Roman period at Mursa (Bulat 1989a: 21-22) and for several north-Pannonian towns (Póczy 1980: 249-250, 262), but this feature has neither been researched in detail nor commented upon.

The most controversial issue of this section is an analysis of early Christian church typology: we know of only one securely Christian church (Varaždinske Toplice) in the area. If a generally held assumption is accepted that the basilica at Aquae Iasae was first endowed with an apse at the beginning of the 4th century and remodelled into a Christian church

only in the second half of the century, it would typologically be insignificant. Contrarily, it is possible to assume that the addition of an interior apse to a formerly apseless building was a consequence of its adaptation for Christian use as early as the time of Constantine. In this case the basilica from Aquae Iasae would be attributable to an outstanding type of the so-called box-churches of early Christian architecture, typical of the Alpine-Pannonian and other regions (see I.b.1). Only chancel sections of other supposedly Christian churches are documented, which as a rule feature a semicircular eastern (Ludbreg: I.a.4; Sisak: I.a.3.; Čečavac - Rudina: I.c.2.) or western (Osijek: I.a.1.) projecting apse. The northern orientation of the basilica at Varaždinske Toplice has no such typological significance, its basic plan having been layed out prior to its reconstruction for Christian purposes. Hypothesized differences in the orientation of early Christian churches in northern Croatia are yet to be proved, as are their very existence and lay-outs. If actually they were oriented so differently, it would only fit happily with the ecclesiastical architectural thinking of the 4th century: the orientation of early Christian churches towards east was brought into effect only in the 5th century (Krautheimer 1963: 69; Menis 1976: 395).

Another detail of the basilica at Varaždinske Toplice - a subsequently added narthex - is potentially significant in terms of typology. According to the excavator's opinion (Vikić-Belančić 1978: 590-591) the adding of the narthex was contingent to the Christianization of the building in the second half of the 4th century. If, on the contrary, the basilica was Christianized under Constantine and reconstructed only later, a subsequent adding of the narthex would be exactly correspondent with an axiom of early Christian church architecture - that the narthex frequently postdates the essential core of the building (Ovadiah 1970: 199; Bovini 1974; 132; Chevalier 1995: 92).

A typological variety of south-Pannonian churches, if correctly hypothesized, would in principle correspond to a similar variety in the territory of northern Pannonia and in a measure to the early Christian architecture on the whole; with no hard and fast rule governing 4th century church architecture, solutions to similar situations were at times strikingly different (Krautheimer 1963: 42, 68; Gough 1973: 59-63). Yet extreme caution is required with northern-Pannonian parallels, given that Hungarian archaeology has not yet reached definite conclusions about seemingly quite rich remains of early Christian church architecture on northern-Pannonian soil. Data on this topic are quite often contradictory in the literature, while a few buildings, formerly considered to be Christian churches, are now viewed differently (Kádár 1969: 180-182; Thomas E B 1980a: 197; Hicke 1985: 165-166; Thomas E B 1987: 285; Tóth 1994: 247; Gáspár 1995: 116, 119).

Adaptations of churches in previous thermal complexes is an axiom of the early Christian architecture (Dumaine 1925; Zellinger 1928; Stommel 1959a; Krautheimer 1963: 8; Vaes 1989: 301); whether this is also true for northern Croatia, as at this stage seems likely (see I.a.4; I.b.1.; I.c.1.), has yet to be proved.

II Structural Church Members, Fittings and Decoration

II.1. Round stone table (mensa?) I

Provenance: Štrbinci (Certissa?); chance find of the mid 19th century.
Location: AMZ (366)
Description: Marble; 15 x 17 cm, thickness 3 cm. A fragment of a round table with a grooved border, broken in several pieces and restored. On the upper surface a chi-rho with expanded terminals and a hooked open rho-loop is rather clumsily carved. Of the two palm branches, one at each side of the device, the left one is barely visible.
Dating: 2nd half of the 4th century/1st half of the 5th century.
Literature: Brunšmid 1909: 102, n. 366; Vikić-Belančić 1978: 593-594, n. 7; Katalog: n. 114.
Commentary: This fragment, in addition to a few more inscribed stones, had for a long time been considered to derive from Osijek (Mursa) (Katalog: nos. 114-118). All of them were donated to AMZ in the mid 19th century by a higher priest Pavić from Đakovo, some 60 kilometres south of Osijek. While the early Christian bishopric in Mursa was a famous historical fact for the local public, hardly anything was known at that time about the site of Štrbinci (most probably Roman Certissa) in the immediate vicinity of Đakovo. However, given the current knowledge of the site (Katalog: 155-163; Migotti 1997: 213), it is almost certain that the foregoing stone fragments, including nos. II.1., III.c.2. and III.c.5. here, donated to AMZ, had originally been found at Štrbinci.

The round shape of this object points to a circular altar table (mensa), but the lack of data on the context precludes any reliable suggestion about its precise function. It might have been placed above a grave or fixed on the wall of a grave chamber, serving thus either as a funerary banquet table or a real altar or else as a marker of the grave respectively. It could have further been used as an altar or an offering table in a church (Barb 1964; Hicke 1985: 148-160; Salona I: Pls.

33-40). Whatever the case, an architectural setting was still the most probable context for this object.

Its symbolic device - a chi-rho surrounded by two palm branches - is by far the most frequent means of decoration on early Christian epigraphic and artistic monuments, especially funerary. The chi-rho (a blend of Greek letters X/chi/ and P /rho/, representing Christ's abbreviated name) appears in Christian iconography for the first time on a medallion of Constantine in 315, soon to spread to various objects and in different media (coinage, gravestones, small objects etc.). Its popularity was overwhelming during the 4th century, eventually to diminish in the 5th and later centuries when it was replaced by the cross. This, however, is not an absolute and unviolable sequential scheme, the chi-rho appearing frequently as late as the 6th century and at times alternately with crosses. The most profound symbolic association of this motif is obviously religious, but a magic-apotropaic afterthought is not to be overlooked either (Garrucci 1879, Tav. 337:3; Marucchi 1906: 166-167; Kaufmann 1913: 537-645; Leclercq 1948; Leoni 1950: 966; Vogt 1957: 321-327; Sauer J 1958; Testini 1958: 354-356; Salin 1959: 345, Fig. 142; Fasola 1961: 249, Fig. 7; Huskinson 1974: 77; Arrhenius 1986: 129, Abb. 1). An open rho loop of the chi-rho has sometimes been attributed to oriental influences or stimuli. This speculation should not, however, be very committing, as items with both variants of the device in question appear within a joint context, or even on a single object (Leclercq 1948; Briesenick 1964: 110-111, 173; Kempt - Reusch 1965: nos. 6, 10, 12 ff.; Arrhenius 1986: 137-138; Higgins 1987: 113-116; Mawer 1995: 132-133). On the other hand, it does appear that in terms of a relative chronology the open rho loop is later than the closed one, dating preferably to the end of the 4th century and the first half of the 5th (Leclercq 1948: 1509; Mawer 1995: 71).

II.2. Stone vessel (III)

Provenance: Daruvar (Aquae Balissae); a donation of the management of the Thermal Baths at Daruvar to the Municipal Museum in Bjelovar (midway between Daruvar and Zagreb, somewhat more northerly) in the 1950s.
Location: GMB

Description: Yellowish limestone; height 40 cm, base diam. 50 cm, rim diam. 38.5 cm. A reciptacle in the form of a cylindrical vessel with a threefold profiled rim, lid missing. Outer surface of vessel between upper and lower borders is like a carpet filled all over with various low-relief motifs, rendered by way of flat carving. The upper border features a row of stylized trefoils with pointed leaves, while the lower one bears a motiv reminiscent of a barred chain. In the field in between four pairs of in-turned animals confronting a central element are depicted, twice doves and once peacocks drinking from a deep bowl or chalice, and also a pair of rabbits propped up against a stylized plant with leafy tip. Vessels are all decorated with stylized acanthus leaves; branches and water are springing from the one placed between the peacocks.

Dating: 6th/7th centuries(?)

Literature: Katalog: 112-113, n. 145; Migotti 1994: 195-196.

Provenance: See II.2.

Location: GMB

Description: Yellowish limestone; column height 71.5 cm, column width 20 cm, column diam. 23.5 cm, base width 34.7 cm. Column composed of four equal segments and accordingly four-lobed in section. Two of them were hewn from a single stone block; the remainder were individually worked and joined together with others to form a whole. The top and bottom surfaces of the shaft are both provided with a depression, intended for attaching the base and capital (now missing) to the shaft. The entire surface is covered with an arabesque-like recurrent motif of a plant with fanned pointed leaves and floral calyces, reminiscent of grape bunches. A cushion-like four-leafed base bears decoration in the form of stylized acanthus leaves.

Dating: 6th/7th centuries(?)

Literature: Katalog: 112, n. 146; Migotti 1994: 196.

Commentary on II.2. and II.3.: These two objects were included with much reservation; the essential data on the archaeological context and circumstances of the finds is missing, while their function and dating remain equally dubious and disputed. Although they have never been discussed in literature at any length, opinions on their chronology expressed by personal communications are manifold and quite contradictory: from the early Byzantine period through the Middle Ages up to the present, including afterthoughts of a neo-style or even modern forgery. This commentary should therefore be understood not only as an attempt at an analysis of two potentially early Christian objects, but also as a means of bringing attention to difficulties and hesitances awaiting the researcher of early Christianity in northern Croatia.

The precise find spot at Daruvar or its area is unknown. It is worthy of note in the present context that Daruvar - the Roman Aquae Balissae - is an almost entirely unresearched area despite a few very important and occasionally also very luxurious chance finds from the past. In any event they indicate an exceptional archaeological site with the tradition of a thermal establishment from antiquity up to the present (Szabó 1934; Mócsy 1968). Owing to its location in the bordering region between two *Pannonias, Savia* and *Secunda*, the Daruvar area was also quite important politically in the late Roman period. In the 6th and 7th centuries the Goths and Longobards respectively are supposed to have held strongholds in the area (Degmedžić 1979; Šašel 1992; Christie 1995: 309). Since by that time both peoples were Christianized, adhering mostly to the Arian creed (Thompson 1963; Menghin 1985: 143-188; Pavan 1991: 493 ff.; Giustechi Conti 1994: 146; Christie 1995: 307-310), Christian buildings in their use should plausibly be envisaged in the area.

While the function and use of these objects cannot be established securely, a suggestion for a baptismal font and a column of a baldachin construction or an altar railing appears sufficiently convincing at this stage. This hypothesis is mostly substantiated by the symbolic associations of the pairs of antithetic animals next to a vessel (the font of life) or a tree (the tree of life) essential to baptismal icongraphy (Haberl 1958: 227 ff.; Daniélou 1966: 54-75; Neiman 1969: 116; Velmans 1969; Forstner 1982: 69-73, 149-154). Most significant for a baptismal context are doves (Garrucci 1880: 6, Tav. 406: 12; Salin 1952: 149-151; Klauser 1958: 22; Eizenhöfer 1960: 53-55; Grabar 1968: 122; Gough 1973: 97, Fig. 82; Quacquarelli 1978: 405-406; Forstner 1982: 240-243;) and peacocks (Garrucci 1880: 6, Tav. 406:8; Leclercq 1937a; Salin 1952: 149-151; Haberl 1958: 222-247; Gough 1973: 97, Fig. 82; Bargebuhr 1991: 89; Mawer 1995: 60, passim), while in early Christian iconography hares are somewhat less familiar (Garrucci 1880: 6, Tav. 406:7; Kondić - Popović 1977: 35, Fig. 17; Forstner 1982: 260-261).

While the presumed function of the objects in question is still disputed, both their dating and cultural affiliation remain even more debatable. The motifs and figures depicted on them are deeply rooted in the classical and early Christian repertoire, but the manner and style of execution (accumulation of scenes and carpet-like covering of surfaces in the manner of the so-called *horror vacui*, choice of unusual ornamental shapes like a barred-chain or curious plant motifs, deep bowls instead of a cantahros, naturalistically-depicted animals, deep flat carving, unequal quality of rendering in individual details, etc.) are rather suggestive of the early mediaeval period and the so-called barbarian antiquity (Salin 1959: 442-471; Hubert 1964; Arbeiter 1994: 328-335). The shape of both these objects further point (although not unquestionably) to the early medieval period: four-lobed columns are typical of medieval periods, but in a more monumental appearance. They have, however, sporadically been disovered on Roman and early

Christian sites (Sanquer 1977: 345, Fig. 6; Βοκοτοπουλος 1980: 152, T. 94a). Likewise a carpet-like covering with stylized plant motifs is basically a well-known stylistic approach to the decoration of early Christian church equipment and structural elements (Volbach 1958: 59, Fig. 80). As for the vessel, early Christian baptismal fonts were as a rule dug into the ground, but movable receptacles of various dimensions were also in use (Leclercq 1925: 395-396; Leclercq 1925b: 1223-1226, Fig. 1693; Khatchatrian 1962: 121, Fig. 204; Török 1975a; Wharton 1992; see also II.4.).

In short, I know of no immediate convincing analogies from any period or place. Aproximate parallels that can tentatively be brought up are neither close nor complete. They concern individual details rather than the whole, and are in any case a little forced. It appears accordingly that the objects in question might possibly be unique specimens announcing a transition to mediaeval forms of liturgical fittings; but almost any interpretation is possible and they require further investigation.

II.4. Stone vessel with handles (III)

Provenance: Sisak (Siscia); chance find of the 19th century.
Location: AMZ (685)
Description: White marble; rim diam. 53 cm, height 30 cm. A vessel in the shape of a deep bowl hemispherical internally and conical externally. Along the rim four lug-like oval handels are symmetrically arranged, one of them provided with a groove for pouring out of water.
Dating: 3rd to 7th centuries.
Literature Brunšmid 1911: 102, n. 685; Katalog: 82-83, n. 41.
Commentary: This type of vessel is frequently found on pre-Christian and early Christian sites and is usually termed mortar (*mortarium*). In the former cases it was used variously either in secular (domestic and industrial) surroundings or else in temples, serving probably as a liturgical furnishing (Egger 1963; Török 1975: 120-122; Minguzzi 1983: 178; Sauer E 1996: 25). When discovered at early Christian sites it is preferably interpreted as either a transportable baptismal font or else a vessel for blessed water (Leclercq 1925c: 766, Fig. 1502; Brøndsted 1928: 98, Fig. 93; Ferrua 1963: 183, Fig. 7). It should be noted that portable fonts of various materials and sizes, used alternately with fixed ones, are common in early Christian practices throughout the Christian world (Watts 1988: 216; Mawer 1995: 12, 20); it is obvious then that marble vessels with four

handles passed over from pagan to Christian use. Their precise function can be established only within a familiar archaeological context, not generally. In addition to the specimen from Sisak, a few such vessels are known from MSO, yet data about their possible relation with early Christian surroundings is missing (Katalog: 104, nos. 119a, b; Migotti 1994: 196-197).

Note on the entries II.5, II.6. and II.7.

All of them were found at the site of Kamenica, a hypothetical early Christian memorial-cemeterial complex of Cibalae (cf. I.a.2.). They are accordingly classified in the category II, regardless of the lack of any specific Christian devices applied.

II.5. Fragment of capital (II)

Provenance: Vinkovci (Cibalae); site of Kamenica; chance find during ploughing at the end of the 19th century.
Location: AMZ (526)
Description: White marble; diam. 41 cm, height 14 cm. A lower section of a capital decorated with a single row of eight flat and fleshy tongue-like leaves, bending slightly outwords. Battered are leaves' tips and underside of base, provided with a recess to fit the column shaft.
Dating: 4th/5th centuries.
Literature: Brunšmid 1911: 65, n. 526; Katalog: 100, n. 102.
Commentary: This type of capital is familiar in classical architecture from as early as the 1st/2nd centuries (Kiss 1960: 213, fig. 1; Buršić-Matijašić 1985: 69-74, T. 12) and is retained in late Roman and early Christian surroundings of the 3rd and 4th centuries. The early Christian building at Kamenica was erected on the site of the former Roman villa (Dimitrijević 1979: 249); accordingly the capital could have belonged to a layer of the pre-Christian profane architecture. When once in Christian use, both its fabric and size point to a monumental Christian basilica, rather than a minor mausoleum. The hypothesis about a small mausoleum at Kamenica apparently resulted from the commentators' overlooking the previous find of the large capital.

II.6. (a-c) Fragments of transennas (II)

Provenance: Vinkovci (Cibalae); site Kamenica; trial excavation in 1968.
Location: GMV (3124)
Description: White marble; a) 18.2 x 14.5 cm; b) 9.8 x 6 cm; c) 9.5 x 4.7 cm, average thickness 2-4 cm. Three fragments (two of them fitting together) of an openwork transenna in the form of overlapping arcs reminiscent of fish scales, with the middle of outer surfaces grooved.
Dating: 4th/5th centuries.
Literature: Katalog: 100, nos. 103 a-c.
Commentary: Finds like these are extremely abundant on early Christian sites throughout the Roman world from the 4th to the 6th century. Without a precise archaeological context it is virtually impossible to tell a window transenna from one belonging to an altar screen or a railing. With the ubiquitous frequent occurrence of such fittings in mind I am adducing here parallels from neighbouring areas only (Kempt - Reusch 1965: 19-20, n. 4; Fülep 1984: 279, Pl. 5:5; Knific - Sagadin 1991: 56, n. 18; Salona I: 61-62, Pl. 17: III.d.1, 3).

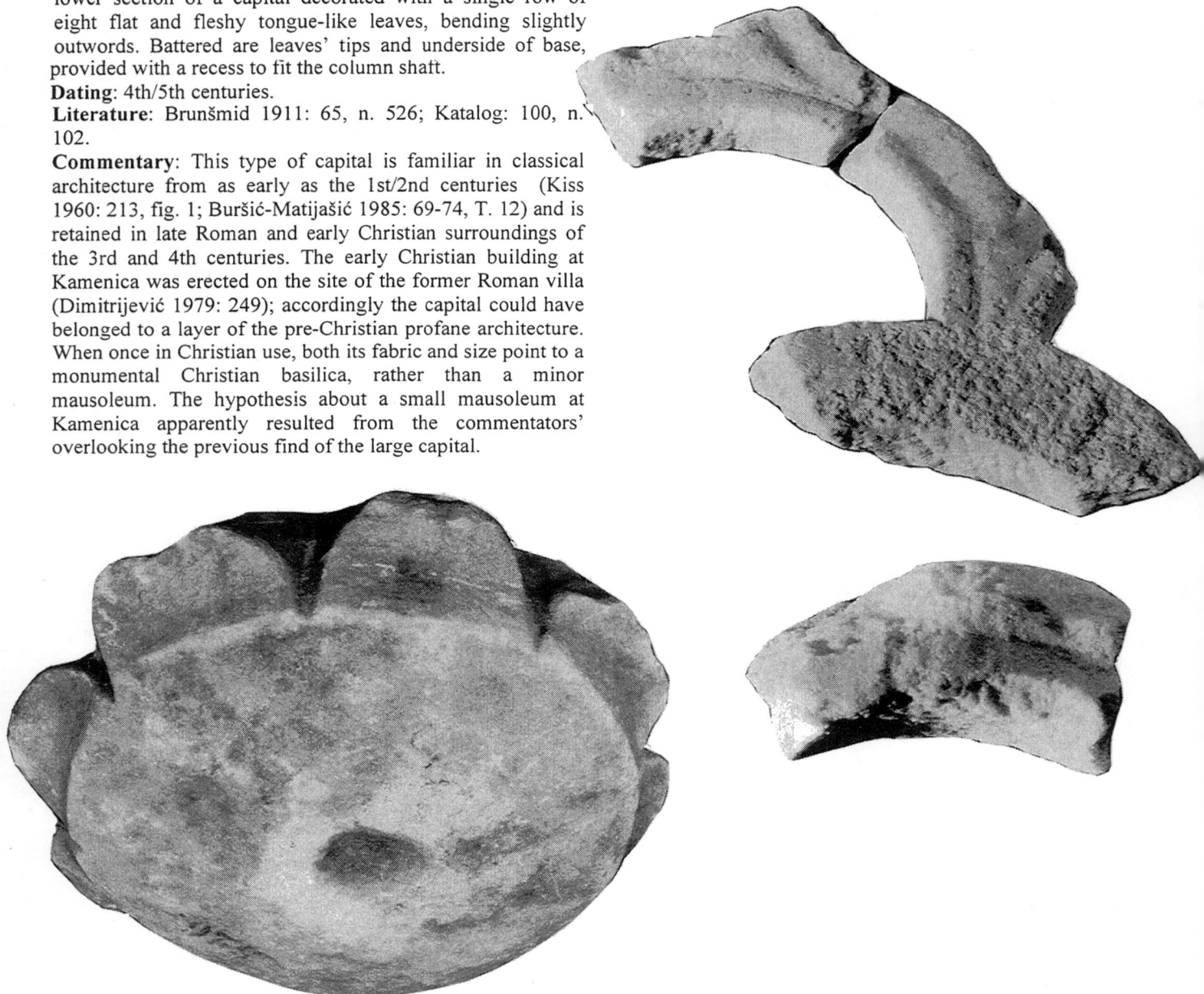

II.7. (a-f) Fragments of revetment stone slabs (II)

Provenance: Vinkovci (Cibalae); site of Kamenica; small-scale trial excavation in 1968.
Location: GMV (3125)
Description: a) Green stone; 16.4 x 6.2 cm, thickness 2.5 cm; b) Whitish stone streaked with brown and grey; 15.8 x 12 cm, thickness 3.2 cm; c) Reddish-ochre stone of various nuances; 14 x 13 cm, thickness 2.1 cm; d) Ochre stone with darkish flecks; 10.2 x 9.7 cm, thickness 2.2 cm; e) Cinnabar stone with darkish flecks; 10.4 x 5.3 cm, thickness 2.4 cm; f) Whitish stone with darkish veins; 9 x 6 cm, thickness 2.9 cm.
Dating: 4th/5th centuries.
Literature: Katalog: 100, nos. 104 a-f.
Commentary: Although these stone slabs have not been subjected to geological-chemical analyses, their colours and hardness qualify them as marbles, at least in the broader sense of the term. Facing of wall surfaces with marble slabs was a very early and widespread fashion in classical times, and one that was cherished even more lavishly in early Christian architecture; this is only natural considering the much greater consideration given to interiors of Christian churches than to their exteriors (Krautheimer 1963: 20; Barkóczi 1965: 236, T. 28:7; Terry 1986; Mainstone 1988: 45, 71; Ward-Perkins 1994: 117, 430).

II.8. Fragment of a ceiling fresco (I)

Provenance: Varaždinske Toplice (Aquae Iasae); systematic excavations 1956-1959; found in the middle of the main basilical hall of the thermal complex in the fill of material from the collapsed walls and ceiling.
Location: AMZ
Description: Plaster with groove-like imprints of reed logs on the back; 43.5 x 26.7 cm, thickness 3.5 cm. The surface layer of plaster was severely deteriorated and cracked, rendering vague the outlines of the depiction. A frontal draped bust with nimbate head of an elderly man in part profile with a beard, moustaches and curled hair is nevertheless discernible; the head with an intense facial expression, belonging apparently to a saint, is slightly bent towards right and down. The upper section of the fresco is dark reddish, as are are saint's face and garments, only the latter are slightly lighter and pale. Hair and beard are rendered in a mixture of grey, brown and greenish nuances, while the nimbus with a section of the background around it is pale yellow. The actual faded nuances must have originally been at least slightly, if not even markedly, brighter. Most affected by damage is the area of eyes, which in any event appear to be less expressively rendered than the mouth; the lips, slightly curved downwards at edges, produce a melancholic or, rather, pathetic expression on this noble and resigned saintly face.
Dating: 4th century.
Literature: Vikić-Belančić 1978: 590-591, Fig. 3; Katalog: 11o, n. 140.

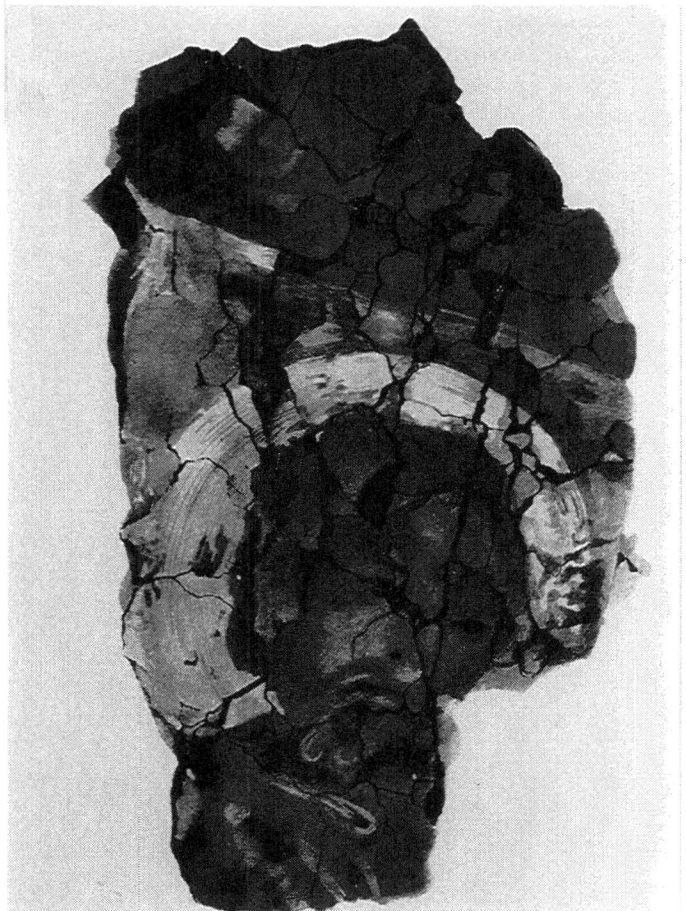

Watercolour by Slavko Šohaj made in imitation of the original fresco from Aquae Iasae (Varaždinske Toplice).

Commentary: Bands of yellow and red behind and above saint's had testify to the placement within a geometrical frame rather than an architectonic or a landscape surrounding. A bust or even a whole figure of a saint might have been depicted in a rectangular panel on the ceiling either as a single figure or as a central one among several. The former hypothesis is much more plausible in the light of the lack of any additional remains on the spot of frescos with human figures. On the other hand, the saint's head, slightly bent down, could be suggestive of his paying attention to another figure in his immediate vicinity. A similar ambiguity attaches to the question of whether a bust or a full figure is depicted. Both hypothesized variants are well-known in early Christian iconography and it would be next to futile, given the lack of data, to make attempts at visualizing the whole of this singular piece of art. The plaster was interpreted as a ceiling fresco, probably on account of its find spot roughly in the middle of the room.

The fresco was dated by the excavator to the second half of the 4th century and related consequently to the conversion of the thermal basilica into a Christian church (Vikić-Belančić 1978: 590). Very complex and complicated archaeological stratification of the site should, however, be borne in mind when considering the fresco in question. Such circumstances, in addition to the scarcity of small finds, render the establishing of a precise chronology and stages of the Christianization of Aquae Iasae next to impossible. If now we consider the possibility of the basilica becoming a Christian church already in the time of Constantine (see I.b.1.), the fresco with the depiction of a saint should preferably belong to this initial stage; the next phase should in this case be represented by the addition of a narthex to the basilica. The former interpretation can tentatively be reinforced by the style of a fresco from the narthex (II.9.), executed in the entirely simplified and stylized manner and therefore possibly later than the ceiling fresco, itself distinguished for the exceptionally high qualitiy of both its execution and style. Although any such estimations are tantalizingly dubious for reason of the lack of the additional diagnostic evidence, the ceiling fresco from Aquae Iasae is possibly attributable to a trend in Constantinian painting, characterized by a preference for dark nuances and melancholic expressions on human faces, and above all by a return to the classical values of beauty in portraits (Dorigo 1966: 124-129). Such revivals in art are recurrent (and therefore perplexing in terms of chronology) throughout the Roman and later periods, one being attested also in the second half of the 4th century, known as the Theodosian renaissance (Dorigo 1966: 227-229; Gough 1973: 107, passim). The most serious handicap in this respect is the lack of immediate parallels within the whole of Roman Pannonia. True, early Christian painting in northern Pannonia (Hungary) is much better researched in comparison with the Croatian section of the province, but comprises mostly funerary settings at the expense of congregational churches (Migotti 1997). Although, then, the chronological, stylistic and cultural appurtenances of the fresco from Varaždinske Toplice remain basically unresolved, one inference can at least be drawn with some degree of certainty: it is highly probable that such a singular high quality painting was executed, especially if this occurred under Constantine, either by a travelling artist coming preferably from Rome or Aquileia, or under his auspices, as was sometimes conjectured for distinguished paintings in northern Pannonia (Kádár 1969: 186).

II.9. Wall fresco (I)

Provenance: Varaždinske Toplice (Aquae Iasae); systematic excavation of the basilical area in 1956-1959.
Location: Faintly visible in situ on the interior surface of the northern narthex wall.
Description: Wall plaster; 35 x 40 cm (total surface of the motif), 36 x 28 cm (saltire cross). A section of fresco bearing a motif of a saltire cross in the form of two obliquely crossed red lines on a background of pale yellow with greenish nuances.
Dating: 2nd half of the 4th century.
Literature: Vikić - Belančić 1978: 590; Katalog: 110, n. 141.

Commentary: The extant saltire was obviously part of an original continuing the motif of lattice rails, which in terms of early Christian iconography is an established convention for the paradisiac fence as pars pro toto of paradise itself. It is a very common motif in early Christian painting, typical in the main of funerary surroundings, although not unfamiliar in churches either (Migotti 1997: 215). It was agreed that the narthex-like room was added to the basilica subsequently, possibly after its having already been in Christian use for a while (see I.b.1.). If this happened in the second half of the 4th century as could reasonably be supposed, it would chronologically be quite compatible with the artistic style of the fresco as rendered by means of unassuming schematic outlines. Basically the fresco is attributable to the so-called green and red linear style typical of 3rd century early Christian painting, but revived in the 2nd half of the 4th century in mainly provincial areas (Dorigo 1966: 227).

III. Funerary Constructions and Furnishings

III.a. Graves

III.a.1. Frescoed grave vault (I)

Provenance: Štrbinci (Certissa?); chance find during excavation of military trenches in 1991; grave was destroyed but fresco survived.
Location: MĐĐ (fresco and grave finds).
Description: A grave in the shape of a chamber with pitched roof (measurements were not taken). Both the walls and floor were constructed of tiles bedded with mortar; the interior was white-washed. Remains of a female skeleton were dislocated as a consequence of plundering in antiquity; all that survived of once apparently rich grave goods are bronze fittings from a jewellery casket, glass-paste and gold beads from a necklace, a pewter ring and a bronze bracelet with terminals in the form of snake's head and tail. The grave was oriented east-west (with head to west, 'looking' towards right), and the inner surface of the eastern gable was frescoed.

The fresco was evacuated to MĐĐ in a fairly damaged state, and was restored in AMZ in a way to permit a nearly complete reconstruction of the figural motif. On a background of pale ochre plaster a drawing was delineated in faded tones of red and brown, with faint traces of the original bright red colour, transpiring in places. A central triangular field is occupied by the well-known early Christian motif of two peacocks next to a vase, enclosed within a cross-hatched framing band featuring occasional dots in the interstices of crossed lines. Peacocks are rendered extremely coarsely and schematically: but for the three conventional feathers and large dotted tails, they look more like quadruped with pointed heads, than birds. The cantharos is unproportionately tiny, with its full shape actually marred by damage to the corresponding area of the fresco's surface. In the triangular field above the peacocks' heads a chi-rho is depicted clumsily, accompanied by two sun discs with wavy rays and two six-pointed stars below them. A rough linear schematization in the manner of the so-called *horror vacui* is apparently the most prominent stylistic element of this piece of early Christian art.

Dating: 3rd quarter of the 4th century.

Literature: Katalog: 117, n. 158, 159: a-e; Gregl 1994; Migotti 1997.

Commentary: The figural motif depicted on the fresco is imbued with the symbolism of death and resurrection in each individual element as well as in its entirety. While a detailed analysis of the fresco was given elsewhere (Migotti 1997), only sketchy outlines of its artistic and symbolic references are adduced here. The bordering cross-hatched band is a schematized paradisiac fence, standing for the allegory of paradise itself, while confronted peacocks feature a well-known Christian metaphor for resurrection and eternal life. A prominent encircled chi-rho symbolizes the essential core of Christian soteriology - victory of life over death through Christ's passion and crucifixion and the ultimate salvation of mankind (cf. II.1.). Christ's sacrifice opens the heavenly doors (latticed fence) to the faithful (peacocks) who, by drinking from the well of life (vase) become participants of eternity (astral bodies).

This fresco has so far been the single known specimen of early Christian funerary painting in northern Croatia. Basically it shares the same essential stylistic and iconographic features of the 3rd to 7th centuries early Christian artistic 'commonwealth' (*koine*). In terms of iconography, however, it displays some traces of singularity as compared with styles of northern Pannonia and the early Christian world in general. It should therefore be perceived as a piece of work of a local painter.

Coins found in graves in the immediate vicinity of the frescoed tomb enabled its very precise dating to the third quarter of the 4th century (Gregl 1994: 185). Exactly concordant with such a dating are some of the iconographic and stylistic details of the fresco, as well as the configuration of the tomb and the typological attributes of the grave finds (Migotti 1997).

Objects recovered from the tomb induce caution to the interpretation of religious affiliation of the deceased on the sole basis of grave goods. But for the fresco, the burial in question would on no accounts, as far as the remains of the goods are concerned, be declared Christian. The presence of a snake-like bracelet is no argument; the snake's attribute of wisdom with appeal also to Christians (cf. Mt 10: 16) is sometimes brought as a corroboration of its Christian symbolic appurtenance (Leclercq 1925f: 1121), but this should relate to only rare and specific instances.

The grave goods from the tomb in question bring into focus yet another essential issue of the late Roman/early Christian archaeology: poverty in grave goods. The tomb from Štrbinci was apparently a rich one: witness the gold beads among the remains of its looted contents. There are numerous references in the literature about possible religious motifs for the poverty of late Roman and early Christian burials (Salin 1952: 233-250; Burger 1966: 159-163; van Doorselaer 1967: 139-145; Lányi 1972: 141; Vágó - Bóna 1976: 150; Nikolajević 1984: 534-535; Schulze-Dörrlamm 1990: 345-348; Salway 1993: 503; Tóth 1994: 251). A fairly unanimous opinion transpires that contrary to luxury-inclined Barbarians, the autochthonous Roman populace gave up rich burials not only for reasons of actual povery but for religious considerations as well. There is also a chronological aspect to the question: in the 4th century, imbued with manifold syncretistic conceptions, rich Christian burials could be expected as a consequence of the fusion of elements of the earlier religion with the not yet finally standardized ways of the Christian church (cf. Mawer 1995: 87-88). However, a question of rich Christian Romano-barbarian burials in the 5th and 6th centuries still remains to be explained; hints of 3rd to 5th centuries rich burials of wealthier Christians are not infrequent in Christian literature (Leclercq 1922). Such procedures might tentatively be explained in terms of Christian religion which, while recomending the virtue of modesty, would not oblige the faithful to an absolute denial of their wealth. In a word, there are obviously not only chronological but also social, religious and ethnical aspects to this complex issue, and no general rule could reasonably be expected as the explanation for every single instance. In fact, each burial should be investigated individually and within its specific archaeological context.

III.a.2. Cross-like grave vault (I?)

Provenance: Štrbinci (Certissa?); rescue excavation in 1966.
Location: grave construction destroyed; grave goods in MĐĐ.

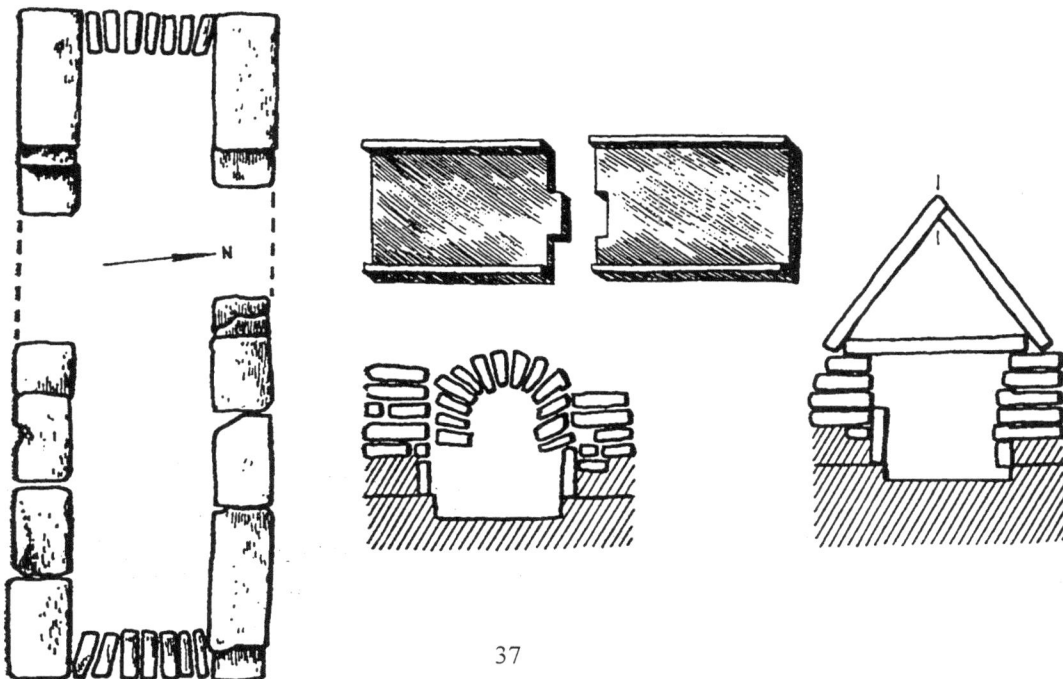

Description: Outer measurements: 210 x 90 cm, recorded height 70 cm; female skeleton aligned west-east (with head to west). Skeleton was placed in the bare ground with no construction save for a shallow pit (about 15 cm deep). Side walls and a barrel-vaulted roof were constructed of tiles measuring 60 x 40 x 3.5 cm. Two lateral niches added to the main oblong produce the grave plan in the shape of a Latin cross, slightly skewed through damage caused by the pressure of the earth from above. Grave goods were abundant: pottery and glass vessels, an iron knife, metal fittings from a jewellry box in addition to various items of jewellery, coinage.
Dating: after AD 320 (based on the most recent issue of Constantine, dated 320).
Literature: Raunig 1980: 151-154, 159, T. 1:3, 2:1-3, 6:8-9; Katalog: 57-58, Fig. 13, 116, n. 156.

III.a.3. Cross-like grave vault (I?)

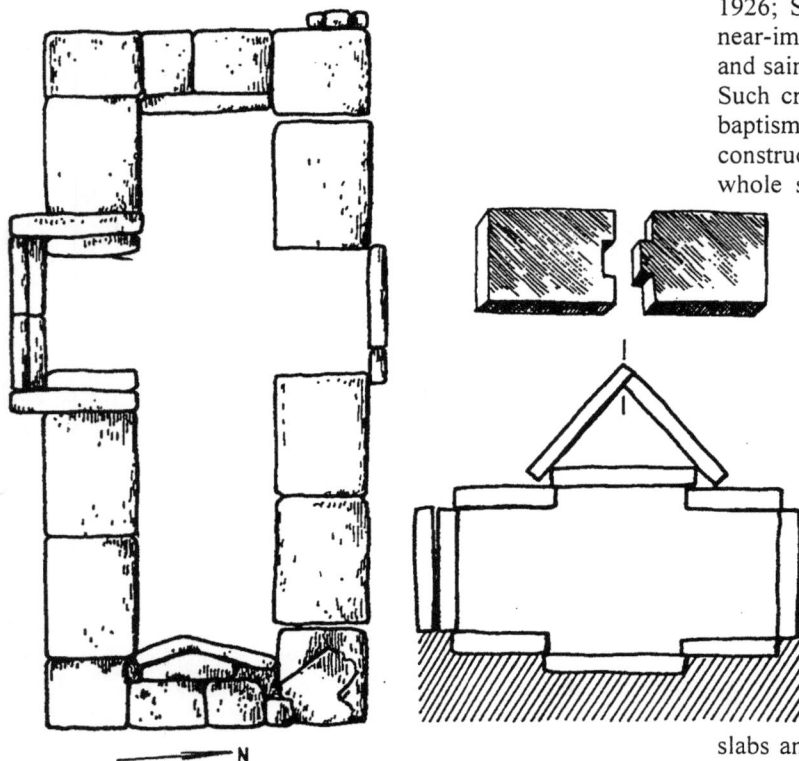

Provenance: See III.a.2.
Location: See III.a.2.
Description: Outer measurements: 220 x 100 cm, recorded height 65 cm; female skeleton aligned west-east (head to west). Much the same construction and shape as grave III.a.2., only roof is pinched instead of barrel-vaulted. Lateral niches are less disturbed, giving the tomb a more precise cross-like plan. Walls, roof and pavement are made of tiles measuring 40 x 30 x 5 cm. Grave goods are abundant, containing glass vessels, metal fittings, indeterminate iron objects, a bronze key, a mirror, a single playing dice, various items of jewellry, coinage.
Dating: After AD 328 (based on the most recent issues of Constantine, Licinius and Crispus, dated from 319 to 328).
Literature: Raunig 1980: 154-158, 159, T. 1:1-2, 2:4-5, 7:8-9; Katalog: 57-58, Fig. 13, 116, n. 157.
Commentary on III.a.2. and III.a.3. The two grave vaults were discovered in a small-scale rescue excavation at a distance of 50 cm from each other; there is no knowing whether these two were detached solitary occurrences or part of a larger cemetery. Having escaped looting in antiquity, they display a considerable wealth in goods, yet without any obvious Christian association. The graves were nevertheless designated as almost definitely Christian; a more plausible explanation for their cross-like plans is altogether missing. The side niches had apparently not been intended solely for grave goods; these were placed at various places within the graves. The W-E orientation with 'sight' of the deceased towards the east points (although not conclusively) to a conception of the Christian afterlife (Salin 1952: 189-192; Burger 1966: 162; van Doorselaer 1967: 83-84; Láyni 1972: 131-132; Forstner 1982: 98; Nikolajević 1984: 523; Salway 1993: 523).

Graves of this type are exceptional not only to Roman Pannonia, but to the Roman world in general. What parallels exist are rare, and are no more than approximations (St. 1926; Sennhauser 1978: 1527-1528, Fig. 8). Alternatively, near-immediate parallels can be found in crypts for martyrs' and saints' relics under the altars of early Christian churches. Such crypts are in turn similar to a type of early Christian baptismal font, while ranging in size from quite small pits to constructions of the shape and size of a grave intended for a whole skeleton (Brenk 1994: 36, Abb. 4; Chevalier 1996: 165-176, 441-443). The similarity of baptismal fonts and graves is only expected in view of the intermingling of associations of baptism and death in early Christian doctrine (Stommel 1959a: 14; Krautheimer 1963: 70; Watts 1988: 214; Wharton 1992: 319-320). A resurrection should therefore most probably be envisaged as the Christian conception underlying the shape of two graves from Štrbinci.

III.a.4. Brick and stone grave vault (I?)

Provenance: The Samobor area; chance find in 1952.
Location: Some of the tiles and stone slabs were reported to be in the museum at Samobor as late as 1993, but cannot be traced there.
Description: A grave constructed of dressed stone slabs and tile roofing. Floor was rendered in the shape of a stone 'bed' with a cushion-like terminal for head; a Latin cross was impressed with a finger-tip or a dull object in the plaster of the 'cushion' (height 20 cm). Roofing was constructed of three tiles measuring 60 x 60 x ? cm. They bore a simple linear decoration in addition to impressions in the form of dog's paws.
Dating: 4th/5th century.
Literature: Sudnik 1993.
Commentary: The grave was classified among the first-category Christian finds, which it should be according to the description; yet some doubts as to its authenticity arise from its being documented merely through a drawing and a very inadequate photograph of the find spot at the time of discovery. No traces exist today and accordingly no possibilities of a verification of either the context or individual sections of the find. Admittedly a stone 'cushioned-bed' figures unfamiliarly within the repertoire of the known shapes of late Roman graves in Pannonia; its configuration cannot be discerned from the photograph either. On the other hand, a relative abundance of late Roman

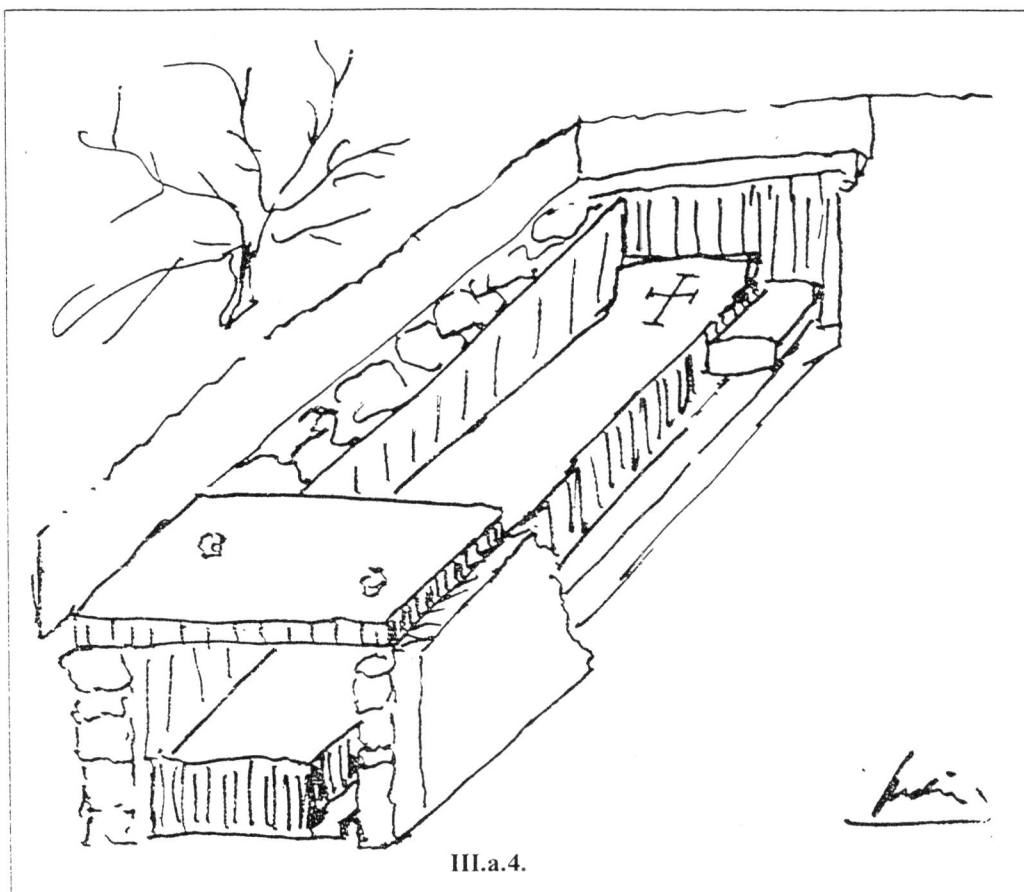

III.a.4.

sites in the area (Gregl 1993: 145; Migotti 1994: 197, note 110) reinforces the interpretation of the find as authentic.

Graves constructed with a combination of stones and tiles are less common in Pannonia than those made of bricks only, but are not entirely unfamiliar (Vágó - Bóna 1976: 142). This one was dated to the 4th century (Sudnik 1993: 493); its flat roofing points rather to the end of the 4th century or the first half of the 5th (cf. Salin 1959: 93, 104; Fülep 1984: 163, 171). The motif of the Latin cross is basically in line with such a dating. As an artistic device the cross was mentioned in the sources as early as the 2nd century. On the other hand, the cross clearly designed in terms of early Christian iconography occurs in its Greek or Latin form first on coins and later on various objects and materials from the 4th century; it gains its utmost popularity during the 5th and 6th centuries, pushing into the background the until then dominating symbolic device: the chi-rho (Marucchi 1903: 285, 529; Kaufmann 1913: 643; Dölger 1958, 1959; Salin 1959: 354-385; Dinkler 1962; Dölger 1963, 1964, 1966, 1967; Sutherland - Litt - Carson 1981: 143, passim; for the chi-rho see II.1.). This, however, is only a theoretical typological-chronological sequence with no absolute regularities implied; to confirm this statement instances may be adduced of occurrences of the chi-rho as late as the 6th century, and also of a cross and a chi-rho found in tandem on a single artefact (Kaufmann 1917: 329; Salin 1959: 345, Fig. 142, 35o, Fig. 145; Fasola 1961: 249, Fig. 7; Briesenick 1964, Pls. 20-33). On the other hand, early examples of the cross in the 3rd century on both funerary monuments and small objects should also be mentioned (Marucchi 1933: 224, Fig. 76; Testini 1958: 296, Fig. 106; Gough 1973: 25-26).

III.b Sarcophagi

Note

The epigraphic material in sections III.b and III.c had all been published previously, but is here given with considerable updating of commentary to meet the modern epigraphical standards; as the author is not qualified in epigraphy, this was carried out through the kind help of Dr. Ante Škegro. On the other hand, very few new expansions or corrections of readings have been attempted, and then have mostly been limited to pointing to out the over-enthusiastic previous readings. Such instances as exist are briefly discussed in commentaries, as are occasional controversial matters or unremarked details of texts if they relate to specific Christian issues.

III.b.1. Sarcophagus of Severilla (I)

Provenance: Sisak (Siscia); chance find of the 16th century in the SE section of town (Fig. 5: 3); donated to AMZ in 1871 by the Zagreb Kapitol.
Location AMZ (351)
Description: Greyish limestone; dimensions of box: 227 x 119 x 90 cm, of lid: 238 x 144 x 55 cm. Sarcophagus is cracked in places, but no part is missing. While pedestal to the box is now missing, extant is heavy gabled lid imitiating a tiled pitched roof with acroteria at its corners; only the sarcophagus's front bears decoration. In the centre is an inscription panel with two small trapezoidal handle-like projections at each side (*tabula ansata*), carrying the inscription. In each of the two *ansae* a chi-rho is roughly carved. Fields left and right of the inscription bear each a

39

motif of a vase with vine and grapes and wheat-ears springing from it; vines are looping around the entire free surface of the front. In the field left of the inscription panel, two birds are depicted perching among the vegetation, and in the lower section among vine tendrils a dog is shown chasing a rabbit. The motifs, filling the entire available space in the so called *horror vacui* manner, are rendered quite schematically in low relief; the same rough manner of execution applies to the inscription containing seven lines, the letters of the two or three last ones awkwardly squeezed. But for the quite spoiled lettering of the last section, a pretty elegant and skilfully executed late Roman *capitala actuaria* is employed. The inscription runs:

Huic arcae inest Seve-
rilla, famula Chri(sti), quae
vixit cum viro novem
continuis annis, cuius
post obitum Marcellianus se-
dem hanc videtur conlocasse meri-
tus.

(This is the chest of Severilla, a servant of Christ, who had lived with her husband for nine continuous years, and for whom after her death the obliged husband Marcellianus provided this resting place.)

Dating: 1st half of the 4th century.
Literature: CILL III: 3996; Brunšmid 1909: 159, n. 351; Vikić-Belančić 1978: 595-596; Katalog: 82, n. 39.
Commentary: The decorative conception of the front displays two different subject matters: pastoral scenery and inscription. The bucolic artistic motifs chosen here are in line with 4th century syncretism and are basically typical of Dionysiac and other mystery religions' iconography. They were also commonly employed in early Christian iconography, but with a new sense - that of peace and happiness in paradisiac surroundings - attached to them (Turcan 1966: 353, passim; Mócsy - Szentléleky 1971: 39-40, 65-73; Provoost 1978; Koch - Sichtermann 1982: 116 ff.; Engemann 1983; Kaiser-Minn 1983: 319; Provoost 1986; Bargebuhr 1991: 19-26; Kühnel 1994: 166-169). Of the bucolic motifs on the sarcophagus's front, particularly

significant is the one featuring a dog chasing a rabbit; it is not quite unfamiliar in early Christian iconography. In Christian contexts the dog and the rabbit depicted individually acquire various, at times contradictory symbolic connotations, pertaining to the spheres of either good or evil (Forstner 1982: 260-261, 266-268). The motif as displayed here probably conveys no deeper or more particular meaning than has usually been attached to the hunting scenes in early Christian surroundings: a struggle of good against evil and sin (see VI.d.8.).

Contrary to the overall basically 'neutral' artistic devices employed, some expressions from the inscription are more symptomatic of early Christian than pagan vocabulary, for instance *arca* and *obitus* (Kaufmann 1917: 40; Testini 1958: 441), while one of them - *famula Christi* - is explicitly so (Kaufmann 1917: 193, 209; Leclercq 1948a: 1758; Testini 1958: 382). Severilla's Christian religious affiliation is further revealed by a chi-rho at each side of the inscribed field (for the chi-rho see II.1.). The names Severilla and Marcellianus have no specific Christian associations. Severilla is common in Gallo-Illyrian regions, Pannonia included. Putative Christian connotations might be conveyed in the stem of the name Severilla, the adjective *severus* corresponding with Christian-like virtues of simplicity, seriousness and even asceticism, the more so as the name is very common among freedmen (Kajanto 1965: 69, 126-127). Marcellianus is a common late Roman name occurring frequently on pagan and Christian inscriptions (Kajanto 1965: 109). A Christian martyr of this name is also known in Rome (Delehaye 1912: 327, 363; Kaufmann 1917: 307).

With the bucolic and syncretistic contents of the pictorial decoration of the front in mind, the possibility cannot be excluded that the sarcophagus was adapted for Christian use at some later stage after its manufacture; this would imply a subsequent addition of both the inscription and chi-rhos (for a similar procedure concernig monogrammatic devices cf. Kaiser-Minn 1983: 320). Equally it is possible that the sarcophagus was originally made for a Christian still imbued with syncretistic religious feelings, typical of the 4th century religious cultures of the Empire.

III.b.2. Sarcophagus of Felicissima (I?)

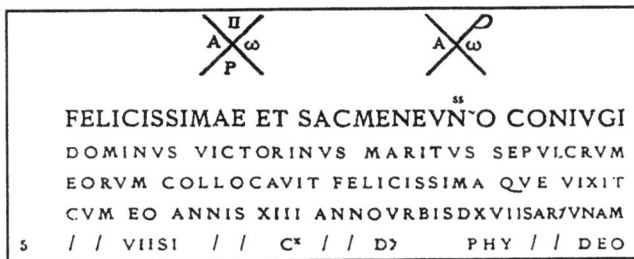

FELICISSIMAE ET SACMENEVŃ̈O CONIVGI
DOMINVS VICTORINVS MARITVS SEPVLCRVM
EORVM COLLOCAVIT FELICISSIMA QVE VIXIT
CVM EO ANNIS XIII ANNOVRBISDXVIISARJVNAM
5 / / VIISI / / Cˣ / / D⁊   PHY / / DEO

Provenance: Sisak (Siscia); chance find in the SE section of town (Fig. 5: 3) prior to 1830 (a datum based on a letter from a correspondent to Theodor Mommsen, witness CIL).

Location: Since lost sight of, with no clues as to its location.

Description: Data on the stone type, measurements and general configuration and appearance of sarcophagus are missing; it had never been published otherwise than in the CIL. Above the five-line front inscription two unusually composed signs were depicted. The left one is basically a saltire cross with an alfa and omega in the horizontal interstices; while the lower interstice bears the letter P, it is not discernible from the CIL copy whether the sign in the upper one is a Π (the Greek P), or just two vertical strokes (II) standing for the Roman numeral 2. The sign on the right side is an oblique rho-cross (monogrammatic cross) accompanied also by an alfa and omega. If copied correctly, the first four lines of the inscription run (only the word Deo is discernible on the fifth line):

Felicissimae et Sacmeneuno coniugi
dominus Victorinus maritus sepulchrum
eorum collocavit. Felicissima quae vixit
cum eo annis XIII, anno Urbis DXVII SARV unam
⁵*[--]VIISI[--]CX[--]D PHY[--]Deo*
(To his wife Felicissima, with whom he had lived for 13 years, and to Sacmenunus, sir Victor commissioned this sepulchre ...)

Dating: second half of the 4th/5th centuries.

Literature: CIL III: 3996a; Migotti 1994: 200, Fig. 3.

Commentary: The question-mark by the category denominator concerns the lack of any uncontestable documentation for this monument, with text from the CIL remaining the only clue; it had obviously never been photographed and is not available for inspection any more. The inscription contains five lines of text covering a greater portion of the front. While the meaning of the first three lines is fairly clear, the fourth one conveys partly unintelligible data on the time of setting up the sepulchre. Contrarily, it is virtually impossible to reconstruct the fifth line at any level, but for the word Deo. The essential core of the inscription clearly conveys the fact that sir Victorinus commissioned a sarcophagus for his late wife Felicissima, after having shared 13 years of matrimony with her. Although the term *dominus* was often attached to church dignitaries and martyrs, sir Victorinus here was most probably a secular dignitary (cf. Delehaye 1912: 17; Leclercq 1921; Kajanto 1965: 96; Mócsy - Szentléleky 1971: 117, n. 161). The name Victorinus occurs quite frequently among pagans all over the Empire, including Pannonia; it has been attested there as early as the 2nd/3rd centuries and mostly among high-ranking military and municipal magistrates (Alföldi 1969: 327; Bratož 1986: 279). The name bears a general emotional connotation on parents' wishes for their descendants to be victorious in whatever they do or experience (Kajanto 1965: 71-71, 98, 278). In Christian interpretation this wish acquires specific overtones bearing on the Christian victory over death and evil. As a result, the name was very common among Christians, who might also have been attracted to it through connotations towards martyrs named Victor or Victorinus (Delehaye 1912: 334, 381, passim; Kaufmann 1917: 36, passim; Leclercq 1936a: 1516; Testini 1958: 375, passim; Kajanto 1965: 98). The name Felicissima, the superlative of felix, is symptomatic of slaves and freedmen, particularly Christian, and was also attested among Christian martyrs (Delehaye 1912: 323, 361; Harnack 1915: 408; Kaufmann 1917: 223; Kajanto 1965: 13, 104, 273). Most problematic in every sense is Sacmeneunus, who is mentioned in the inscription as having shared the sarcophagus with Felicissima. There is no obvious clue as to his relationship with Severilla; a plausible guess would imply a relative. The name is probably of Gallo-Illyrian origin and is unattested elsewhere. Its occurrence here is very curious given the disappearance of autochthonous names from the late Roman epigraphic material (Oliva 1962: 342; Mócsy 1965: 214). Alternately, such a name might have come as a singular consequence of a general revival of native cultural and ethnic attributes during late antiquity (Harnack 1915: 411; Nagy 1945: 275, note 11; Salin 1959: 466-467; Vinski 1971: 378). The inscription probably terminated with a common Christian phrase in Deo (Testini 1958: 141, passim).

Two monogrammatic devices above the inscription display a few peculiarities suggestive of a gnostic-heretical milieu; both are accompanied by the apocalyptic letters alpha and omega. The alpha and omega in conjunction with the chi-rho made their first appearance on coins slightly earlier than the mid 4th century. The most popular variation on the device - the one with the letters placed between interstices of chi - gained ground in time and retained its popularity throughout the second half of the 4th century and well into the 5th (Kaufmann 1913: 644 i d.; Sutherland - Litt - Carson 1981: 43, 251-252). Concurrently it became common in media other than coinage (Cabrol 1924; Leoni 1950: 966; Lohmayer 1950; Sauer J 1958: 1177; Kádár 1969: 179; Forstner 1982: 36). It is commonly held that the chi-rho with alfa and omega should be interpreted in terms of Christian orthodoxy, particularly regarding its struggle with various heretical teachings, above all with Arianism. However, neither historical sources nor archaeological material substantiate this opinion in a conclusive manner (Bratož 1996: 327, note 113). While it is true that the employment of the device in question gained its greatest popularity concurrently with the Arian-orthodox controversies, its appeal for the heretics and gnostics has not been sufficiently pointed out in literature (Cabrol 1924: 17; Sauer J 1958: 1177; Lohmayer 1950: 2). The apocalyptic letters in repeating lines is equally a favourite artistic device with gnostic iconographies and is frequently encountered both in gnostic scriptures and on various artefacts (Cabrol 1924: 17; Leclercq 1924a: 2213, Fig. 750; Testini 1958: 529-532; Craveri 1969: 30). Of the two monogrammatic devices depicted on the sarcophagus in question, the one on the left is based on a saltire cross (see S.3.); two unintelligible signs in the perpendicular interstices of the saltire might tentatively be understood as the Greek letters P and R, and correspondingly related to various religious terms (*protos, presbyter*, etc.). They might equally be interpreted as the Greek and Latin latter P respectively, standing possibly for various terms, primarily *pax* (Kaufmann 1917: 40). It is worth mentioning in this context that a gnostic text from Asia Minor commences with a cross and a letter P at each side (Testini 1958: 529). The device to the right above the sarcophagus's inscription is based on the oblique monogrammatic cross, a sign known in its upright position in the numismatic iconography from the first half of the 4th century (Kaufmann 1913: 642; Sutherland - Litt - Carson 1981: 170). Within a chronological-typological development of early Christian devices the monogrammatic cross is later than the chi-rho and is mostly limited to the end of the 4th century and the first half of the 5th (Leoni 1950: 966; Sauer J 1958; Mawer 1995: 138). The oblique version is a much rarer occurrence and is possibly suggestive of gnostic surroundings (cf. Leclercq 1931a: 1289; Testini 1958: 531).

All the foregoing symbolic devices should date the sarcophagus to the end of the 4th century and the first half of the 5th. Sadly enough, it is exactly the phrase in the fourth line concerning its chronology - *Anno urbis DXVII* - that is rather unintelligible; it is incompatible with both the familiar manners of dating in early Christian epigraphy and with the potential period of the burial: supposing anno urbis relates to Rome and connotes possibly the expression *ab urbe condita* (in 753 BC), it would amount to B.C. 230! While the mentioned chronological phrase is reminiscent of unorthodox datings of Christian inscriptions, expressed by means of various eras (Kaufmann 1917: 42-51; Testini 1958: 403-404), nowhere to my knowledge is there to be found an immediate parallel. In a word, for all its queer and peculiar details this monument should be regarded as possibly pertaining to gnostic-heretical surroundings.

III.b.3 Carved sarcophagus II

Provenance: Vinkovci (Cibalae); chance find in 1881 in the area of the northern Roman cemetery.
Location: GMV (A-770)
Description: Limestone; 201 x 76 x 99 cm. A sarcophagus of the Asia Minor type with plain elongated box bare of postament or crowning moulding. Most of the front is occupied by an uninscribed *tabula ansata* of classical appearance. Each of the two *ansae* bears a motiv of a massive rosette in high relief; triangular spaces between *ansae* and frame of the inscription field are each decorated with a smaller rosette in addition to wavy tendril-like plants,

both carved in low relief. On the free surface of the front right of the inscription field a large, sketchily outlined fish with a differentially hachured body is engraved in relief. In the corresponding field to the left, a rosette and a plant identical to those in triangular sections by the *tabula ansata* are engraved.
Dating: 3rd century (first use); reused at the end of the 3rd or the beginning of the 4th century.
Literature: Vikić-Belančić 1978: 594-595, Fig. 8; Dimitrijević 1979: 227-228, Taf. 11:1; Katalog: 98, no. 95.
Commentary: Contrary to the Norico-Pannonian series, the Asia Minor type of sarcophagus is far less common in Pannonia (Vikić-Belančić 1978: 594-599; Dimitrijević 1979: 227-229; Koch - Sichtermann 1982: 323-332). What concerns us in this context is modification made for the purpose of secondary use of this piece. The manner of execution of various elements of the front decoration reveals two different styles; the original ornamental conception was apparently based on two single plastic rosettes at each side of the inscription field. The remaining motifs - smaller rosettes, plants and a fish - were added later, and were rendered by means of a deep engraving of the outlines with a chisel to effect a low relief. This procedure was amply used in early Christian sculpture at the end of the 3rd and the beginning of the 4th centuries in various regions, northern Pannonia included (Tòth 1972: 62-63).

A prominently situated motif of a fish was unanimously taken by scholars to represent a cryptic Christian emblem, which would date the secondary use of the sarcophagus to prior to 313 at the latest. The hypothesis is convincing enough despite the fish motif being always, and with good reason, subject to verification. The fish is imbued with manifold symbolic connotations in various pagan religions, but hardly anywhere is it so deeply rooted as in Christianity (Leclercq 1927; Klauser 1958: 22; Salin 1959: 176-180; Eizenhöfer 1960: 55-62; Engemann 1969; Forstner 1982: 248-249). It is therefore hard to conceive of a more natural religious milieu than the Christian for a single fish added to the already existing decoration. Two different symbolic meanings of the fish should then be considered in this context. The first one relates to Christ himself and has its justification in the fish's relative size and prominence among the other motifs of the sarcophagus's front. The second, induced by the occurrence of three rosettes, should imply eucharistic associations; of the total of the three rosettes at least the one on the left, acting as a counterpart to the fish, appears to represent a loaf. Rosettes in question are represented neither in a monogrammatic form as occurs frequently, nor naturalistically as real loaves; nevertheless, this is not an indispensable condition for interpreting them as

eucharistic devices, since in this capacity they are quite often represented as either geometrically or florally stylized (Garrucci 1977: Tav. 262:1, 266; Garrucci 1880: Tav. 477:43, 486:6; Gough 1973: 47, Fig. 8; Cambi 1975: 65; Thomas E B 1980a: 198-199, Pls. 139, 140). The eucharist as represented in this context should understandably be enriched with eschatological overtones. A very close analogy in regard to the symbolic decoration of the piece from Vinkovci is to be found on a north-Italian sarcophagus dated to the end of the 3rd century and the beginning of the 4th (Toynbee J M C 1975: 14-16, Pl. 5:a-c). Finally to tip the balance in favour of the Christian interpretation of the secondary use of the sarcophagus under discussion is its find spot in the area of the northern cemetery of Cibalae, in the immediate vicinity of another Christian burial (III.c.1.).

III.b.4. Carved sarcophagus (I?)

Lesbyan cyma). Within a tripartite division of front (to be visualized as a far echo of the clear architectonic scheme, symptomatic of the Norico-Pannonian sarcophagi) the central plainly framed rectangular section was intended as the inscription panel. This inscription was either never executed at all, or has disappeared as a consequence of having been painted instead of cut. In the niches left and right of the central field, standing portrait-figures of the deceased (in the guise of *palliati*) were carved in high relief. On the left side a woman is depicted (head missing) with her left hand resting on her abdomen and the right pointing to a round object, probably an amulet box (*bula*). The man on the right side is shown holding a scroll in his left hand and pointing to it with the right. The right short side of the sarcophagus is occupied by a motif of two panthers seated on their hind legs by a vase filled with fruit; vines and grapes are springing from it. Two panthers with heads slightly bent down and touching the vase

Provenance: Veliki Bastaji near Daruvar (Aquae Balissae); amateur excavation in 1842; found in a grave chamber in tandem with a stone slab (III.c.3.).
Location: AMZ
Description: White marble; dimensions of box: 232 x 128 x 78 cm, of pedestal: 261 x 147 x 35. Box and base are damaged and cracked in several places; a section of front is missing, as is also the lid, which had previously been attached to the box, as evidenced on the old photographs. The pedestal is decorated with two superimposed ornamental bands, the upper bearing zig-zags and the lower a simple leaf pattern (a stylized version of the leaf and dart or the so-called

with lifted outer front legs are placed against a background of two tiny leafed trees. The left short side of the sarcophagus is completely filled with arabesque-like images of vines and grapes and two trees identical to those on the right short side. Vines are growing prolifically in all directions from the central stem, producing the effect of the overwhelming domination by a single motif. Scenes on both short sides are rendered in low and flat relief, reminiscent almost of wood-carving.
Dating: End of the 3rd century/beginning of the 4th century.
Literature: Szabó 1934: 83-84; AIJ: 272-273, no. 589; Vikić-Belančić 1978: 597-598, Figs. 12-14; Migotti 1996.

Commentary: The question-mark by the classification number denotes the lack of any blatant or indisputable Christian elements in the decorative scheme of the sarcophagus, whose Christian religious background is corroborated only by the context; it was discovered in conjunction with the indisputably Christian inscriptive slab (III.c.3.). For the peculiar context, the precious material (marble) and a singular decorative repertoire, this is one of the most outstanding early Christian sarcophagi of the Norico-Pannonian series in the whole of Pannonia, unparalleled elswhere in the region (Koch - Sichtermann 1982: 329-330; Migotti 1996: 146-150). Although at first glance blatantly Dionysiac in its subject-matter, the decorative scheme as a whole should, given the context, be interpreted in terms of syncretistic mystery religions' conceptions, with hints of Christian hopes and expectations for a resurrection (cf Turcan 1966; Mócsy - Szentléleky 1971: 39-40; Gough 1973: 80; Forstner 1982: 174-176; Koch - Sichtermann 1982: 57; see also III.b.1.). Such an interpretation is bolstered also by the fact that it was exactly the Dionysiac cycle that was most often and with a least embarrassment taken over for use in Christian funerary contexts. For instance, the mausoleum of Constantine's Christian daughter Constantia, decorated in the same line, was known to the Renaissance as the temple of Bacchus (Gough 1973: 80). A further corroboration of a Dyonisiac/Christian blend can be observed in two significant elements concerning both the general layout and some details of the decorative scheme of the monument from Bastaji; while in Dionysiac surroundings vines and grapes are no more than a background for the god and his retinue (Koch - Sichtermann 1982: 420-421; Bielefeld 1993; Cambi 1993), here they are the essential core of the decorative composition of the sarcophagus's right short side and the sole motif on its left. The motif is here important in itself and was not employed as a mere background to other figures. A further element suggestive of Christian interpretation is the gesture of two docile seated panthers with heads bent down. In pre-Christian funerary contexts in Pannonia and elsewhere the motif of heraldic panthers with a central element occurs frequently, but with the animals' heads unexceptionally straight and their gaze directed towards the vase as a symbol of life and strength (Migotti 1996: 143, note 71; abundant literature on various aspects of the religious symbolism employed in this context can also be found there). Conversely, the gesture as contrived here should justifiably be explained as a metaphor for the defeated paganism or the converted sinners in a penitent attitude; such an interpretation was convincingly proposed for the motif of a panther with head bent down on a coin struck by Constantine (Forstner 1982: 279).

The virtually insoluble issue of the sarcophagus's original religious background (its possible manufacture for a Christian burial or a subsequent re-use for the same purpose) is understandably connected with the dating of the archaeological context as a whole. This, unfortunately, emains insecure; it rests upon the palaeographic and epigraphic characteristics of the inscribed stone slab, found in conjunction with the sarcophagus. Features as occur on the inscription extend through the whole of the 4th century and appear to be even more typical of its second half (see III.c.4.). However, on grounds of the physiognomy of the deceased man it was possible accurately to date the sarcophagus to the end of the 3rd century and the beginning of the 4th (Migotti 1996: 140, notes 56-58). All that can safely be stated is that the underlying conception of the sarcophagus' symbolic scheme ultimately bore on eschatological and soteriological ideas with Christian overtones, either conceived from the start or achieved later.

There are no immediate analogies to the sarcophagus from Bastaji; it is different from the related Pannonian monuments in both style and carving technique and is unique in the choice of themes. The reliefs on short sides are very flat, reminiscent almost of wood-cutting and depending for their colouristic effect on an interplay of light and shade; while universally used in the 6th century, such an artistic feature contains oriental overtones at this early date (Gough 1973: 167). The animals' bodies are filled with engraved circles, which is a typical late Roman artistic device, but one applied usually to bone and metal objects (Migotti 1996: 145, notes 84-87) and only quite exceptionally stone.

Roman marble monuments in Pannonia, sarcophagi included, were manufactured in Noric marbles (Migotti 1996: 147:99). This one was made of marble from the quarries near Ptuj, the Roman Poetovio, on the border of Pannonia and Noricum; it can reasonably be assumed that it was also sculptured in one of the Poetovian workshops, as is further suggested by its artistic style. The mentioned peculiarities of the style further suggest a carver who came to work in the area from outside, possibly from the eastern parts of the Empire.

III.b.5. Fragment of carved sarcophagus(?) (II)

Provenance: A mediaeval hillfort site Rudina near the village of Čečavac in the Požega valley; excavation in 1986.
Location: MPKP
Description: Sandstone; 72 x 44.5 cm, thickness 8-13 cm. A sub-trapezoidal stone slab with a lightly-engraved fish covering most of the surface. The fish is rendered very sketchily and is geometrically stylized, featuring angular

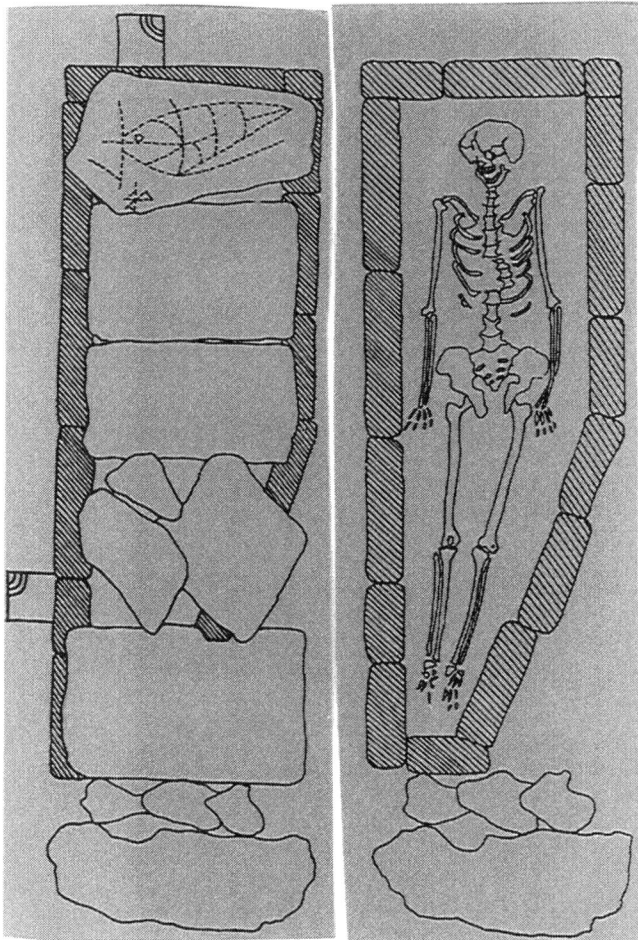

Christian connotation (of the many attached to the fish motif) employed here remains disputed. In any event funerary (and by implication soteriological) associations (if this be part of a sarcophagus) are to be expected. Additionally, the trefoil above the fish might possibly be symbolic of the Trinity; there are some hints in early Christian epigraphical and historical sources at the number three bearing associations with the Trinity. As a result, objects featuring triple shapes or elements are at times hypothetically given orthodox Christian meaning, embodying essentially the conception of the Trinity (Cabrol 1924: 18; Engemann 1976; Giordani 1978; Quacquarelli 1978: 405-406; Higgins 1987: 121, Fig. 44; Watts 1988: 220, note 40). The nearest analogy, although not exactly an immediate one, is to be found in the Archaeological Museum in Istanbul. A stone slab from the altar-screen there, dated to the 5th/6th centuries, bears a flat relief motif of a fish between two trefoils within a rhombic frame (Fıratlı 1990: 160, no. 316). Curiously enough, among the Romanesque sculpture from the site some pieces were recognized as featuring the Trinity in various ways; should it be too enthusiastic to search for the continuity of the symbol on this site, connected possibly with a tradition of worship of the Trinity?

III.c. Inscriptive tombstones and stone slabs

III.c.1. Tomb stone of Venatorinus and Martoria (I)

Provenance: Vinkovci (Cibalae); chance find in 1956 in the area of the northern Roman cemetery.
Location: GMV (A-736)
Description: Limestone; 58 x 45 cm, thickness 16 cm. A massive stone slab slightly damaged on the edges. The upper third of the field is occupied by the four-line inscription executed in a fairly good late Roman *capitala actuaria*. The inscription runs:
Hic sunt positi
Venatorinus et
Martoria innocen-
tis.

outlines and an impressed annular circle for an eye. It is placed next to a trapezoidal shape projecting from a side of what appears to be part of an inscription field (*tabula ansata*). Should this perception be correct, this is a fragment of a sarcophagus' front. Above the fish's head a trefoil composed of triangular leaves is depicted.
Dating: 3rd/4th centuries.
Literature: Sokač-Štimac 1987: 151; Katalog: 125, no. 177.
Commentary: The slab was discovered as used secondarily as part of the covering of a Romanesque grave vault. It was placed right above the head of the deceased, with depiction on the innerside, suggesting obviously origin earlier than the grave itself and probably prior to the mediaeval period in the first place; similar procedures with presumably an apotropaic function were at times employed in early Christian burials (Salin 1959: 384). Next to the head and feet of the skeleton, fragments of Roman bricks were found; the site as a whole abounds in building materials and small finds of the Roman period (see I.c.2.). With this in mind, the hypothesis for figured slab as a witness to the early Christian layer of this primarily mediaeval site is additionally reinforced. The basic argument for this case rests, however, on the stylistic features of the fish depiction. This is completely different from the remainder of the well-known Romanesque relief sculpture recovered on the site of the mediaeval monastery of Rudina. Furthermore, both the motif and the manner of execution of the fish are typical of early Christian artistic expression (see III.b.3.). Given the fragmentary state of the piece in question, a specific

Below the inscription a large encircled monogrammatic device is neatly and skilfully incised, composed of a chi and a monogrammatic cross, both with expanded terminals and with a slightly open and hooked rho. The alfa and omega are inconspicuously incised within two horizontal sections of the device.

Dating: second half of the 4th century/first half of the 5th century.

Literature: Vikić-Belančić 1978: 593-595, Fig. 6; Dimitrijević 1979: 230, Taf. 12:4; Katalog: 98, no. 96.

Commentary: This piece is significant in both its symbolic and epigraphic aspects. It is the single instance of this type of monogrammatic device in northern Croatia, while other, simpler forms of kindred devices occur frequently in archaeological material. Both its characteristic features - a compound shape and an open hooked rho loop - are sometimes ascribed to oriental influences. This appears to be true in a measure, but not absolutely. The dating of the device in question is, however, more secure; both its shape and the accompanying letters point to the end of the 4th century at the earliest (see II.1. and III.b.2.).

The epitaph was composed in a quite simple and lapidary manner, typical otherwise of Christian inscriptions prior to the advanced 4th century (Kaufmann 1917: 56; Testini 1958: 367). There is no mention here of the date of the departure or the age of the deceased or who commissioned the inscription, which might suggest that the buried persons were somehow well-known to the community, and maybe honoured as martyrs or confessors of the Christian faith. This conjecture should, however, be supported on other grounds; lapidary inscriptions occur not infrequently in later periods, particualrly in northern provinces (Kaufmann 1917: 85; Kempt - Reusch 1965: 25). The official persecutions of Christians in Pannonia terminated in AD 308 (Jarak 1994: 171). Hostilities arose again during the orthodox and Arian or other religious controversies (Delehaye 1912: 71 ff.; Demandt 1989: 460, 467; Bratož 1996: 322-323) and the emperor Julian's pagan revival (see IV.1.), but actual killings were exceptional. There is yet another slight possibility of Martoria and Venatorinus being martyrs: their putative martyrdom might have occurred in the period of Diocletian's persecutions, with the relics discovered only later in time, as was a familiar procedure in the 4th century (Delehaye 1912: 86-109). Given all the possibilities, however, these two Christians were probably not martyrs at all. The name Martoria is possibly a reference to Christian martyrdoms having occurred at Cibalae in the 3rd and 4th centuries (cf. Jarak 1994: 170). Martoria derives obviously from the corrupted term *mártyros*, and is, together with those of similar origin, typical of the second half of the 4th century Christian onomastics (Leclercq 1936a: 1514; Testini 1958: 363, 369; Kajanto 1963: 99-100; Marucchi 1974: 182-190). True, certain virtual martyrs bore the name derived from this term (Delehaye 1912: 167-168; Leclercq 1932a: 2497; Barton 1975: 102; Cavada 1994: 226), but this should be perceived as a sheer coincidence, unrelated to any specific meaningful event. The name Venatorinus - a derivative of the professional term venator - occurs rarely (Kajanto 1965: 324; Mócsy - Szentléleky 1971: 115). It is by no means a specifically Christian name, but counts among those with putative Christian connotations, bearing on strength and courage and leading ultimately to the Christian victory over death and evil, like Victorinus, Bellator etc. (Kaufmann 1917: 36; Leclercq 1936a: 1516; Grabar 1968: 53; Craveri 1969: 84; for the Christian symbolism of the hunt see VI.d.8.).

The term (*de*)*positus* is typical of early Christian conceptions in its pointing to the overcoming of death and emphasizing a temporary rest in expectation of the resurrection (Leclercq 1920). It occurs frequently in Rome, but seems to be familiar in Pannonia as well (Kaufmann 1917: 88; Thomas 1980: 119-123).

Venatorinus and Martoria were denoted as innocent on their epitaph. This is a common Christian expression related to either children or the Christian righteous, in other words, all those as innocent as children (Kaufmann 1917: 43, passim; Leclercq 1926a). There is a typical palaeographic error of mistaking the letter *i* for *e* (cf. Kaufmann 1917: 33-34; Testini 1958: 363-364), giving the word *innocentis* instead of *innocentes*. (A slight possibility should also be considered of the word in question denoting filiation and giving the name of the deceased's parent - Innocens, as in III.c.4. and VI.b.3.). In all other aspects of execution this inscription counts among the average, or slightly above average, of the early Christian epigraphic material in northern Croatia.

III.c.2. Stone slab of Flavius Maurus (I)

Provenance: Štrbinci (Certissa?); chance find of the mid 19th century.

Location: AMZ (361)

Description: Grey marble; 50.5 x 39 cm, thickness 4.5 cm. A fragment of upper left hand section of an inscriptive stone slab with inconspicuous traces of a Christogram above the text. The inscription, executed in a fairly good late Roman *capitala actuaria* with no apparent errors, runs as follows:

Fl(avio) Mauro f[ilio ---]
nis bene[merenti---]
fedeliq[ue---]
an(norum) X[---]
⁵m[emoriae causa?]
coll[egae---]
f[ecerunt ?---]

Dating: 4th century.

Literature: CIL III: 4002; Brunšmid 1909: 98, no. 361; Katalog: 116, no. 155.

Commentary: The only indisputable Christian element on this slab is the chi-rho above the inscription (for the chi-rho see II.1.). With this in mind, two terms from the text - *collegae* and *fedelis* - further to be discussed, probably carried Christian connotations.

This inscription should not be dated later than the 4th century, as suggested by the onomastic formula, which contains a family name (*nomen gentile*) Flavius and a personal name Maurus, derived from a nickname (*cognomen*). Such a formula is in fact typical of the 3rd century, while expiring during the 4th (Leclercq 1936a: 1492; Testini 1958: 368). In the late Roman period the nomen Flavius relates to the house of Constantine and occurs frequently all over the Empire during the course of the 4th century. It has been observed that the family name Flavius was as a rule attached to high-ranking civil, military or ecclesiastical officers (Kaufmann 1917: 45, 155-156; Testini 1958: 368-369; Mócsy 1965: 215-218; Mócsy - Szentléleky 1971: 33). The cognomen Maurus is evidently of geographical (African) origin; it was very common among Christians, who might have been additionally attracted to it for its saintly connotations (Kaufmann 1917: 190; Kajanto 1965: 49-50, 206; Delehaye 1912: 314).

Fedelis can possibly denote any religious affiliation of the deceased, but is most common on Christian inscriptions (Kaufmann 1917: 35, passim; Testini 1958: 381, passim; Kempt - Reusch 1965: 25, 33, nos. 12, 23). The most interesting term from the point of view of the social history of early Christian Pannonia is *collega*. It has fortunately not been expanded only tentatively on this inscription; the section of slab now missing must have been attached to the whole in the last century, and Mommsen appears to have been able to read as much as *colleg* (CIL III: 4002). The colleagues from this inscription were evidently responsible for setting up of Maurus's funerary stone. They were probably members of a humanitarian-religious, or rather, professional-religious association - a fraternity or a corporation. Both these related institutions have existed in an apparently stationary form or with some insignificant alternations from antiquity to the present day (Waltzing 1948; Alföldi 1958; Kurz 1960; Pavan 1955: 211-214, 330-335; Migotti 1987). Curiously enough, a missing link in this hypothetical line of continuity appears to be exactly the late Roman/early Christian period.

It is a commonly-held opinion that up to the 4th century the only legal form of Christian associations of any kind were the so-called *collegia funeratica* - associations providing for Christian burials and cemeteries in general. True, this suggestion seemed to be reinforced by the lack of epigraphical evidence for Christian fraternities or corporations other than funerary, at least for a very early period (Kaufmann 1917: 125; Waltzing 1948). However, professional Christian corporations are first mentioned in 6th century sources (Thomas J P 1987: 75), while the syntagm *collega in Christo* is known from Christian literature as early as the 3rd century (Delehaye 1912: 27). The opinion of the non-existence of early Christian collegia therefore requires a scrutiny from the general point of view as well as concerning the province of Pannonia, which has so far produced two inscriptions with a probable mention of Christian professional associations (the second stemming from Savaria in *Pannonia Prima*, see Thomas E B 1980: 119). This is a surprising and at the same time a revealing fact, given that even neighbouring Dalmatia, with its profusion of epigraphical material, seems to be lacking in evidence for Christian corporations. On the other hand, the existence of early Christian professional associations should not be doubted, also on the grounds of the common features of related mediaeval institutions, preserving a continuity with all the essentials of their Romano-Christian predecessors (Migotti 1987).

III.c.3. Funerary slab with versed inscription (I)

Provenance: Gornji Bastaji near Daruvar (Aquae Balissae); amateur excavation in 1842; found in a grave chamber in tandem with III.b.4.

Location: Built into the wall of the Janković manor house at Daruvar.

Description: Grey limestone; 92 x 100 cm, thickness 2.5 cm.

A stone slab damaged at upper section, with a triangular right hand side portion actually missing. Also missing are the two last bottom lines of the inscription, apparently walled in. At first discovery these two lines were still visible, but unintelligible (Kukuljević 1891: 32, no. 108). The hexametric inscription, containing currently visible 18 versed lines, was executed skilfully in the best tradition of the elegant late Roman *capitala actuaria*. Elongated and squeezed letters (height 4 cm) are spaced along equally distanced lines with no stops between the words or ligatures within them; letters A, E, F, H, L and T feature significant characteristics. The text is composed of regular hexametres, distorted at only two points, the first being *caelique* instead of *caeli* in the 10th line and the second *promere* instead of *promerere* in the 13th line. The inscription (with now missing upper portion included) runs:

Tartareis ruptus forna[cibus implicat omn]em
perpetuum vitae, quondam da[tum, nunc rap]it acr[is]
aeternum poenis factum pro cr[imine fl]amm[a].
Hic simili natos meritis pro ta[libu]s igni
^{5}*ante obitum genuit perituros tabe parentum,*
donec cura Deum miserandi cepit et atro
nunc tulit exitio simulacrum pendere semper
poenas indigne suum et premi nocte maligna.
Nam, Dominum puro velamine semper amictum,
^{10}*adque inmortalem, caelique regionibus usum,*
et culpa vacuum portantem insignia natum
cuncta patris pressis humano crimine membris
induit; et nulli orso, sic fas promere, verbum
hunc umquam pecasse, Deum tamen omnia magnu[s]
^{15}*alterius delicta tulit. Sic corpore sumpto,*
demissus caelo terras petit, haut secus artu[s]
induit humanos, qua, ut tellus ferre vale[bit],
membrorum mediante Deum de visce[re]

(Occasional allegories and metaphors render this text somewhat unintelligible and an accurate and incontestable translation hardly possible. Here is a possible version of it: A fire bursting from the furnaces of Tartarus embraces him entirely, him that once had been endowed with eternal life; but now a severe blaze reaches him as a punishment for his crimes. Before dying he had generated sons that would perish in a similar manner; until God took mercy on him and let his image expiate for ever in the dark and shameful disaster, oppressed with sinister night. Lord, namely, appeared clad in clean garments, immortal and sinless, with his residence in Heaven and with all the inherent tokens of his father, yet oppressed with sins of humanity; no one with such a descent can be blamed for ever having sinned; yet in his greatness he atoned for others' sins. Delegated from heaven, he thereby assumed a human body and ascended to earth and with his human body the earth was able to support...).

Dating: 4th century.

Literature: Kukuljević 1891: 32, no. 108; Szabó 1934: 84-85; Katalog: 122, no. 171; Migotti 1996: 131-135.

Commentary: This unique monument was allegedly discovered in a grave chamber in tandem with two sarcophagi, one being III.b.4,, while another has subsequently been lost trace of.

The chronological ambiguities of the contextual unity of sarcophagus and slab have already been mentioned (see III.b.4.). While no single parallel from any place or period for the subject matter or style of the verses inscribed on the slab are known, epigraphical-palaeographical references from the Pannonian region are many (AIJ: 260, no. 564; Barkóczi - Mócsy 1972: 52-53, 80-81, nos. 48, 83; Barkóczi 1973: 78; Soproni 1980b: 236, Pl. 8). The text in question exhibits traces indicative of a long time-span from the 3rd to the 5th centuries (Kaufmann 1917: 25; Marucchi 1933: 297, passim; Petrović 1975: 108-120); yet kindred inscriptions have in Pannonia mostly been assigned to the second half of the 4th century. With the sarcophagus securely dated to the end of the 3rd century and the beginning of the 4th, the second half of the 4th century for the slab would be acceptable only in case of a secondary use of the sarcophagus. Contrarily, should sarcophagus have original Christian associations, the slab would also have to be dated to the beginning of the 4th century at the latest.

The inscribed limestone slab must have been fixed onto the inner wall of the burial chamber, as were probably several other marble specimens, whose fragments were discovered in the same chamber. The versed text was first published within a collection of mediaeval and later inscriptions, and with the contingencies of the find inaccurately explained (Kukuljević 1891). This was the most probable reason for its omission from the CIL or any of the numerous collections of early Christian epigraphic verses. As a result, it has never been subjected to analysis by experts in relevant fields (epigraphy, classical phylology and early Christian doctrine and literature). True, this inscription was perfunctorily mentioned in the literature on several occasions, but its mysterious contents and overall intelligibility deterred commentators from more committed involvement.

The verses represent a liturgical hymn whose essential core is straightforward, alluding to the Christian dogma of original sin and redemption through Christ's sufferings - a theme perfectly appropriate for the funerary ambience within which it was found. In a few of its expressions it leans apparently on thoughts from the Scriptures, particularly the works of St Paul and St John's Revelation. The air of mystery and allegory evident in the verses from Bastaji is in effect most reminiscent of Revelation; it is worthy of mention that similar attributes were primarily responsible for a long-time stigma of heresy and apocrypha associated to Revelation itself (Demandt 1989: 442).

It seems that the verses under discussion were never recorded epigraphically or literary in any other place except in this archaeological context (Prof. Dr. Kurt Smolak pers. comm.); two possibilities appear to be acceptable in terms of the nature of the inscription. First, it might have been contrived by a local anonymous versifier, well-instructed in Christian doctrine, for the purpose of the burial of the rich and demanding owner of the sarcophagus from the Aquae Balissae area (III.b.4.). However, the very high artistic level of accomplishment of the verses would militate against this case; it is more plausible to hypothesize a passage from early Christian literature used as a model or simply copied for the needs of a burial settings, and apparently recorded in this sole instance.

As stated above, the hymn is preoccupied with original sin and the sacrifice of Christ the Redeemer, bringing consequently to mind canonical literature as the most probable source of inspiration. On the other hand, a number of heretical gnostic sects, notably the Basilidians and the Ophites, include among their doctrines the dogma of the Fall and Redemption (Stutzinger 1983: 88). Given some gnostico-heretical overtones in the occasionally allegorical and metaphorical wording of the hymn, a conjecture appears to be plausible for its basically syncretistic and possibly gnostic and heretical surroundings. Such a possibility would also be in keeping with the features of religious syncretism so explicitly displayed on the sarcophagus (III.b.4.) from the same context.

Although still unresolved and disputed in many of its detail, this find (both sarcophagus and slab) is as a whole unique not only to Pannonia, but to early Christian archaeology in general.

III.c.4. Stone slab of Paulinus (II)

Provenance: Sisak (Siscia); chance find of the 19th century.
Location: AMZ (348)
Description: Grey marble; 55 x 32 cm, thickness 2.7 cm. A fragment of a tombstone split in two, with much of left section missing. The inscription containing seven probably hexametric lines is executed in a fairly debased *capitala actuaria*. The letters are of various size and unevenly spaced; triangular stop-marks are occasionally placed in unexpected places. The inscription runs as follows:

[O]pt(imae)[mem(oriae)?]
[---]Paulini Lucerinis
[---]ab omnibu(s)
[---]r operav
5[---]e benedict
[---]X et tu

[---]ris
[---gra]tias ag[a]

Dating: 4th/5th centuries.
Literature: CIL III: 3991; Brunšmid 1909: 156, no. 348; Katalog: 82, no. 40.
Commentary: The inscription is too fragmentary for any attempt of a convincing expansion and reading as a whole; even its Christian context remains slightly dubious. Two terms and expressions point, however, to probable Christian contents. The invocation formula behind the extant letters P and T was expanded as *optimae memoriae*, but this does not seem to be convincing enough. A little more plausible, but still far from certain, is the possibility of the reading as *Pax tibi* or *tecum*. While the term *pax* is in Latin epigraphy sometimes abbreviated as P (Kaufmann 1917: 20, Fig. 40, 85; Marucchi 1974: 97), the formula *optimae memoriae*, however common in inscriptions otherwise, is not familiar in the form as displayed here. Bringing the name of the deceased person and his father's name in the genitive is a usual manner of expressing filiation in the early Christian epigraphy (Testini 1958: 371; Kajanto 1963: 5). The name Paulinus is a common late-Roman personal name, particularly symptomatic of Italy and Gallo-Illyrian provinces (Kajanto 1965: 41, 244); its great appeal for Christians was in a measure certainly induced by imitation of the saintly name Paul (Delehaye 1912: 226, 326, passim; Kaufmann 1917: 35, 185; Kajanto 1963: 96; Kajanto 1965: 244). The name of Paulinus's father bears no Christian connotations and is of geographical origin (Apulian town of Luceria) (Kajanto 1965: 193).

A fragment of a word *bened* in the 4th line can be expanded equally plausible as a name (Benedictus) or an adjective (*benedictus*) or an adverb (*benedicte*). This term bears pagan connotations as well as Christian, and is accordingly also attested in pre-Christian epigraphy. It is, however, by far more familiar in Christian surroundings, particularly in the role of an attribute of martyrs (Deelahye 1912: 5, note 6; Leclercq 1925d; Macrea 1959: 333; Marucchi 1974: 97-105; Mawer 1995: 141). Despite its very frequent occurrence in the Christian liturgical phraseology, the term is fairly rare in epigraphical material (Leclercq 1953: 2282; Testini 1958: 254). A fragment of a word terminating in *tias* in the bottom line was given an acceptable expansion: *Deo gratias* - a known Christian exclamation formula symptomatic of Gallican, African and Roman liturgies and frequently used in martyrs' legends; they were the most probable source for its wide application in funerary epitaphs. The formula *Deo gratias* is often interpreted as a token of the Christian orthodoxy contrary to Donatism with its favourable formula *Deo laudes* (Cabrol 1920; Testini 1958: 489, 532).

III.c.5. Stone slab (II)

Provenance: Štrbinci (Certissa?); chance find of the mid 19th century (see II.1.).
Location: AMZ (367)
Description: White marble; 23 x 17 cm, thickness 2.3 cm. A fragment of the right hand section of an inscribed tomb stone with four lines of the partially extant epitaph. It was executed skilfully in a fairly high-quality late Roman *capitala quadrata* with deeply cut and equally spaced serifed letters and with a lightly incised ancillary outlining of courses. The

inscription runs as follows:

[--- in pa]ce
[---q]ui vi[c][xit---]
[---u]s Adri[---]
[---qui] vi[c]xit [---]

Dating: 4th/5th centuries.
Literature: CIL III: 4004; Brunšmid 1909: 101, no. 363; Katalog: 103, no. 115.
Commentary: Except for emperors' inscriptions (IV.1.,2.), this one is surprisingly well executed in relation to average south-Pannonian standards; the cutter even went to trouble of using lines to improve on the accomplishment of the

inscription, a procedure not unfamiliar with either the imperial or the late Roman epigraphy, although more typical of the latter (Kaufmann 1917: 22; Testini 1958: 344, 376). Despite such qualities, a typical late Roman epigraphical error of confusion of letters is observable: it seems that the verb *vixit* is even twice written as *vicxit*, certainly in the fourth line and possibly in the second. The monument was classified as probably Christian on account of a fragmentary form of the key-term for the Christian attribution - *pace*. letters c and e contained in the first line were convincingly (a slight reservation is still appropriate) expanded as *in pace* (in peace). This is by far the most significant and extremely frequent formula of Christian epigraphy, denoting the serene tranquillity of Christian death in hope and expectation of eternal life (Kaufmann 1917: 134-135; Leclercq 1948a: 1757). The name Adrianus can tentatively be presumed in the third line.

III.c.6. Stone slab (II)

Provenance: Vinkovci (Cibalae); chance find during building works in 1858.
Location: AMZ (371)
Description: White marble with reddish-brown streaks; 15.5 x 10.5 cm, thickness 3 cm. A fragment of probably central portion of a tomb stone with remains of an inscription in two lines, the upper one unreadable. It had been executed in a good *capitala actuaria* and reads as follows:

[---]o cl[---]
[--- ?dep]osit[---]

Dating: 4th/5th centuries.
Literature: CIL III: 10252; Brunšmid 1909: 107, no. 371; Katalog: 98, no. 97.
Commentary: The object was categorized as only probably Christian on account of a very slight possibility of an incorrect reading of the letters *osit* in the second line. The proposed expansion *(de)positus* or *(de)positio* is, however, convincing enough; Christian associations of the term *(de)positus* are well known (see III.c.1.).

III.c.7(a-d). Stone slabs (II)

Provenance: Vinkovci (Cibalae); found during field surveys in 1974 and 1976.
Location: Private possession (Dimitrijević collection, Zagreb).
Description: White marble; four very similar small inscribed stone fragments. Inscriptions are quite fragmentary and unintelligible, and are executed in a very debased *capitala actuaria*.
a) 5.1 x 2.5 cm, thickness 2.1 cm; read as:

[---]tio[---]
[---]ae[---]
------

b) 12.5 x 16.5 cm, thickness 3.6 cm; read as:

[---]ael
[---]x et ec[---] vel *[---]nec f[(ecit)---]*
------

c) 16 x 15.2 cm, thickness 3 cm; read as:

[---eccle]sia v[---]
[--- pa]ter vel *[--- ma]ter* vel *[--- fra]ter*
------

d) 11.5 x 13.5 cm, thickness 4 cm; read as:

[---]tua c[---] vel *o[---]*
[---]a[---]

Dating: 4th/5th centuries.
Literature: Dimitrijević 1979: 249-250, Taf. 25:1-4; Katalog: 99, nos. 98-101.
Commentary: Despite the lack of any specific Christian words or devices, these pieces were classified in the category based on probable Christian associations; this can be excused on the account of their find-spot, commonly considered to be a very probable early Christian memorial-cemeterial complex of Cibalae (see I.a.2.). A typical word *vixit* possibly appears in the third line of the inscription III.c.7.b if *x et c* is read *vixit* instead.

III.c.8. Stone slab (III)

Provenance: Sisak (Siscia); chance find of the second half of the 19th century.
Location: AMZ (misplaced).
Description: White marble; 13.5 x 13.8 cm, thickness 1.5 cm. A fragment of a stone slab inscribed on both sides. One of the sides bears larger and more skilfully executed letters of the original inscription, while the other features an unintelligible fragmentary inscription cut in a slightly debased *capitala actuaria*. The former can be read as follows:

[---]sia [-]cn[---]
[---] plus m[---]
[--- v]ixit civ[---]

Dating: 4th/5th centuries.
Literature: Brunšmid 1909: 161, no. 354.
Commentary: The probable Christian appurtenance of this inscription is deduced on the basis of the formula *vixit plus minus (annos)*, referring to the Christian disregard for the duration of earthly life (Kaufmann 1917: 38, passim; Testini 1958: 373, passim; Frend 1964: 125; Salway 1993: 498). It should be noted that opistographi (stones inscribed on both sides) like the one here are on the whole quite familiar in early Christian funerary epigraphy (Kaufmann 1917: 17; Testini 1958: 338, 341).

III.c.9. Stone slab (III)

Provenance: Sisak (Siscia); southern Roman cemetery (Fig. 5:6) on the right bank of the Kupa; chance find during ploughing in 1901.
Location: AMZ (misplaced).
Description: Grey limestone; 54.5 x 56 cm, thickness 3.6 cm. A fragment of a funerary stone slab with the upper right portion missing. The inscription in 6 lines is executed in a fairly high-quality late Roman *capitala quadrata*. Letters are of roughly the same size and words are divided by leaf-stops. Lines are not quite equally spaced, and the inscription can be read as follows:

Dom(us) aet(erna) [---]
Gaudenti[o---]
filio piisi[mo---],
qui vix(it) an(nos) VI[---],
m(enses) VI, d(ies) X, h(oras) n(octis)
VIII. Fati m(unus) c(omplevit).

(Eternal home. To pious son Gaudentius who had lived for 6 years, 6 months, 10 days and 8 night hours. Fate has been fulfilled.)
Dating: 4th century.
Literature: CIL III: 15181[2]; Brunšmid 1909: 153, no. 344.
Commentary: While palaeographic features are basically not in themselves sufficient to produce a sound base for chronology in any period (Kaufmann 1917: 54, Fig. 47-56; Testini 1958: 345. note 1; Kempt - Reusch 1965: 35, no. 25; Ševčenko 1992: 39-40; Sartori 1994: 15), certain characteristics of this piece seem to date it convincingly to a period not later than the 4th century. Such a date would in this instance be substiated on the ground of both the quality of the execution and the form of the cross-bar of the letter a: after the 4th century the letter a with a straight cross bar peters out, developing on the contrary either a slanted bar or one in the form of the letter v (Kaufmann 1917: 447-457; Petrović 1975: 109-110).

The symbolic vocabulary of this inscription is at a first sight totally pagan, particularly as concerns the formula *muni fata complevit*. It should, however, be borne in mind that the pagan phraseology, like for instance the invocation formula *D(iis) M(anibus)*, was not altogether banned from the early Christian epigraphic vocabulary; it was variously considered either as something in the nature of a camouflage in unfriendly surroundings or as a meaningless relic of the traditional way of thinking (Delehaye 1912: 35; Kaufmann 1917: 37, passim; Testini 1958: 497, passim; Barton 1975: 66-67; Frend 1964: 125). If taken literally, the opening syntagm *domus aeterna* should imply pagan connotations, as indeed it often does. Alternatively, it bears religious and apotropaic associations symptomatic of Jewish or/and Christian, rather than pagan surroundings; when employed in a funerary context, Christian overtones of the term eternity are only understandable (cf. Eliade 1987: 169-170). In Christian usage, preoccupied with faith in resurrection, the expression *domus aeterna* implies either a place for a temporary rest while awaiting resurrection, or, more generally, the eternal home with God in Heaven (Altmann 1931: 119; Nagy 1945: 277; Stommel 1959). The syntagm in question passed into Christian usage in the course of the 4th century and was rather typical of the West (Testini 1958: 440-445).

A further corroborative element for the Christian basis of this inscription should be the name Gaudentius; on the ground of both its suffix *ius* and its connotations of the joyful participation in life with God, it is usually, although not unanimously, ascribed a Christian appurtenance (Kaufmann 1917: 36; Testini 1958: 531; Kajanto 1963: 70-89; Kajanto 1965: 59, 260; Mócsy 1965: 219; Mócsy - Szentléleky 1971: 33). It should be admissible to consider this inscription as a result of a syncretistic line of thinking with some Jewish-

Christian overtones, as typical of the overall religious air of the 4th century.

The second line was originally expanded as Gaudentius (Brunšmid). This, however, is apparently a misconception to be replaced by Gaudentio, denoting the son's and not the father's name.

III.d. Other monuments

III.d.1. Decorated grave tile (I)

Provenance: Štrbinci (Certissa?); chance find of the mid 19th century (see II.1.).
Location: AMZ
Description: Brick; 31.5 x 30.5 cm, thickness 7 cm. The whole of the upper surface is decorated with a precisely and skilfully engraved motif of an encircled chi-rho with the closed rho loop, accompanied by a conspicuous alfa and omega. The engraving was effected by means of short notches or strokes on both sides of the main line to the effect of a barbed wire or a vestigial herring bone.
Dating: second half of the 4th/5th centuries.
Literature: Ljubić 1876: 44, no. 14; Katalog: 130, no. 192.
Commentary: Late Roman tiles bearing Christian devices are familiar parts of funerary constructions everywhere, yet with particularly high frequences in Gallia and Pannonia (Cabrol 1924: 14; Burger 1966: 120, Figs. 91, 92; Dölger 1966: 36; Sági 1968; Fülep 1984: 47-48;). Although at times inscriptions and various figural depictions occur on tiles, by far most common are those bearing a chi-rho with or without an alfa and omega (see III.c.1.).

The ornamented tile from the site of Štrbinci is the only one so far known from the territory of northern Croatia. With this in mind it is particularly curious that, contrary to the average undistinguished artistic standards for such objects, this one should be executed very skilfully and neatly. A special technique employed of short strokes branching off from the main lines gives the impression, at least regarding the circle, of a schematized wreath round the chi-rho. The wreath is a very common Christian device stressing on one side the conception of victory over sin and death, as well as resurrection (if employed together with a chi-rho or a cross) on the other (cf. Rev 1: 10; Kaufmann 1917: 205-206; Bagatti 1958: 125-127; Testini 1958: 361, 437; Daniélou 1969: 262; Gough 1973, Figs. 158-160; Forstner 1982: 379-381; Watts 1988: 213-214). The suggestion of a wreath is here supported by instances of of clay lamps bearing on their discs similarly stylized chi-rhos encircled by wreaths (VI.c.2,5).

IV. Imperial Inscriptions

IV.1. Building inscription of Constantine the Great (II)

Provenance: Varaždinske Toplice (Aquae Iasae); chance find prior to 1600.

Location: Built into the wall of the County Museum at Varaždinske Toplice.

Description: White marble; 160 x 70 cm, thickness 6 cm. A building inscription set up by a provincial governor of Pannonia Superior to honour Constantine's munificences on behalf of the town of Aquae Iasae. It was executed in a fairly good *capitala quadrata*, as befits an imperial inscription of the early 4th century; yet certain mistakes concerning both the cutting of individual words and styling of the composition were not escaped. Words are separated by stop-marks in the form of triangular dots, omitted at places. The cutter apparently had difficulties with the composition as a whole, so he either squeezed individual words or else left them with too much free space, primarily in the right section of the inscription. It runs as follows:

Imp(erator) Caes(ar) Fl(avius) Val(erius) Constantinus, Pius, Felix, Maximus, Aug(ustus), / Aquas Iasas olim vi{i} ignis consumptas cum porticibus / et omnib(us) ornamentis ad pristinam faciem restituit. / Provisione etiam pietatis su(a)e nundinas / die Solis perpeti anno constituit. / Curante Val(erio) Catullino, v(iro) p(erfectissimo), p(raeside) p(rovinciae) P(annoniae) P(rimae) Super(ioris).

(Flavius Valerius Constantinus, pious, felicitous, the greatest and August Emperor, restored to a former shape the baths of Aquae Iasae, previously destroyed in a fire, together with its porches and all their decoration. Induced by his pious providence he also introduced fairs to be held regularly on the day of Sol throughout a year. This inscription was set up under the auspices of most distinguished Valerius Catullinus, governor of the province of Upper Pannonia).

Dating: Between 321 and 324/326.

Literature: CIL III: 4121; AIJ: 210, no. 469; Katalog: 110, no. 139.

Commentary: The only significant detail in the present context concerns the statement on the introduction of fairs to be held on Sundays. A probable religious background to this act was guaranteed by its being induced by 'pious providence'. While the syntagm *dies Solis* bears obvious religious connotations, this is no less true for the fair itself (Delehaye 1907: 265; Barnish 1987: 170; Salway 1993: 194). To find out the true nature of the mentioned religious background, presumably Christian, a variety of possible arguments might be considered. First, only with Constantine

did the week consisting of seven days come into official use, and with it Sunday as the first day and a day of both rest and attending of fairs. While seemingly a reflection of Christian attitudes, it requires a further substantiation in that we should be able to prove that at the beginning of the 4th century the syntagm *dies Solis* was perfectly acceptable for Christians and identified by them with *dies Dominica*, a true Christian holiday; this in fact transpires in literary sources, in epigraphic evidence and above all in various legal acts of Christian emperors (Kaufmann 1917: 47; Dumaine 1920; 858-875; Testini 1958: 398-399, Fig. 183; Kempt - Reusch 1965: 38, no. 29; Kühnel 1994: 16). The issue of the possible Christian significance of the inscription, when once proved possible, depends ultimately on the emperor Constantine's religious affiliations, divided, as known, between Sol and Christ (see Introduction to S.1.-5.). This, unfortunately, is a question unlikely to ever be resolved beyond doubt, for all the immense scholarly discussion and literature on the theme (cf. Vogt 1957; Winkelmann 1961; Jones 1963: 33-34; Halsberghe 1972: 167-171). However, subtleties such as Constantine's deepest perceptions on the nature of Sol or Christ are less important here than is his overt and official support of the Christian Church and its eventual legalization in 313. Particularly interesting in the present context is his decision of 321 to proclaim Sunday a holiday for all the inhabitants of the Empire. Even more significant is the fact that in a legal act Sunday was termed *dies Solis* when *dies Dominica* was clearly implied (Dumaine 1920: 874-875; Vogt 1957:335). Equally significant in this context is the fact that after 323 the image of Sol disappears from the imperial numismatic iconography (Alföldi M R 1964; Heintze von 1983: 146). It follows, therefore, that at least a hint of Christian affiliation should be observed in the wording of Constantine's inscription from Aquae Iasae.

IV.2. Milestone inscription of Julian the Apostate (II)

Provenance: Osijek (Mursa); chance find in 1889 outside the town walls.

Location: MSO (664)

Description: Limestone; height 207 cm, diam. 42 cm. A milestone containing as many as three imperial inscriptions from the 4th century, two of them Diocletian's and the third one of Julian the Apostate. The latter reads as follows:

Bono r(ei) p(ublicae) nato D(omino)
Fl(avio) Cl(audio) Iuliano,
[c]vm max(imo) triunf(o), semp[er]
Aug(usto), ob deleta vitia

[5]*temporum preter(i)*
totum.
(To the emperor Flavius Claudius Iulianus, who was born for the well-being of the Empire and has always proved a great winner, for having eradicated vices of bygone times).
Dating: A. D. 361
Literature: CIL III: 10648; Pinterović 1978: 95-96, T. 19: 2; Katalog 1994: 103, n. 113.
Commentary: Although the primary function of Roman milestones was to yield information on distances between various settlements, they assumed an additional role of medium for dedicatory inscriptions in later periods. Not infrequently, particularly in Africa, they expressed religious subject matters and feelings (Oliva 1962: 326; Salama 1967). The apposition to Julian's name speaks for itself of his religious affiliation and his devotion to revivifying the pagan religion is well-known. The inscription in question conforms to others of this kind in that its sole intention was to point out the fact of the emperor Julian's dtrive against Christianity, denoted here as 'the vice of past times' (Salama 1967: 280). It was classified here as only probable evidence for Christianity; it cannot be certain beyond doubt that specific references to Christianity of the area around Mursa were implied in addition to the general perception of Julian as a militant for the pagan cause. However, given the rich history of Christianity (both Arian and orthodox) in Mursa during the whole of the 4th century (cf I.a.1.), this suggestion is highly probable.

V. Small Objects of Ornament

Introduction

In keeping with the overall Christianization of spiritual and material aspects of daily life, introduced by Christian emperors of the House of Constantine from approximately the mid 4th century, early Christians applied Christian devices either cryptically stylized or overtly expressed to a wide range of personal ornament and accessories. They seem to have been more devoted and zealous in this respect than the pagans (Dölger 1958; 7-8; Dölger 1963: 22-23; Dölger 1966; Demandt 1989: XVII; Mawer 1995: 59, passim). There are sound reasons for viewing thus applied devices as both ornamental and symbolic, the primary one being their frequent placement on objects that contain symbolic attitudes in their very shape or position of wear. This is particularly relevant for brooches, arm-rings, finger-rings and belt fittings; most usually they bear devices with combined religious and apotropaic symbolism, hard to differentiate in any event (Testini 1958: 487; Salin 1959: 101 ff.; Dinkler 1962: 99; Dölger 1964: 24-26; Kyll 1966: 58-62; Huskinson 1974: 77; Engemann 1975: 42-48; Forstner 1982: 331-344, 416-428; Mawer 1995: 59, 139).

Two levels of artistic stylization within early Christian iconography can basically be perceived: one cryptical, allegorical and syncretistic and the other intentionally stylized as a consequence of artistic will. It is not appropriate here to dwell on the insoluble issue of the dichotomy between the 'pure' or the symbolic decoration, whatever it means, of artistic devices applied to various objects and in different media of Romano-Christian art (see chapter 4. of the main Introduction). The commentator on symbolic associations of whatever work of art should essentially bear in mind that these imply attitudes of both the author and the perceiver (Pillinger 1989: 92; Migotti 1994: 192). Most conspicuous Christian artistic stylizations of the period after 313, containing primarily manifold cross-like compositions, can be observed in various monumental media, most of all mosaic (Gough 1973: 71; Engemann 1975: 46-48, Abb. 14, Taf. 16; Klein-Pfeuffer 1993, Abb. 73; Kühnel 1994: 167). They are as a rule rooted in pre-Christian art and are retained as late as 7th century 'Barbarian Christian antiquity'; they should be taken into account when appreciating possible Christian associations of devices on small objects (see V.a.14.).

V.a. Brooches (fibulae)

V.a.1. Cross-bow brooch with three knobs (I)

Provenance: Osijek (Mursa); chance find during building works in 1934; north-west section of town where a Christian church was conjectured (Fig. 1:2; Fig. 3).
Location: AMZ
Description: Gold-plated bronze; 10 x 7 cm. A brooch with a seemingly massive, yet hollow-cast short bow and a flat rectangular catch-plate, both lavishly ornamented by engraving and niello technique. The catch plate has 'pelta-scroll' designed borders in the form of openwork lace and upper surface filled with floral and geometric motifs of alternating roundels and rhomboid shapes. The bow bears all over a geometric decoration, in addition to a frontal male

bust in the middle and a chi-rho at either end.
Dating: second half of the 4th century.

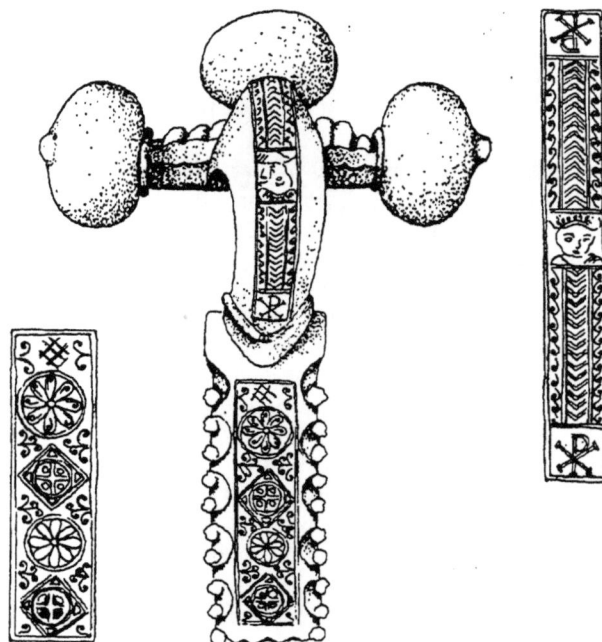

Commentary: This type of brooch, related almost exclusively to the male dress of state officials and military, is of interest here from the point of view of both its shape and provenance. While occurring in large numbers everywhere in the Empire, this type appears to stem from the Illyrian provinces, Pannonia being most probably the particular area of its origin (Lányi 1972: 140-141; Vinski 1974: 7-9; Koščević 1979: 54; Vágó - Bóna 1976: 166-167; Bojović 1983: 82, 173; Pröttel 1988: 347-348). The chronological sensitivity of cross-bow brooches has understandably been their most often discussed archaeological aspect; no discussion has arisen on symbolic associations of the cross-like shape, despite its being implied in the very name of the brooch. Most commonly used in recent literature are derivatives of the German term *Zwiebelknopffibel*, related to three knobs on the bow (Pröttel 1988). The formerly popular term - cross-bow brooch, referring to the cross-like bows - has been retained mostly in the English speaking areas. Contrarily, the prevalence for the German term has been explained in Croatian literature as a means of avoiding confusion with types of plate cross-shaped fibulae (Vinski 1974: 53, note 32; for plate cross-like fibulae see Bierbrauer 1992). It can be presumed that the avoiding of the term cross-bow fibulae has also to do with a reluctance to recognize religous symbolic implications in the very shape of these objects. Such implications, however, remain a real possibility, the more so as the period of their appearance in the 3rd century corresponds to the begginings of the Christian art in the proper sense of the word. On the other hand, it is only understandable that by seeking to establish a possible Christian origin of the artistic conception of these objects, an uncontested Christian affiliation of their owners would not be claimed.

Yet another interesting question imposes itself in relation to cross-like fibulae when compared with the plate cross-like types, symptomatic in principle of female dress (Vinski 1968: 138, 147; Bierbrauer 1992: 2): Would it be too bold to envisage the cross-bow fibula of the male dress as the counterpart of the 'female' cross-like type? This suggestion unfortunately loses much of its appeal when dating is considered; it appears that by the time the cross-like plate fibula gained in popularity in the 6th century, the cross-bow type had become outmoded. Whatever the case, the brooch from Osijek was in any event designated as Christian on account not of its shape, but its device, and the remainder of the discusion stays in the domain of hypothesis.

V.a.2. Cross-shaped openwork fibula (I)

Provenance: Osijek (Mursa)
Location: MSO (3437)
Description: Bronze; diam. 2.8 cm. An openwork brooch in the shape of an equal-armed cross with expanded terminals.
Dating: second half of the 6th century.
Literature: Vikić-Belančić 1978: 602, Fig. 21; Katalog: 106, no. 124.

V.a.3. Cross-shaped plate fibula (I)

Provenance: Mediaeval castle of Ozalj; found during excavation in 1992 on the site of the Romanesque church and possibly parts of masonry of early Christian architecture.
Location: ZMO
Description: Silver-plated bronze; 3.4 x 2.6 cm. A fibula in the shape of an equal-armed (most of the right arm is missing) cross with expanded terminals. Each arm bears a decoration in the form of three impressed circles with a dot in the centre, with an additional circle in the middle of the cross.
Dating: second half of the 6th century.
Literature: Čučković 1994: 9; Katalog: 114, no. 147.

V.a.4. Cross-shaped plate fibula (I)

Provenance: Sisak (Siscia); chance find possibly from the south-eastern Roman cemetery (Fig. 5:5).

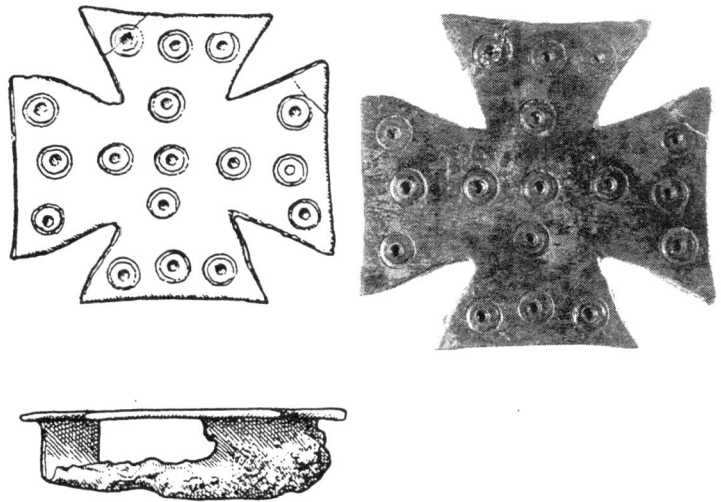

Location: AMZ (1926)
Description: Silver; 3 x 3 cm. A brooch in the shape of an equal-armed cross with expanded terminals. The upper surface is decorated with impressed dotted circles, with each of the arms bearing three circles along its edges, in addition to a cruciform arrangement of four circles in the middle of the brooch.
Dating: second half of the 6th century.
Literature: Vinski 1968: 107, T. 5:8; Simoni 1989: 122, T. 4:4; Katalog: 85, no. 49.

V.a.5. Cross-shaped plate fibula (I)

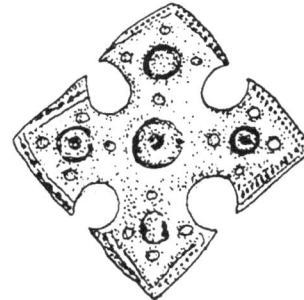

Provenance: Sisak (Siscia); chance find.
Location: AMZ (misplaced).
Description: Bronze; 4 x 4 cm. A brooch in the shape of an equal-armed cross with triangular or, rather, anchor-like terminals devised by four semicircular indentations of the four edges of a rhombic plate. The upper surface is decorated with four conspicuous, probably impressed (the artefact is only known from a drawing) cruciform arranged dotted circles, each in turn encircled with four smaller dots.
Dating: second half of the 6th century.
Literature: Vinski 1974: 22, T. 14:8; Katalog: 62, Fig. 15.
Commentary on V.a.2.3.4.5.: Cross-like ornaments in various forms and media are of the Roman artistic and cultural heritage, but one that subsequently gained much popularity with Christianized Barbarian peoples, who settled down on Roman soil during the 5th and 6th centuries. This type of jewellery was most typical of the greater Alpine area and Dalmatia and, as it appears, southern Pannonia as well. The Romano-Christian tradition here is mirrored in the choice of motif (about the cross see III.a.4.), while Barbarian

attitudes can be perceived in a somewhat rustic execution and irregular employment of precious metals (Vinski 1968: 119 ff.; Bierbrauer 1992: 17-18). This type of brooch can then safely be considered as a product of 'Barbarized late antiquity' and was accordingly favoured by both the Romans and Barbarians. Most of the known objects of this group were recovered from graves of as late the second half of the 6th century (Vinski 1968: 129; Bierbrauer 1992: 11); the lack of finds from the 5th century and the first half of the 6th remains as yet unexplained. Curiously enough, all types of cross-like personal ornaments, brooches included, are related to exclusively female burials (Vinski 1968: 147; Bierbrauer 1992: 2).

Within the group of items under discussion here brooch no. V.a.2. should be singled out as the sole specimen featuring a Christian variation on the so-called solar cross, known within Christian iconography as the coronated cross (crux coronata). It ocurrs as early as the 4th century on not only small objects, but also on items of church furniture, sarcophagi, mosaics and paintings, to gain its utmost popularity in the 6th century (see S.1.). The type of personal ornament in the form of an encircled cross, whether it be on a fibula or a pendant, is generally less frequent than the type featuring a cross free of the circle (Vinski 1968: 129-130; Schretter 1993: 188-190). However, the specimen from Osijek is by no means unique and has many immediate parallels (Anamali 1971: 220, T. 7:6; Nedved 1981: 176, Fig. 7:280; Menghin 1985: 174, Abb. 165).

V.a.6. Liturgical(?) plate brooch (I)

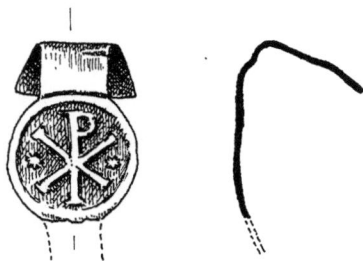

Provenance: Sisak (Siscia)
Location: MS
Description: Gold-plated bronze sheet; diam. of the roundel 1.7 cm, dimensions of the trapezoidal section: 2.4 x 0.9-1.6 cm. The upper section of a brooch in the form of a trapezoidal plate with a roundel attached to its lower part; trapezoidal section has been crooked and recurved, as is visible on the drawing. The round plate with slightly moulded bordering bears a chi-rho with serifed arms and two stars in the horizontal quarterings of chi, executed in very low relief. On the underside vestiges of the catch-pin in the form of a stunted swelling are visible.
Dating: second half of the 4th century.
Literature: Katalog: 90, no. 72.

V.a.7. Liturgical(?) plate brooch (I)

Provenance: Probably Sisak (Siscia); reported to have been seen in AMZ in the 1930's.
Location: No data available.
Description: Gold-plated bronze sheet much the same as the previous item; dimensions (according to a drawing taken

from the literature as the sole record of this object): diam. of the roundel 2.9 cm, overall dimensions of the extant portion: 8.3 x 0.6-2.2 cm.; preserved upper section was subsequently pierced for an unknown purpose. Also extant are a circular plate and approximately a third of the original lower section of the brooch in the form of an elongated sub-trapezoidal plate tapering towards the base. Within a slightly moulded circle in roundel a chi-rho with serifed arms is depicted, while faint traces of accompanying stars are likewise discernible.
Dating: second half of the 4th century.
Literature: Tóth 1988: 59, Abb. 26.

Commentary on V.a.6.7.: Only three specimens of this unusul type of brooch have so far been found in the territory of Roman *Pannonia* (I know of no examples from elsewhere), two under discussion here stemming from *Pannonia Savia*, and the third one from *Pannonia Prima*, modern Hungary (Tóth 1988: 58-59; Tóth 1994: 254). All the three are nearly identical in shape and size (except for the Hungarian specimen lacking stars by chi-rho) and probably constitute a type unique to Pannonia. With two of them stemming from Sisak, their Siscian manufacture can reasonably be suggested, and to no surprise: Siscia was the well-known production centre in various branches of metal-work (Koščević in: Koščević - Makjanić 1995).

These objects were securely dated not only on grounds of their decoration, but also by analogy to the archeological context of the Hungarian find (Tóth 1988: 60-61). As for the motif, its iconographic model should be sought for in the Urbs Roma type of Constantine's issue with on the reverse a depiction of the Capitolian wolf and above it a chi-rho with a star at either side. As early as the mid 4th century this motif became widespread on other types of small objects of glass, clay and metal. It gained its utmost popularity in the second half of the 4th century and in the 5th; this is on the whole true of all artefacts bearing a chi-rho with additional elements like alfa and omega, stars, animals, birds etc. (Garrucci 1873, Tav. 189:6, 192:2; Garrucci 1880: Tav. 481:27; Sauer J 1958; Rigoir - Rigoir - Meffre 1973: 254, no. 2293). The motif of the chi-rho accompanied by two stars is usually interpreted symbolically as representing Christ's redemptive power over the Universe (Leclercq 1924f: 3016-3017; Forstner 1982: 103-106).

A precise purpose for which these objects were intended remains fairly obscure; nowhere they were found in an undisturbed context. As already mentioned, the Hungarian specimen stems from a site dated securely by coins, which was an argument sufficient for dating also the brooch. The brooch, however, was a chance find prior to the excavation on the site and therefore devoid of its own context. The site in question is Alsóhetény in Pannonia Prima, where recently a late Roman fortified settlement has been excavated in addition to a cemetery with a lavishly decorated early Christian mausoleum; these contingencies urged Hungarian archaeologists to seek there the much disputed location of the see of Iovia (Tóth 1988: 61; Tóth 1989; cf. also hereI.a.4.).

With both the fineness and delicacy of these brooches and their decoration in mind, Tóth suggested their use as safety-pins on a bishop's pallium, made of some light material. Although as yet unattested either archaeologically or in the sources, this suggestion is not to be altogether discarded. Whatever the case, the use of these brooches was manifestly more decorative than functional.

V.a.8. Brooch in the shape of dove (II)

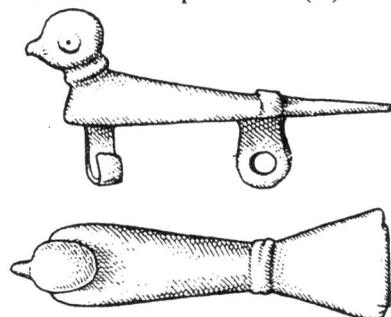

Provenance: Sisak (Siscia)
Location: AMZ (1928)
Description: Silver; 3.4 x 1.7 cm. A full cast brooch in the form of a dove. On the rounded head the eye is rendered by means of an engraved dotted circle, while the junctions of the elongated body with neck and tail are marked by annular mouldings.
Dating: 4th/6th centuries.
Literature: Simoni 1989: 109, T. 2:8; Katalog: 84, no. 43.

V.a.9. Brooch in the shape of dove (II)

Provenance: Sisak (Siscia)
Location: AMZ (3918)
Description: Bronze; 2.9 x 2.9 cm. Nearly identical in shape with previous one, but for the material and a rougher execution; tail section is missing.
Dating: 4th/6th centuries.
Literature: Simoni 1989: 109, T. 2:7; Katalog: 84, no. 44.

V.a.10. Brooch in the shape of peacock (II)

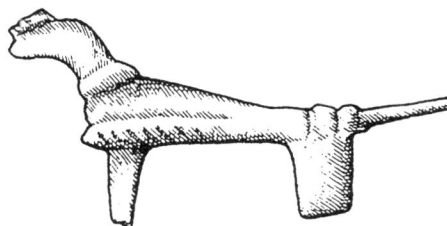

Provenance: Sisak (Siscia)
Location: AMZ (3396)
Description: Bronze; 4.2 x 2.1 cm. Full cast brooch in the shape of a peacock. The slightly elongated head bears a crest, while the bordering lines between body and neck and tail are marked by annular mouldings. The tail is fluted, and the lower section of the body is hatchured with short oblique strokes. Part of the fastening device is preserved in the form of two stumps.
Dating: 4th/6th centuries.
Literature: Simoni 1989: 110, T. 2:6; Katalog: 84, no. 45.

V.a.11. Brooch in the shape of peacock (II)

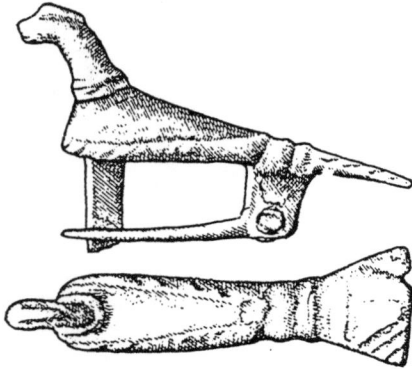

Provenance: Sisak (Siscia)
Location: AMZ (3397)
Description: Bronze; 3.7 x 2.3 cm; nearly identical with the previous specimen, only the fastening device is completely preserved.
Dating: 4th/6th centuries.
Literature: Simoni 1989: 110, T. 2:10; Katalog: 84, no. 46.

V.a.12. Plate brooch in the shape of eagle (II)

Provenance: Sisak (Siscia)
Location: AMZ (1994)

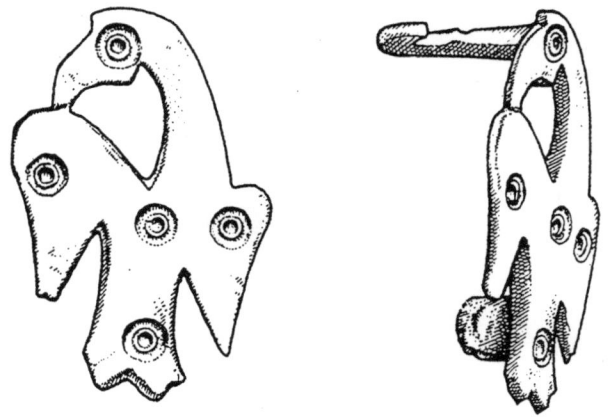

Description: Bronze; 3.7 x 2.5 cm; a brooch cast as a fairly thin plate in the shape of an eagle. The bird's body is frontal with spread wings, while the head in profile is bent down towards the right wing which he is touching with his beak. The tail section is missing. The upper surface of brooch is decorated all over with a cruciform arrangement of five impressed dotted circles, one of them standing for the bird's eye. On the back, vestiges of the fastening device are visible.
Dating: 6th century.
Literature: Simoni 1989: 114, T. 4:5; Katalog: 85, no 5.

V.a.13. Plate fibula in the shape of eagle (II)

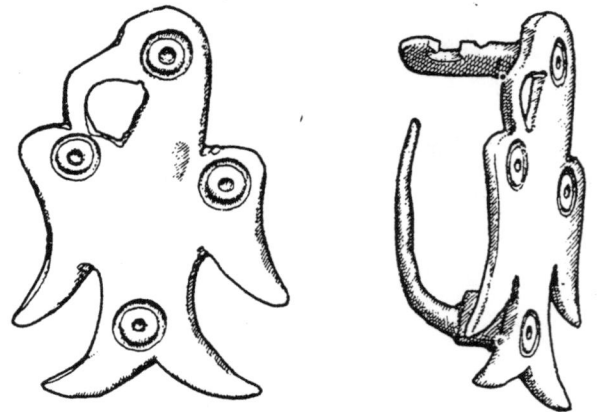

Provenance: Sisak (Siscia)
Location: AMZ (1927)
Description: Bronze; 3.7 x 2.6 cm; nearly identical with previous specimen, except for the decorative scheme lacking the central circle, and wings sligtly curled outwards. This artefact has suffered no damage and even the fastening device is completely preserved on the back.
Dating: 6th century.
Literature: Simoni 1989: 114, T. 4:6; Katalog: 85, no. 51.
Commentary on V.a.8.9.10.11.12.13.: All the items were classified as probably Christian, despite the lack of any manifestly Christian devices. This comes as a result of a general attitude of early Christian thinking and iconography towards the three specific birds: in the period between the 5th and 7th centuries the dove and the peacock, and to a slightly less measure the eagle, were very frequently found in undoubtedly Christian contexts. Consequently, they are usually assumed to have Christian associations even when found in isolation from other diagnostic motifs or without a corroborative context, as is the case here (Leclercq 1926: 29-31; Werner 1962: 128; Knfic - Sagadin 1991: 108, Fig. 75,

nos 69-75; Mawer 1995: 60). All the three of them represent known Christian allegories, confirmed time and again in both the documentary sources and the archaeological evidence. The dove stands for a variety of Christian conceptions, for instance Christ, Holy Spirit, Church, soul, peace, innocence, deliverance, fidelity etc.; the peacock, with its supposedly incorruptible flesh, is the metaphor for eternity, immortality and ressurrection (see II.2.3.). The type of brooches in the form of dove or peacock, very similar in style and technique to those under discussion here, are most typical of North Italy and the Alpine and Subalpine areas.

The eagle is the *par excellence* solar bird and a symbol of immortality (Halsberghe 1972: 78), acceptable accordingly to Christian conceptions; in pagan and Christian thinking alike it is an emblem of ruler of both Heaven and Earth, and of Jupiter and Christ alike. Christian iconography has further attached to the eagle virtues of righteousness, generosity, heartiness and bravery, and has ultimately related him to the divine inspiration of St John the Evangelist (Salin 1959: 197-200; Grabar 1968: 113; Klein-Pfeuffer 1993: 146; Forstner 1982: 220-22). Concerning, however, the secular (imperial) symbolism of the eagle, no more than a possible Christian affiliation should be attached to objects featuring the image of this bird, but lacking a context. Yet in the instances of items V.a.12. and 13. this possibility was felt to be enhanced by the decorative scheme of cruciform arranged dotted concentric circles, which are likely to convey basically solar conceptions (Salin 1959: 122). Identical arrangements on some cross-shaped brooches and other objects (see V.a.4.5., V.g.1.;) speak in favour of this feature as a thought-out symbolic device, and not a mere coincidence or the artist's whim. Certain general analogies for Christian-aquiline symbolism from the repertoire of 'Barbarian antiquity' are even more telling than the two specimens from Sisak (cf. Bierbrauer 1994: 196, Fig. III.74a).

Brooches in the form of dove and peacock, very similar in style and technique to these here, are typical of North Italy and the Alpine and Subalpine areas. They are perceived as the autochthonous Romano-Christian heritage, taken up subsequently by Christianized tribesmen (Knific - Sagadin 1991: 107-108, nos. 72-75; 1993: 195-198). If found without a determining context, they are virtually undatable more precisely than within the span of two centuries, the 5th and 6th. Brooches in the shape of the eagle are even more ambiguous in this respect: a specimen from Dura Europos, identical with those from Sisak, was dated to the 2nd century or the 3rd, and was observed as typical of the eastern provinces and the Balkans (Schulze M, in: JRGZM 32/1985: 738-739, Abb. 52:7). True, zoomorphic plate fibulae, those in the form of eagle included, are typical of the imperial period (Böhme 1972). These early specimens were, however, far more often decorated by means of enamelling than engraving or impressions; a continuous line between early brooches and those from the late Roman period cannot be proved beyond doubt (Böhme 1972: 40; Schretter 1993: 197-198; Koščević in: Koščević - Makjanić 1995: 20). Additional proof for a 6th century date for specimens V.a.12. and 13. has been established by a type of decoration in the form of impressed dotted circles, identical with those on the more securely dated cross-shaped brooches (V.a.3.4.5.). It should also be borne in mind that the 6th century is the period of the eagle gaining its utmost popularity as a

Christian symbol (Leclercq 1926: 29-31)

V.a.14. Longobard bow fibula (III)

Provenance: Sisak (Siscia)
Location: AMZ (1920)
Description: Gold-plated silver; 5.5 x 3.5 cm; a brooch with three-knobbed terminals on a semicircular head-plate and with short bow and rhombic catch-plate. The head and bow bear spiral motifs, while the catch plate is decorated with a chip-carved meandering swastika/cross.
Dating: mid 6th century.
Literature: Simoni 1989: 113, Taf. 4:1; Katalog: 85, no. 48.
Commentary: The meandering swastika on the catch-plate may freely be perceived as a mere decoration; yet in various media of early Christian art, it was widely used as an emblem of the cross (Eizenhöfer 1967: 61, Taf. 1a; Engemann 1975: 42-43, Abb. 11, Taf. 16c; Plesničar-Gec et al. 1983: 18; Pillinger 1989: 95; Lucchesi-Palli 1990: 120-121). Correspondingly the possibility should not be discarded of the meandering swastika here representing a cross. To reinforce this interpretation, religious conceptions of Christianized Barbarians can be mentioned, characterized profoundly by the inclination towards syncretism and simulation in displaying religious symbols (Arrhenius 1986; Bierbrauer 1994: 179, 189, 198, Figs. III.41, III.65; Ripoll López 1994: 307-309, Figs. IV.11.,13.).

V.a.15. Horse-head swastika fibula (III)

Provenance: Probably Sotin (Cornacum).
Location: MSO (1134)
Description: Bronze; 3.4 x 3.1 cm. A plate fibula in the form of a rounded swastika with horse-head terminals. The horses' eyes are marked by incised circles with a central dot, as is the

junction of their necks in the the middle of body. The upper surface is smooth and shiny, while the back, with traces of a fastening device, is rough.

Dating: 3rd/4th centuries.

Literature: Vinski 1068: 132, T. 18:41; Katalog: 106, no. 121.

Commentary: A Christian identification of this object could only be attested by a determining context, which in this case is missing altogether. To both the swastika and the horse have been attached religious, magical and apotropaic symbolic associations, primarily solar, reaching as far back as the prehistoric periods. All three symbolic components of horse and swastika blend during the late Roman period into specific Christianized conceptions (Salin 1959: 200). It was exactly solar attitudes from which Christianity took over a conception of the horse as a divine creature endowed with an august nature and capable of overwhelming wordly deficiencies and evils (Leclercq 1948b; Kantorowicz 1964; Forstner 1982: 282-285). Correspondingly the swastika had been given attributes of an emblem of the solar cult *par excellence*, reinforced quite often by concentric circles of undoubtedly solar inspiration (Salin 1959: 122; Buora 1992, Pl. 1, 2). As a religious and magical-apotropaic metaphor for life, the swastika was continuously present in Roman art and artistic conceptions of the peoples on the fringes of the Roman empire, particulary Germans, from the 1st/2nd centuries onwards (Bóna 1963: 262; Thomas S 1967: 54, 71; Ellmers 1974: 236, Taf. 98:6). The swastika was in early Christian art from the 2nd/3rd centuries down to the 6th employed variously as an overt or a disguised emblem of the cross, covering all its manifold meanings (Garrucci 1873: 50, Tav. 1, passim; Kaufmann 1917: 64-67; Leclercq 1953b; Salin 1959: 121-128; Forstner 1982: 20; Bastien 1988: 161-163; Schultze-Dörrlamm 1990: 368; Klein-Pfeiffer 1993: 94, Abb. 17).

V.a.16. Anchor and S-shaped fibula (III)

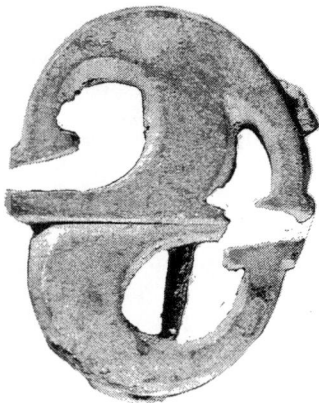

Provenance: Novačka, site of Gradina; a cremation burial in a tumulus excavated in 1980.

Location: MGK (2846)

Description: Bronze; 2.8 x 2.1 cm. A plate fibula in the shape of the reversed letter S with an anchor-like lower section.

Dating: End of the 2nd century/3rd century.

Literature: Šarić 1981: 79; Katalog 76, no. 15d.

Commentary: This item constitutes an exception, and hopefully an excusable one, to the practice (as imposed by the overall scheme of the catalogue) of shunning too remote possibilities in the III category of the material evidence. Two finds from Novačka (a brooch and a terra sigillata bowl) were included with the intention of discussing certain debatable issues of early Christian funerary practices (see VI.d.9.). The brooch is a mixed variation of two different types, the trumpet and anchor fibulae, dated to the end of the 2nd/3rd centuries. Like the swastika brooches this type is typical of the Danube provinces and the Balkans (Böhme 1972: 43-44, Taf. 29:1143). The object under discussion displays two specific features with possible Christian symbolic associations: the anchor and the shape of the letter S, which gives the overall form to the artefact. In both pagan and Christian iconographies the anchor symbolizes consistency, steadiness, tranquillity and fidelity. Christian thinking adds to these meanings a specific connotation of the cross and through it of salvation and ressurection, as attested in the words of St Paul to the Hebrews (6: 19); the anchor was thereby turned into one of the most frequent symbolic depictions in the Christian funerary iconography (Kirsch 1924; Stumpf 1950; Testini 1958: 220, Fig. 64, pasim; Eizehöfer 1960: 67-68; Forstner 1982: 399-401; Higgins 1987: 116). Concurrently in early Christian symbolic thinking the letter S comprises a variety of meanings (see G.4). In the present context the term *spes* (hope) appears to be particularly significant in view of its possible relation to the above-mentioned quotation from St Paul, where the word *spes* is perceived metaphorically as the anchor of soul; in funerary art (possibly as an echo of these words) depictions of the anchor were occasionally acompanied by the word hope in its Latin or Greek form (Forstner 1982: 401). It follows therefore that a possibility exists, if slight, of the brooch in question having been designed to associate certain Christian meanings. Understandably the issue of the original symbolic conception of this, as any other object, does not automatically include the correspondent religious affiliation of its owner (see VI.d.9.). As concerns the hypothetical symbolism of small ornamental objects at the level of their basic design, it is interesting to observe that a 'pure' version of the anchor fibula from the 2nd/3rd centuries appears to be originating in south-Pannonian territory (Koščević in: Koščević - Makjanić 1995: 19; Katalog: 78, no. 21).

V.b. Belt fittings

V.b.1. Buckle plate (I)

Provenance: Sisak (Siscia)
Location: AMZ (1938)
Description: Bronze; 4.5 x 2.5. An openwork sub-triangular plate with three perforations, one of them heart-shaped and two round, featuring a human face in the guise of a mask. At the lower edge, possibly in the place of a beard, a plate disc has been attached with an equal-armed cross incised within a barely visible circle.
Dating: 7th century.
Literature: Vinski 1974: 25-26, T. 18:7; Simoni 1989: 117, Taf. 6:9; Katalog: 86, no. 52.
Commentary: This artefact is part of a belt buckle of the Corinth type, typical of the Mediterranean and surrounding areas in the 7th century and considered to be a Byzantine product intended for both Roman Christians and the Christianized Barbarians (Vinski 1974: 25-27; Ripoll López 1994: 307, Fig. IV.11). It was suggested that the specimen in question reached Siscia after the destruction of the town by the Avars (Vinski 1974: 26), which in terms of chronology would disqualify it as evidence for Christianity in the present context. However, it was included for consideration on the grounds of both its configuration and symbolic associations. This artefact appears to be a good case in point for the illustration of the survival of Christian artistic features at the dawn of the as yet pagan Avar Middle Ages (the Avars being Christianized only in subsequent centuries, see Bálint 1985: 214). Its decorative conception further displays an accomodation of Christian features to Barbarian styles. This is evident in the fusion of the cross and the openwork technique as Romano-Byzantine features (but those widely accepted by the Barbarians, see Salin 1959: 327, 368; Schulze-Dörrlamm 1990: 243) with the mask as typical of Barbarian fashions. The mask, basically an apotropaic device in Barbarian artistic conceptions, assumes in time the role of an emblem of either the Christian ruler or Christ himself (Salin 1959: 258-281; Milojčić 1968: 238 ff.; Vinski 1974: 33, note 335; Arrhenius 1983: 141-145; Bierbrauer 1994: 198-199). In a word, a Christianized Barbarian can be envisaged as the owner of the buckle plate from Sisak.

Paraphrased Christian elements are well-known features of Christianized Barbarian art (Arrhenius 1983). Curiously enough, they seem to reflect a process from the formative periods (2nd/3rd centuries) of Christian art, the most conspicuous feature of which was Christianization of pagan subject-matters.

V.b.2. Belt mount (I?)

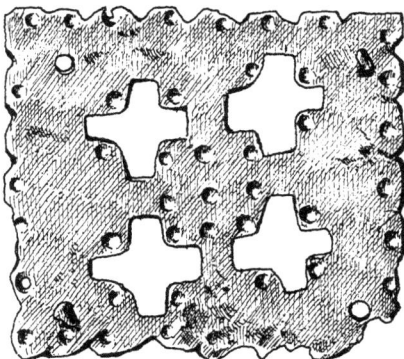

Provenance: Sotin (Cornacum)

Location: AMZ (15)
Description: Iron; 5.2 x 4.7 cm. A roughly executed openwork plate in the form of a near-square frame with notched edges. Within the frame is a solid central equal-armed cross with rectangular expansions of terminals and a rectangular plate at the intersection of the arms. In the quarterings between the arms of the central cross and frame, an additional four equal-armed crosses figure as coarsely executed openwork shapes. The surface is completely filled with regularly spaced small shallow pits, intended probably for inlay (enamel or glass-paste) filling. The plate was secured by four rivets at the outer corners, with two of them misssing and the stumps of the remaining two still in place.
Dating: 6th/7th centuries(?)
Litrature: Katalog: 127, no. 182.
Commentary: Within the late Roman 'military' style of belt fittings, predominant are objects decorated with a well-known repertoire of chip-carved linear and curvilinear motifs. They are usually accorded Germanic affinities and are concomitantly ascribed to German mercenaries in the Roman military (Bullinger 1969; Böhme 1983). Whether all such items belonged to military or even to male wear is a debatable question (cf. Mawer 1995: 60), but one outside the scope of this study. On the other hand, openwork items of belt fittings are a rarity in comparison with those chip-carved, the specimen from Sotin being moreover unique (for the openwork technique see V.b.1.); it can be classified among a broader group of cross-like ornaments and fittings (see V.a.2.-5.; V.f.1.).

The motif shown features five crosses, a central one surrounded by four smaller ones. It is known as the cross of Jerusalem, perceived as symbolizing the five wounds of Chris, and is basically an artistic device of mediaeval and later Christian art (Forstner 1982: 21; Higgins 1987: 123, Fig. 40:C). In any event, the origin of this motif should ultimately be late Roman, as is evident from many similar, although not identical, depictions on barbarian objects of the 6th/7th centuries, either manufactured for them in Byzantium or produced among them in imitation of Byzantine models (for a relief specimen see Ellmers 1974: 236, Taf. 98:6). Circular seats for a filling should also be interpreted as a concession to Barbarian tastes. The almost identical motif of five crosses appears on a key from Maastricht dated to the 4th century (Leclercq 1948c: 1861, Fig. 3010), but the date seems to be disputable. Near (although not immediate) parallels are frequently met in various media (stone relief, metal-work, mosaic) of the late Roman/early Christian art of the 5th to the 7th centuries and in areas of the conspicuous fusion of Romano-Germanic artistic styles (Lassus 1935: 88, Fig. 98; Bassier - Darmon - Tainturier 1981: 139-140, Fig. 13; Sage 1984: 115-116, Taf. 49:21; Demandt 1986: 115, Fig. 4; Schulze-Dörrlamm 1990: 241-243, Taf. 47).

A question-mark by the classification number denotes a possible slight hesitance about this object being authentic at all, since both the context and the exact parallels are missing.

V.b.3. Strap end (II)

Provenance: Sisak (Siscia); dredging of the river Kupa in 1912.
Location: AMZ (1933)
Description: Bronze with glass inlay; 3.2 x 1.6 cm. A full cast U-shaped strap-end, with lower edge semicircular and the upper one notched and provided with a rivet for securing to a leather belt. Engraved in relief on the upper surface is a motif consisting of two perpendicular triangles and two horizontal circles in a cruciform arrangement, featuring approximately a stylized equal-armed cross; both the triangles and circles are inlaid with red glass settings. The cruciform motif is encircled with four sinuous lines reminiscent of a tendril.
Dating: 7th century.
Literature: Vinski 1974: 30, T. 21:18; Simoni 1989: 117, T. 6:12; Katalog: 86, no. 53.
Commentary: This type is another of a mass of late Roman/Byzantine products accommodated to barbarian tastes, but equally favoured by the autochthonous 'barbarized' Romans (see V.b.1.2.). The central cruciform design is most probably intended for a cross, a concession to Barbarian affinities being mirrored in the specific cruciform stylization and the colourful effect produced by the inlays. The putative cross might possibly have derived from a mask motif, as indicated by side tendrils (vestigial hair and beard?), well-known from similar renderings (see V.b.1.) The whole of the decorative conception would then amount to a representative and meaningful blend of the mask and the cross, symptomatic in principle of Barbaro-Christian iconography (Milojčić 1968: 235; Arrhenius 1986: 141-145).

V.b.4. Strap end (II)

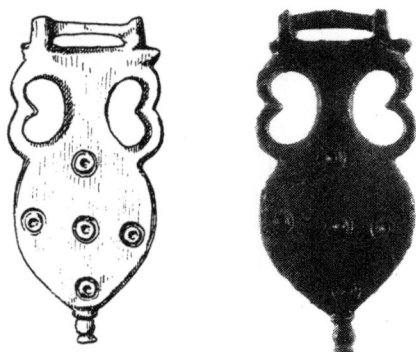

Provenance: Štrbinci (Certissa?); excavation in 1993; found in a grave next to head of a male skeleton.
Location: MĐĐ
Description: Bronze; 4.5 x 2.1 cm. A full cast strap-end in the form of a small amphora. On the upper surface five dotted circles in a cruciform arrangement are impressed.
Dating: 4th century.
Literature: Katalog: 118, no. 161; Gregl 1994: 185, T. 5:7/3.
Commentary: For a variety of reasons the cruciform design on this item should be understood as probably symbolic, i.e. Christian. First, the grave was placed in the immediate vicinity of the early Christian frescoed tomb (III.a.1.). Second, the design was not adjusted to the shape of the object and is accordingly not a 'structural' decoration. Third, parts of belt-fittings are known as objects most frequently given to symbolic decoration and finally, this kind of stylization of the cross is fairly common in early Christian iconography (see V.e.5. and V.g.1.).

V.b.5. Strap end (II)

Provenance: Sisak (Siscia)
Location: AMZ (6375)
Description: Bronze; 6.7 x 1.9/2.3 cm. An openwork strap-end in the form of an elongated sub-rectangular plate with two holes for now missing rivets and with a geometrically stylized floral finial at one end. The space within the solid frame is filled with openwork motifs of equal-armed crosses and gradation-shapes.
Dating: End of the 2nd century/3rd century.
Literature: Košečvić 1991: 140, T. 29:400; Katalog: 79, no. 16.
Commentary: This item is a good illustration of the ambiguities concerning the problem of the (un)suitability of attaching symbolic meaning to early instances of iconographically clearly designed cross-like shapes; such renderings are mainly observed as purely decorative (see chapter 4. in the main Introduction). True, taking the 4th century as a chronological limit to allow for Christian artistic symbolism is a safe choice; in dealing with various small finds in studies other than those specifically devoted to early Christian themes, the issue of possible early Christian appurtenances has as a rule been avoided (cf. Oldenstein 1977: 194-195). Considering, however, all the historical and artistic contingencies, the 3rd century should not be discarded in this respect (see III.a.4.).

This 'minimalistic' attitude deserves a reconsideration for another reason: the general lines of the organization of industry and manufacture in the imperial period. The imperial industry of military equipment in the period of the 1st to the 3rd centuries was, for instance, only partially managed and supervised from the centre of the Empire (Oldenstein 1977: 76-85); at the level, not only of practical execution, but also of artistic and symbolic design, local craftsmen were allowed considerable independence. Artistic conceptions reflecting a specific religious symbolism in the design of small objects might therefore have easily originated in local surroundings, provided these were touched with Christian attitudes prior to the 4th century. In other words, an inconspicuous group of people or even an individual could have been responsible for such 'freaks', with the remainder of the community completely indifferent to or even ignorant of them. It is also worth noting in this context that as early as the 3rd century, Christian communities were documented in even more backward provinces of the Empire, Pannonia included (Frend 1964; Jarak 1994: 158). To reinforce the interpretation of the item in question as evidence for Christianity, a near identical decoration on various objects of barbarized Christian antiquity of the 5th/7th centuries can be mentioned (Leclercq 1938: 2958, Fig. 10065; Cavada 1994: 230, Fig. III. 132).

V.b.6. Buckle loop (II)

Provenance: Sisak (Siscia); dredged from the river Kupa.
Location: AMZ (3088)
Description: Iron, silver-inlaid; 3 x 1.55 cm. A D-shaped buckle-loop with the edge of the tongue bent over the loop. The loop is decorated all over with silver-inlaid parallel strokes, while a saltire cross is executed in the same manner on the quadrangular base of the tongue.
Dating: End of the 5th century/6th century.
Literature: Simoni 1989: 115, Taf. 5:10; Katalog: 86, no. 54.
Commentary: The type constitutes part of the Roman heritage popular with both the Romans and the barbarians from the end of the 5th century onwards (Vinski 1991: 15-16, T. 17:2). An item of a very similar shape and design, only without a saltire on a tapering tongue, was found in the grave of a Christian Gothic woman, dated to the end of the 5th and the beginning of the 6th century (Cavada 1994: 228-231, Fig. III.136). Belt fittings are well-known as very obvious vehicles for symbolic depictions displaying religious, magical and apotropaic conceptions (Salin 1959: 105-108; Forstner 1982: 420-421; Mawer 1995: 59-60). With the context missing in this instance, it would not be of much use to speculate upon one of the three mentioned specific symbolic conceptions of the saltire on tongue base (for the saltire see S.3.). Given the date of the artefact, the motif in question probably stood for a cross as did some of its equivalents (swastika, duplex knot, cross of Solomon), which occur quite frequently on similar objects during the 5th and 6th centuries (Salin 1959: 270, 274, 323, Figs. 82, 86, 123; Vinski 1991: 16, 17, Pls. 15:6, 17:2, 24:1). As this item could easily have been Gothic propriety, a marked barbarian affinity for the crosses so stylized and employed particularly on items of belt fittings, come to mind (Ripoll López 1994: 307-309, Figs. IV.11., IV.13.).

V.b.7. Belt mount (III)

Provenance: Osijek (Mursa); amateur excavation around 1900; found in a detached rider burial outside town walls.
Location: AMZ (1759)
Description: Gilded bronze; 2.1 x 1.7 cm. A rectangular moulded belt mount decorated with the low relief motif of a duplex knot (the cross of Solomon).
Dating: mid 7th century.
Literature: Vinski 1958: 26, T. 12; Katalog: 107, no. 129.
Commentary: This is another instance of a common motif in Roman art, Christianized in later times of 'barbarized antiquity', on the verge of the mediaeval period (cf. V.b.1., V.b.3.). It was very frequently employed on all kinds of artefacts and in various media, particularly mosaic, painting and stone sculpture throughout antiquity. Its symbolic connotations, more pronounced in the late Roman period than previously, were mostly related to magical-apotropaic conceptions, but were in time Christianized. Christian associations of the cross of Solomon have been attested by both archaeological evidence and documentary sources related to biblical stories about king Solomon and his seal (Briesenick 1964: 174; Engemann 1975: 37-48, Taf. 16b; Fülep 1984: 61-62, Fig. 20; Vikan 1984: 75-80; Higgins 1987: 123, Fig. 54; Lucchesi-Palli 1990: 116, Taf. 22:5,6). The motif in question is usually termed the duplex knot or the knot of Solomon, but at times also the cross of Solomon (Knific - Sagadin 1991: 30-31, Fig. 71). The issue of the exact period and circumstances of its Christianization can by no means be resolved generally and can only be pursued on the level of each particular circumstance. Significantly enough, in late antiquity the cross of Solomon was often applied to ornamental items in a manner suggestive of Christian associations, i.e. in the positions reserved as a rule for symbolic devices, primarily the cross (Salin 1959: 129-130; Milojčić 1968, Taf. 25:3; Klein-Pfeuffer 1993: 121-123, Abb. 32).

V.b.8. Strap end (III)

Provenance: Sisak (Siscia); chance find in recent years on the riverbank of the Kupa.
Location: MS
Description: Gilded bronze; 7.1 x 2.2 cm. A strap end made from a plain thin sheet outlined in the form of fish. Its oval upper section tapers towards the lower part ending in a slightly expanded tail. A suspension loop is attached direct on the upper part of body.
Dating: 4th century.
Literature: Katalog: 77, no. 18.
Commentary: Previously inaccurately dated and hypothesized to be an undefined pendant (Migotti 1994: 191), this object is now securely established as a strap end on the basis of persuasive analogies (cf. Mawer 1995: 63-65, D2.Br.9). Its putative Christian associations are based on two preconditions, one being the fish-like outline; the other relates to the nature and function of this type of belt fitting, usually decorated with almost incontestable Christian imagery. Certain of these objects were also made in the form of fish, and one of the closest parallels for the item from Sisak is at the same time the only one decorated with a definite Christian device - a chi-rho (Mawer 1995: 65, D2.B3.9). An interesting suggestion has been put forward about these objects: that they constituted part of the official apparel of lay Christians involved with the administration of the church (Mawer 1995: 60).

V.c. Horse equipment

V.c.1. Decoraive mount (III)

Provenance: Sisak (Siscia); dredging of the Kupa in 1912.
Location: AMZ (1921)
Description: Gilded bronze; 5.4 x 4 cm. A Longobard decorative plate mount in the shape of an equal-armed (lower arm missing) cross with a large central boss. The boss is encircled with a continuing line of small birds' heads and the arms bear deeply carved geometrical motifs, primarily meander.
Dating: mid 6th century.
Literature: Simoni 1989: 113, T. 4:2; Katalog 86, no. 55.
Commentary: For two reasons a hypothesis can be put forward for the cruciform shape of this mount as representing not only constructional or technical features, but also symbolical. First, the Longobards, settled temporarily in Pannonia (526-568), were already partly Christianised touched with both Arian and orthodox affiliations (Menghin 1985: 143). Second, a specific Christian symbolism has often been attached to the horse, while depictions of horses marked with Christian devices are well familiar in early Christian art (Garrucci 1880: 151, Tav. 487:23; Vinski 1974, T. 9:8, 11; Forstner 1982: 182-185; Clover 1986: 4; see also V.a.15.).

V.d. Pins

V.d.1. Pin with bird-shaped head (II)

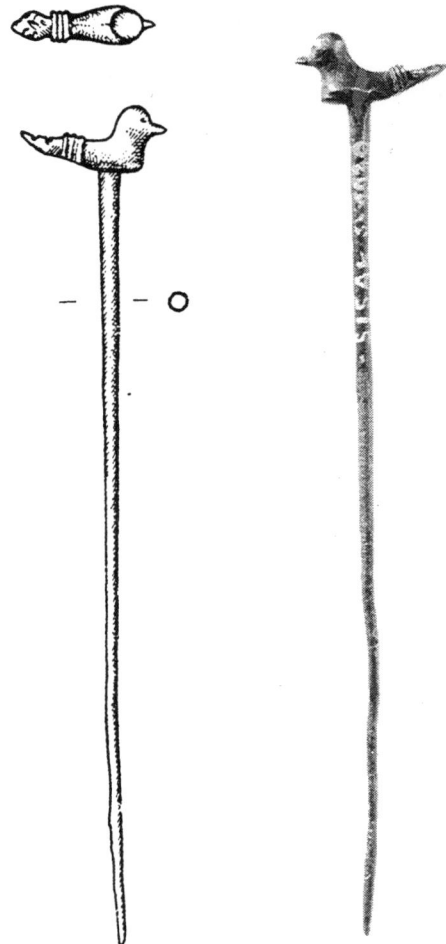

Provenance: Sisak (Siscia)
Location: AMZ (1930)
Description: Bronze; total length: 8.2 cm, head: 1.4 x 0.7 cm. A pin with a head in the form of a schematically

66

rendered sitting bird (dove?). Two annular mouldings mark the junction of body and tail.
Dating: 4th/5th centuries.
Literature: Simoni 1989: 109, T. 2:2; Katalog: 87, no. 56,

V.d.2. Pin with bird-shaped head (II)

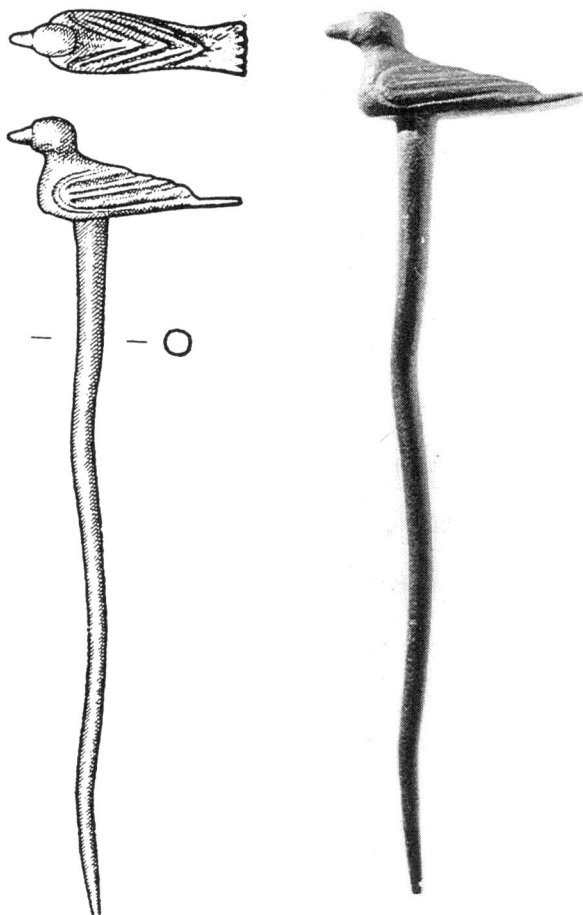

Provenance: Sisak (Siscia)
Location: AMZ (1931)
Description: Bronze; total length: 7.75 cm, head: 2.2. x 1 cm. A pin with a head in the form of a sitting bird (dove?), rendered slightly more naturalistically than the previous entry. The wings are marked with deep horizontal scoring.
Dating: 4th/5th centuries.
Literature: Simoni 1989: 109, T. 2:3; Katalog: 87, no. 57.

V.d.3. Pin with bird-shaped head (II)

Provenance: Ludbreg (Iovia?)
Location: Private possesion (inaccessible).
Description: Documented only by a photograph and a drawing made on its model (measurements unknown). The lower section of the shaft is missing, while the upper section is decorated with four annular mouldings. The bird (dove?) is also decorated with mouldings on the junctions of body with neck and tail; tail is marked by plastic ribs. The head is clumsily rendered, resembling more an insect's than a bird's head.
Dating: 4th/5th centuries.
Literature: Gorenc - Vikić 1986: 66, 69, Fig. 19; Katalog: 111, no. 144.
Commentary on V.d.1.-3. Of all late Roman pins with zoomorphic terminals, the type with birds, particularly the dove, is probably the most widespread (Cüppers 1983: 277-279, Fig. 241; Biró 1987: 176-182, Fig. 15:77; Burger 1987: 83; Schulze-Dörrlamm 1990; Taf. 17:9; Koščević 1991: 11, no. 14). Usage of such objects in fastening dress or else as hairpins can only be established by context, which for the items under discussion is misssing. Although there is no hard and fast rule, larger items are commonly held to have been used in clothing, while more delicate ones, especially bone, are envisaged as hair-pins (Biró 1987: 176).

What concerns us here is the religious symbolism of the most prominent artistic feature of these objects – the dove terminals (for the dove see II.2.3. and V.a. 8.-11.). The motif of a dove perched on the shaft of a pin is connotative of an apocryphal episode relating to the Virgin Mary's suitors: on entering the temple with staffs in their hands they found that from Joseph's staff a dove came out as a token of God's blessing and approval (Craveri 1969: 14). Despite the bird having a prominent role in the religious symbolism of barbarian peoples, it seems that this type of personal ornament did not gain popularity with either the Goths or the Longobards, remaining rather in the domain of religious symbolism of the Roman Christians. The artefacts here were classified as only probable evidence for Christianity on account of the lack of definitely diagnostic contexts.

IV.d.4. Pin with swastika head (III)

Provenance: Sisak (Siscia)

Location: AMZ (5920)
Description: Bronze; total length: 2.7 cm, head: 1.1 x 0.95 cm. An object in the form of a long distorted wire or shaft with a swastika-shaped head.

Dating: second half of the 2nd century/3rd century.
Literature: Koščević 1991: 11, 118, T. 2: 29; Katalog: 78, no. 22.
Commentary: Distortion of one of the two components of this objects precludes securely establishing its nature as an ear-ring or a pin, the latter being more probable (Koščević 1991: 11). At the given time, the swastika was quite a popular motif for jewellery decoration, particularly fibulae (Böhme 1972: 45, Taf. 30: 1179-1183, Taf. 31: 1184-1208). Without a corroborative context, however, its possible Christian associations remain dubious (see V.a.15.).

V.e. Rings and gemstones

V.e.1. Rho-cross(?)-decorated ring (I/II)

Provenance: Sisak (Siscia); dredged from the river Kupa.
Location: AMZ (4805)
Description: Bronze; diam. 2 cm. A ribbon hoop with a slightly rounded expansion in the middle of front section, bordered on either side by parallel perpendicular grooves. On the expanded plate two diagonally-crossed lines are incised, with a circular ending of the upper terminal of the right-hand stroke.
Dating: 3rd/4th centuries.
Literature: Katalog: 88, no. 64.
Commentary: It is unfortunately impossible to establish with any certainty whether the circular end of the arm of the 'x' was an attempt at a chi-rho or was simply an accidental feature due to a raised strip of corrosion (for similar features on various small metal objects see Mawer 1995: 84, 99). Should it be a loop, the ring would be first-rate evidence for Christianity, decorated with an oblique rho-cross identical to the one on sarcophagus III.b.2. A date later in the 4th century should in that event be more appropriate than the 3rd/4th centuries, postulated otherwise on account of the shape and geometrical decoration (see V.e.2.). If there were no loop there remains only a saltire figuring prominently on an expanded plate and featuring most probably a disguised cross.

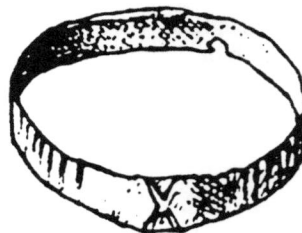

V.e.2. Saltire-decorated ring (II)

Provenance: Sisak (Siscia); dredged from the river Kupa.
Location: AMZ (4807)

Description: Bronze; diam. c. 1.6 cm. A ribbon hoop tapering towards the ends is slightly deformed and a section is missing. It has a prominently engraved saltire cross within a rectangular panel at the centre and geometrical branch-like motifs at each side of the panel.
Dating: 3rd/4th centuries.
Literature: Katalog: 88, no. 62.
Commentary: The plainness of this shape prevents its more precise dating on the basis of typology; a combination of a ribbon hoop and a specific geometrical decorative scheme points broadly to the 3rd and 4th centuries (Marshall 1907: 191, Pl. 29: 1209; Guiraud 1989: 189, 196-200, Typ 8d, Figs. 28: 4e, 50:8). The saltire as a cryptic emblem for the cross would also be in line with such a date (Forstner 1982: 21, 37; for the saltire see also S.3.).

V.e.3. Iota/chi-decorated ring (II)

Provenance: Sisak (Siscia); dredged from the river Kupa.
Location: AMZ (4808)
Description: Bronze; diam. 1.7 cm. A ribbon hoop tapering towards the ends with the central field engraved with a motif of a iota-chi within a rectangular panel and two saltires at each side.
Dating: 3rd/4th centuries.
Literature: Katalog: 88, no. 63.
Commentary: For the dating of the type see V.e.2. Given the iota-chi (cf. Mawer 1995: 6 ff.; Forstner 1982; also S.5. here) in addition to saltires, Christian symbolic associations here are even more probable than with the previous item.

Similarities in the style, decorative scheme and technique of the execution of specimens V.e.1-3. point to their manufacture in a single, most probably Siscian, workshop. If the first in the series was indeed provided with a rho loop, the three of them produce an interesting developmental scheme of putative Christian devices, ranging from saltire through iota-chi to monogrammatic cross (see drawing below).

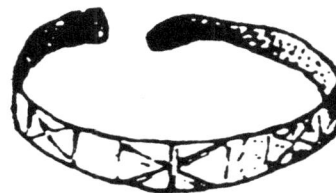

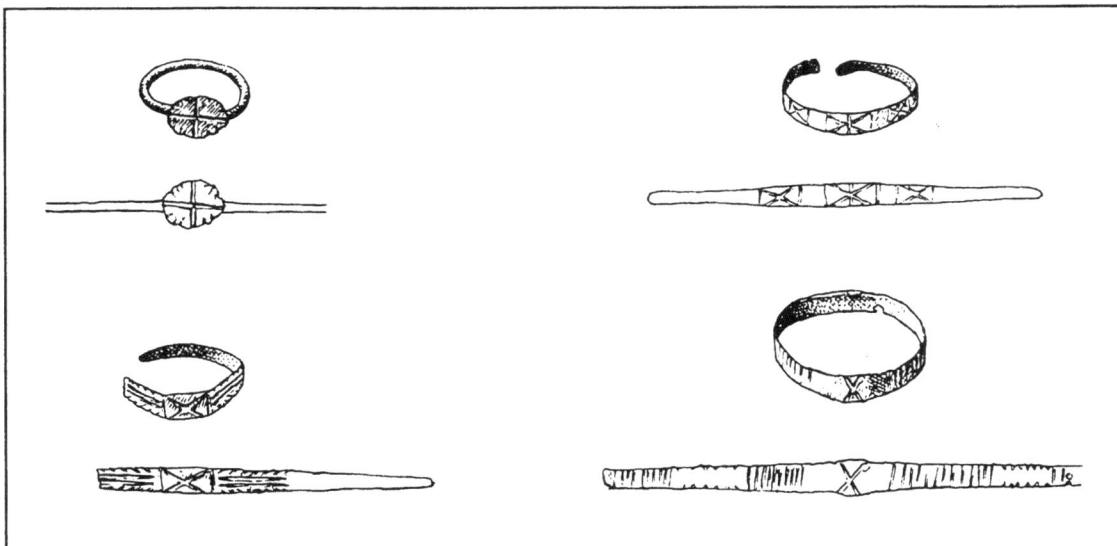

V.e.4. Cross-decorated ring (II)

Provenance: Sisak (Siscia); dredged from the river Kupa.
Location: AMZ (4952)
Description: Bronze; diam. 1.2 cm, bezel: 0.8 x 0.7 cm. To an annular-section hoop a circular plate bezel is soldered bearing an engraved equal-armed cross with arms intersecting at slightly irregular angles; the rims of the thus obtained interstices have each three notches.
Dating: 3rd/4th centuries(?).
Literature: Katalog: 88, no. 61.
Commentary: The small size of the ring points either to its belonging to a child or to its being worn on the tip of the finger (Marshall 1907: XXV). The cross on the bezel was engraved so as to resemble more a kind of technical device than any of the known iconographical versions of cross (see III.a.4.). On the other hand, a pure decorative or even technical device featuring so prominently and covering the entire surface of the bezel is hardly conceivable; a Christian symbolic association is therefore much more appropriate in this instance. A loosely delineated shape of the cross would be in line with the 3rd/4th centuries not yet rounded Christian iconography of the cross. It must, however, be admitted that this item is by no means securely dated: both the plain shape and the roughly executed cross cover a long time-span from the 3rd to the 7th century (Marshall 1907: 32, Pl. 5:191; Henkel 1913: 111, Taf. 47:1214; Hicke 1985: 176, Abb. 18; Guiraud 1989: 176, Fig. 26, Typ 4; Knific - Sagadin 1991: 69, no. 56).

V.e.5. Key-ring (I)

Provenance: Sisak (Siscia); dredged from the river Kupa.
Location: AMZ (4089)
Description: Bronze; diam. 2.1 cm. From the middle section of a ribbon hoop a perpendicular plate roundel rises, provided with two side wing-like projections and decorated with five round holes in the the shape of an equal-armed cross.
Dating: 3rd/4th centuries.
Literature: Koščević 1991: 124, T. 11:164; Katalog: 89, no. 65b.

V.e.6. Key-ring (II)

Provenance: Sisak (Siscia); dredged from the river Kupa.
Location: AMZ (4120)
Description: Bronze; diam. 2 cm. A key-ring with a roughly D-section hoop flattened at the frontal portion, to which a plate is attached rising perpendicularly in the form of an irregular equal-armed cross. The lower arm is solid and the remainder is openwork.
Dating: 3rd/4th centuries.
Literature: Katalog: 89, no. 65a.
Commentary on V.e.5. and 6.: Variously decorated key-rings are typical of the 3rd and 4th centuries, but continue to be produced in later times as well (Guiraud 1989: 191-192, 203; Milošević 1981: 60, no. 109; Koščević 1991: 41). An equal-armed cross composed of five circles or holes (see V.e.5 and V.g.1.) is a recognized iconographical version of the cross on late Roman and mediaeval Christian material (Garrucci 1873: Tav. 95, 97, ff.; Cabrol 1924: 14; Noll 1954: 82-83; Whitting 1973: 190, 286, nos. 311-314, 454, 456; Buhagiar 1986: 322-323, Fig. 105 D; Higgins 1987, Fig. 19, no. 70; Schulze-Dörrlamm 1990, T. 48: 16; Knific - Sagadin 1991: 56, 70, nos. 19, 58). It is nevertheless safer to consider item V.e.6. as only most probably Christian. On the other hand, instances of 'true' crosses in such places reinforce the Christian interpretation of the item from Sisak (Leclercq 1924a: 2197, Fig. 701; Milošević 1981: 60, no. 109; Gáspár 1986: 322, Taf. 273:1144).

V.e.7. Inscribed ring (II)

Provenance: Osijek (Mursa); chance find at the end of the 19th century.
Location: MSO (2308)
Description: Gold; diam. 1.8 cm; width of bezel: 0.5 cm. An elliptical D-section hoop is expanding triangularly into a slightly raised rectangular bezel. Equally spaced along the triangular shoulders and the bezel are 6 letters of the engraved inscriptipn *ev/se/bi* or *Ev/se/bi/*.
Dating: 3rd century.
Literature: Pinterović 1965: 49, no. 33; Katalog 107, no. 125.

Commentary: The inscription was read as an exhortation: 'Be pious /religious!' (Pinterović), implying that the Greek verb *eusebeo* was employed in its transliterated Latin form. As is known, possibilities of various and different readings of inscriptions, particualrly on small objects, are a common fact conditioned by not only obvious mistakes or misapprehensions of wording or writing but also by inherent confusing of transliterated Greek and Latin words (Testini 1958: 339-345; Mawer 1995: 53, passim). The given inscription might therefore alternatively be understood as the genitive of the Greek name Eusebios in its Latin form Eusebius (cf. Tóth 1979: 164; Ševčenko 1992: 47-48). Both variations - exhortations and owners' names in the genitive - are broadly attested on Roman rings (Marshall 1907: XXVIII-XXIX; Leclercq 1924b). Despite the noted ambiguities, putative Christian connotations remain inherent in both the name and the verb based on the term 'pious'. The name Eusebius counts among those with definite, although not specifically discriminating religious connotations; it is in any event more frequently met in Christian than pagan surroundings (Harnack 1915: 13, note 3; Kaufmann 1917: 36; Testini 1958: 487-488; Kajanto 1963: 47; Alföldi 1969: 197). The same is true of the noun and the verb *eusebeia* and *eusebeo* respectively (Kaufmann-Büchler 1966). The first known south-Pannonian bishop in the 3rd century - Eusebius from Cibalae (Jarak 1994: 161) - might possibly point to the popularity of the name in Christian circles of the area in the given period. If not exactly to the Cibalitan bishop, such a sumptuous specimen must have belonged to a high-ranking, possibly eccclesiastical personality of Mursa (cf. Marshall 1907: XX-XXI; Leclercq 1924a: 2181-2187; Mawer 1995: 66).

V.e.8. Monogram-decorated ring (II)

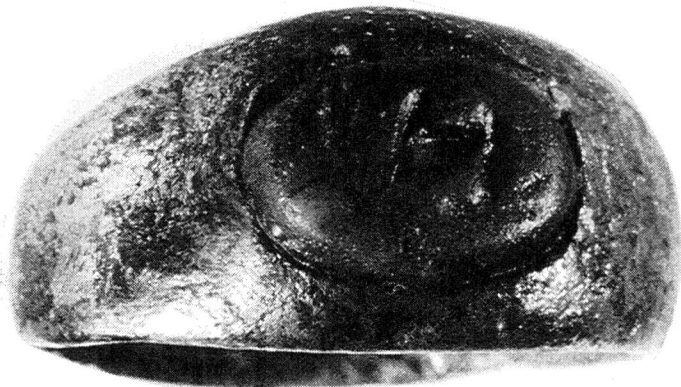

Provenance: Fortified complex on the hill Kuzelin above the village of Donja Glavnica; excavation in 1982.
Location: MPS (58/94) (misplaced).
Description: Silver; diam. 2.1 cm. A ribbon hoop expands into an oval bezel, set with a reddish stone. Engraved carelessly on the gem are the letters I and H.
Dating: 3rd century.
Literature: Katalog: 114, no. 154.
Commentary: Although allegedly found in a 5th century layer (Vladimir Sokol pers. comm.) the type is typical of the end of the 2nd and 3rd century (Guiraud 1989: 181, Fig. 11:d; Koščević 1991: 39, no. 182). This chronology fits well with the reading of the inscription as a monogrammatic contraction of Christ's name, reduced to the first two letters of its Greek form IH(σους). This contraction is far less frequent than other monogrammatic devices; it nevertheless occurs in literary sources from the 2nd and 3rd centuries and on archaeological artefacts from the 3rd century (Kaufmann 1917: 39; Leclercq 1924c: 610; Leoni 1950: 965; Testini 1958: 357, Fig. 154; Forstner 1982: 39-40).

V.e.9. Monogram(?)-decorated ring (II)

Provenance: Cave Vrlovka above the village of Kamanje; excavation in 1983; found together with pottery sherds in a 3rd century layer dated by coins of Valerianus and Claudius.
Location: ZMO
Description: Bronze; 2.5 x 2.75 cm. A D-section elliptical hoop with carinated shoulders expands to a flat oval surface with a slightly raised and somewhat irregularly shaped octagonal bezel. Engraved on the bezel are four intersecting lines, three of them in the form of iota-chi and the fourth one cutting across the lower section of the putative monogrammatic device.
Dating: 3rd century.
Literature: Čučković 1994: 4: Katalog: 129, no. 190.
Commentary: The type is typical of the 3rd century (Guiraud 1989: 185, Fig. 21:e,f; Koščević 1991: 38, nos. 172, 173). This proposed date would fit well with the motif on the bezel featuring possibly a debased iota-chi or maybe a cross-chi (an eight-pointed star). Such a device would at this date represent a cryptic metaphor for the cross (see S.5.). The former possibility - a depiction of the iota-chi - is more plausible; superfluous strokes are quite common on often debased attempts at Christian devices on small objects, metal and ceramic alike (Kempt - Reusch 1965: 265; Sági 1968: 398; Mawer 1995: 19, passim). On a slight possibility of symbolic associations contained in the octagonal bezel see G.5.

V.e. 10. 'Architectural' ring (II)

71

Provenance: Samobor; an individual chance find during digging of a well in 1913.

Location: AMZ (3370)

Description: Gold; diam. 2.4 cm. A luxury massive solid-cast ring made of high-quality gold. A ribbon hoop with triangular upper sections expands towards a slightly raised hexagonal bezel; this in turn is surmounted by an elaborate crown in the shape of two storeys of differently stylized arcades rendered by means of pseudogranulation, on which a smooth undecorated plate (flattened dome as it were) rests.

Dating: 6th century.

Literature: Vinski 1955; Katalog: 129, no. 191.

Commentary: The ring was interpreted as a Longobard jewellery item either manufactured in a Byzantine workshop or at least designed on the model of Romano-Byzantine iconographical conceptions (Vinski 1955: 39-40). This type was labelled 'architectural' on basis of its unique shape and is unanimously considered to be a Byzantine product accomodated to the tastes and fashions of barbarian customers. Also widely accepted is a hypothesis of its form being designed in imitation of early Christian and Byzantine circular buildings, columnar and domed, mostly baptisteries and mausoleums (Vinski 1955: 36-37; Tóth 1979: 178-180). Consequently this type of ring would embody the symbolism of death and ressurection and life eternal. Despite a pronounced resistence to attaching Christian symbolic associations to artefacts' shapes in themselves (cf. Mawer 1995: 66), such a possibility should still be taken into consideration in particular single instances.

V.e.11. Inscribed ring (III)

Provenance: Vinkovci (Cibalae); chance find during building works in 1895 outside the south town wall; found with the upper part of a gold amulet box.

Location: AMZ (misplaced).

Description: Gold with silver-inlaid letters; outer diam. 2.5/2.6 cm. A polygonal ring composed of 11 facets of 2 - 3.5 cm thick gold sheet; each of the eleven fields contains a silver-inlaid letter of the Greek inscription amounting to CAPIWN ZECAI.

Dating: 3rd/4th centuries.

Literature: Brunšmid 1902: 144, 150, Fig. 69: 4,5; Koščević 1991: 36, Fig. 149.

Commentary: This type of finger-ring is typical of the 3rd/4th centuries (Guiraud 1989: 196-198; Koščević 1991: 36). The letter alpha, however, with a V-shaped cross-bar (typical of the 4th century rather than earlier periods) makes a later date more plausible, although by no means secure (see III.c.9.). The inscription Σαριων ζησαι relates to the well-known wish for a long life and is found frequently on all kinds of small Roman artefacts from the 2nd/3rd centuries onwards. Significantly, it is mostly objects constituting grave finds that contain the phrase in question. It should also be observed that either a Latin or a Greek version of the basic motto zeses/vivas in conjunction with mostly personal names and other words is excessively found in Christian contexts. This fact alone should justify attaching to such objects putative Christian connotations even when found outside a

meaningful context or devoid of diagnostic expansions, such as in Deo or in Christo. The *vivas/zeses* formula occurs on small items, mostly jewelry, as early as the 2nd century, to gain the utmost popularity in late Roman period, when it becomes imbued with pronounced Christian overtones. For pagans life is basically a subject-matter of daily procedure, while for Christians it acquires overtones of the afterlife in Christ; this idea was particularly apposite to and probably often present in Christian funeral surroundings, even if not manifestly expressed in words (Garrucci 1880: 99, Tav. 464; Kaufmann 1917: 141-142; Leclercq 1924f: 3018; Leclercq 1939; Behrens 1950: 10-11; Kempt - Reusch 1965: 223; Kajanto 1967: 70-72; Février 1977: 41; Tóth 1994: 247-248; Mawer 1995: 44-49, 71). Of major importance in the present context are instances of objects with unexpanded *vivas* formulas in unquestionable Christian surroundings (Garrucci 1880: 99, Tav. 464; Testini 1958: 487-493; Bagatti 1958: 131); the prevalently funerary contexts of these finds (providing this is not only an accident of archaeology) should also argue in favour of Christian connotations of the formula *vivas*: its presence would hardly make any sense in pagan burials. Finally, it has been hypothesized that particularly susceptible of possible Christian associations are phrases containing only a wish and a name in the vocative (Mawer 1995: 44-49), which is exactly the case here. Given, however, their undeniable presence in pagan surroundings, more than a strong possibility of Christian significance cannot be inferred for objects with unexpanded *vivas* formulae (Behrens 1950: 10-11). Numerous artefacts from northern Croatia bearing the formula *utere felix* have been omitted from this work (cf. Migotti 1994: 204). Although possibly containing symbolic associations similar to those of *vivas*, this formula has usually been perceived as less significant and more neutral, lacking therefore necessary prerequisites for Christian attribution when without a context or a diagnostic expansion (cf. Mawer 1995: 1).

V.e. 12. Gemstone (III)

Provenance: Osijek (Mursa); found in a lead sarcophagus in the southern part of town (possibly within a Roman cemetery, see Fig. 1:1) during building works in 1921. Also found in the sarcophagus was another gemstone (G.6).

Location: Private posession at Osijek (the original); MSO (a gypsum impression). Neither the original nor a photograph of gem are available today, leaving the gypsum impression the only record to be used for study.

Description: Pale yellow transparent cornelian; 1.5 x 1.1 cm. Engraved crudely on the oval surface of the gem is a standing male figure (head and legs in profile, body in three-quarters profile) leaning on a staff and surrounded by a ram and one or possibly two sheep at either side of his feet.

Dating: 3rd/4th centuries.

Literature: Pinterović 1965: 43-44, T. 3:15; Katalog: 107, no 127.

Commentary: There exists an immense literature on the issue of distinguishing Christian pastoral scenes with references to the Good Sheperd from pagan ones with associations of hardly anything more than peaceful happiness in bucolic surroundings. While specific diagnostic contextual or artistic-symbolic details, implying possible religious connotations, relate to each individual case alone, the problem on the whole remains virtually insoluble (cf. Klauser 1958: 24 ff.; Cambi 1975: 60, Fig. 9; Murray 1981: 74-75, 92-93; Cambi 1994: 39-53). The gem from Osijek is apparently devoid of diagnostic symbolic details; yet the circumstances of discovery - lead sarcophagus with a putative gnostic gem - might tentatively speak in favour of its gnostic-Christian, rather than pagan surroundings. While the motif of the Good Sheperd is not quite unfamilar in northern parts of Pannonia (Tóth 1972: 65), the reverse is apparently true of its southern regions. Surprisingly enough, this area also shows a total lack of early Christian gemstones.

V.f. Pendants

V.f.1. Circular cross-like pendant (I)

Provenance: Sisak (Siscia); dredged from the river Kupa in 1912.

Location: AMZ (6585)

Description: Lead; 2.8 x 2.2 cm. A pendant in the form of an openwork equal-armed cross in a circular frame. The frame is grooved and arms of the cross bear each two pellets, with the additional central one, more conspicuous than the others.

Dating: 5th/7th centuries.

Literature: Katalog: 89, no. 68.

Commentary: A model for this apparently Christian motif can be found in solar iconography (see S.1.,2.). With the autochthonous Roman Christians, pendants in the shape of Christianized solar crosses were in use as early as the 4th/5th centuries, as attested by discoveries of both artefacts and corresponding mouldings (Vinski 1968: 129-130, note 145; Schmitz 1993: 57). This would imply their use previous to other types of cross-like ornaments, primarily fibulae (cf.

V.a.2-5.). Pellets on the specimen from Sisak are faithful if less sumptuous imitations of gems employed on a type of luxury early Christian cross - the so-called *crux gemmata* (gemmed cross). The type appears to be mentioned in the literary sources as early as the time of Constantine, to became widespread from the end of the 5th century onwards. Contrary to the plain cross associative primarily with Christ's sufferings, the sumptuousness of the *crux gemmata* is believed to mirror a corresponding symbolism: the Christian triumph over death and evil (Salin 1959: 370-372; van der Meer - Mohrmann 1959: 83, fig. 210; Dinkler 1964). This should also be a probable conception behind the artistic design of the pendant from Sisak which, however, is intriguing from yet another aspect: magical-apotropaic. Magical and apotropaic elements, inherent to cross-like jewellery on the whole (Dinkler 1962: 99; Barb 1963: 106; Dölger 1964: 24-26; Engemann 1975: 42-48), are in this instance further attested by the fabric (lead) employed (c.f. Leclercq 1939a: 1216).

V.f.2. Inscribed pendant (I)

Provenance: Sisak (Siscia).

Location: MS

Description: Low-quality silver; diam. 1.8 cm. A thin, solid pendant, circular in form, with a thickened rim and inscriptions in low relief on both sides. On the obverse is written: IN DEO SPES, and on the reverse: MPER ES.TSE. The total of the inscription amounts to: 'In Deo spes semper est'. Below either inscription a wreath with fillets is depicted in low relief.

Dating: 4th century(?)

Literature: Katalog: 90, no. 69.

Commentary: Pendants with inscriptions on both sides instead of depictions (see V.f.3.) are familiar features of early Christian applied art (Marucchi 1903: 289; Marucchi 1906: 73). The specimen here is, however, unique; the subject matter of its inscription is in no way unusual, but its rendering is both curious and meaningful. The section on the obverse (In Deo spes) has a normal wording and relates to a familiar early Christian phrase associating liturgical and epigraphical texts, particularly African (Leclercq 1953a; Testini 1958: 533; Mawer 1995: 97-98). Contrarily, the text on the reverse, although a natural continuation of the obverse, was rendered enigmatically with words split and written backwards.

The formula 'Spes in Deo' is believed to allude to a hope for salvation in trouble (Cabrol 1924a: 247-253); historical reminiscences of a Christian martyrdom might have therefore been implied here, reinforced by the presence of another symbol of martyrdom - the wreath (see III.d.1.). This would only be natural in a town that at the beginning of the 4th century produced a martyr famous throughout the Christian world - bishop Quirinus (Jarak 1994: 164 ff.)). Quirinus was not martyred at his see in Siscia, but at Savaria in northern Pannonia; his relics are believed to have been translated to Rome probably at the end of the 4th century (Roncaioli 1981). It is, however, hardly imaginable that Siscia would have neglected the memory of her famous saint and a probability of this town becoming one of the centres of Quirinus's cult and possibly of pilgrimage too remains much more plausible. Small objects like the one in question here would in this case have been very much in demand.

In terms of its depiction and its inscription this pendant represents a common Christian ornamental item. Yet the text on the reverse was not rendered as an inversion or a reversal as a consequence of common errors in such inscriptions; the letters and words were mixed in such a manner as to deliberately conceal the sense of the phrase semper est and to induce guessing. This feature might possibly be interpreted in terms of magical-apotropaic and gnostic attitudes. Procedures such as the one described, in addition to the employment of unintelligible syllables and words and their unexpected combinations, aimed at the prevention of straightforward understanding of the text, are all features typical of the magical and gnostic components of early Christianity (Leclercq 1924g; Hopfner 1928: 341; Leclercq 1931: 1101-1102; Testini 1958: 524-525; Salway 1993: 489; Mawer 1995: 85-86; for magic and superstition within Christianity see Leclercq 1931; Barb 1963; Engemann 1975; Philipp 1983; Stutzinger 1983).

The pendant was tentatively dated to the 4th century on the basis of putative magical and apotropaic attributes, symptomatic of the 4th century rather than of later times.

V.f.3. Chi/rho-decorated pendant (I)

Provenance: Sisak (Siscia); chance find on the riverbank of the Kupa (site of Mali Kaptol) in the 60s.
Location: Private collection - Sisak (only a photograph has been available).
Description: Bronze; diam. 2 cm. A round cast pendant with a massive ribbed loop; spaced beading on the rims and depictions on both sides. A serifed chi-rho with a close rho

loop is depicted on the obverse in slight relief. In the fields between the arms of the chi-rho, two crescent shapes and four irregular saltires are shown. The reverse has a butterfly or a kindred insect with hatchured wings spread all over the surface.
Dating: 4th century(?)
Literature: Vikić-Belančić 1978: 600-602, fig. 20; Katalog: 90, no. 70.
Commentary: When first published (Vikić-Belančić) the pendant was dated to the 5th century on account of the depiction with two crescent shapes on the obverse, as understood to be a vestigial and debased alfa and omega device; the colateral saltire-like signs remained at the same time unexplained. In view of their conjoined appearance, the saltires should most probably be interpreted as stars and the crescents as moons, which ultimately would amount to the overall astral-solar symbolism of the motif. It is just these apparently syncretistic features that speak in favour of an earlier dating (for syncretism see III.b.1.,III.b.4. and also IV.a. of the Concluding Discussion). Given the chi-rho (see II.1.), the two depictions would on the whole be rooted in conceptions of solar Christology, primarily those implying victory over death and achievement of ressurection and immortality, as well as God's power over the universe (Migotti 1995: 278-284; Migotti 1997: 216-217). The image of a butterfly or possibly a bee as an emblem of the immortal soul, cherished in various pagan mystery religions, fits well in the given conception; it was subsequently enriched by Christian associations of resurrection (Cumont 1944: 176-183; Gough 1973: 44; Forstner 1982: 292-294).

V.g. Objects of uncertain use

V.g.1. Decorative rivet (I)

Provenance: Sisak (Ssicia); dredged from the river Kupa.
Location: AMZ (6166)
Description: Gilded bronze; 1.1 x 1 cm. A rivet-like object in the shape of an equal-armed cross with rounded terminals on the arms. The upper surface is decorated with five deep engraved gem-like circles arranged in cruciform. On the back a short pointed wire is visible.
Dating: 5th/7th centuries.
Literature: Katalog: 90, no. 71.
Commentary: Judging by the wire on the back, this item was a kind of rivet to be hammered into another object with a purpose which apparently was more decorative than functional. It might have stemmed from the intersection of the arms of a larger cross or a cross-like ornament (cf.

Milojčić 1963: 131-132, Abb. 5:16; Dannheimer - Kriss-Rettenbeck 1964: 193, Abb. 1:3; Hayes 1972, Fig. 56: m, r). In terms of chronology and symbolism this object is apparently related to cross-shaped fibulae (V.a.2-5.) and is also akin to the gemmed-cross pendant V.f.1., sharing with it the symbolism of triumph; spaced gems instead of lines of abutting ones constitute on the whole a common variation on the decorative conception of the gemmed cross (Hayes 1972, Fig. 56: i-m; Lyon-Caen - Hoff 1986, 114, no. 114; Bierbrauer 1992, Abb. 3:3).

V.g.2. Lamb figurine (II)

Provenance: Osijek (Mursa); rescue excavation in 1977; southeastern part of the town (Fig. 1:4).
Location: MSO (18720)
Description: Bronze; 4.8 x 3.1 cm, thickness 1.6 cm. A figurine of a seated lamb (a young ram in fact, as attested by two short horns coming out on top of its head) with frontal head, body in profile and crossed legs. The solid cast head and legs indicate a conjectural free-standing position for the figurine; a large cavity on the back of the body definitely attests its position of half standing on a flat horizontal base and half leaning on an upright surface. The lamb's coat was rendered by means of an overall mass of engraved, or rather, impressed circles.
Dating: first half of the 4th century(?)
Literature: Katalog: 107, no. 128.
Commentary: Despite its discovery in a rescue excavation, no specific indicatory data are available that would enable a secure judgement of the nature and possible use of this object. The dating rests on stylistic grounds and is in the main supported by the typical late Roman artistic device of crowded circles. With the proposed dating in mind, this figurine should be considered as an object with probable Christian symbolic meaning; lambs of the appearance similar to the one here have been attested in catacomb paintings (Garrucci 1873: 88, Tav. 77:1; Leclercq 1924h: 881-882). The lamb as an emblem of victimisation was a commonplace of various pagan cults, notably Dionysiac, but nowhere outside Jewish-Christian circles was this role so pronounced and so often displayed artistically (Leclercq 1924h; Grabar 1968: 115; Forstner 1982: 268-273; Craveri 1969: 495, note 5). In early Christian thinking and iconography the lamb connotes a variety of metaphorical roles - Christ, believers (although the faithful were more likely to be represented by sheep), apostles and prophets. When Christ himself was intended, a seated lamb would symbolize him as a Saviour

and a standing one would be more appropriate for a victorious Redeemer.

The image of a lamb with a cross is considered not to be typical of the period before the 5th century; it was allegedly inspired by a relevant quotation from the Church father Peter Chrysologus (Leclercq 1924h: 879-893). On the other hand, the situation relating to a lamb shown in tandem with a chi-rho is different as regards chronology (see VI.b.1.,2.). On balance, it is reasonable to expect depictions of Christian lambs bare of specific religious devices in the period prior to the developed 4th century. No substantial clue exists as to the nature and use of this curious artefact. Would it be too bold to hypothesize its having been designed after the fashion of modern Christmas crib accesories? True, the Christmas crib of modern appearance is a mediaeval issue; yet not less true are both the mention of the crib in documentary sources and depictions of it in early Christian art from the 4th century onwards (Barb 1964: 23-25).

V.g.3. Lead tablet (III)

Provenance: Sisak (Siscia); dredged fom the river Kupa and donated to AMZ in 1904.
Location: AMZ (7142)
Description: Lead; 2.1 x 1.9 cm. A tiny lead tablet of sub-trapezoidal form cut or broken with a slant at the lower edge, apparently part of a larger whole. In the rectangular panel on the upper surface two fish-like creatures are depicted neatly in low relief, rendered by means of sharp and precise undercutting and reminiscent of wood-carving. The creatures are obviously dolphins shown next to a trident, with heads down and tails curled outwords.
Dating: 3rd century(?)
Literature: Katalog: 77, no. 19.
Commentary: The motif of two sea-creatures - mostly dolphins - next to a trident is well-known in pagan religious iconography. It is, however, much more prominent in the Christian symbolic vocabulary, where ti represents the faithful in search of salvation, associated by a trident as the metaphor for the cross (Leclercq 1924a: 2184; Din 1957: 673; for fish generally see III.b.3., for the trident G.1.). The lack of any contextual references precludes establishing either an accurate dating or a probable use for this object. It is most closely (although not exactly) parallelled on a tomb stone in the Roman catacombs, dated to the second half of the 3rd century (Kirsch 1924: 2011, Fig. 562). Although basically cryptic in terms of early Christian iconography, the motif retained its popularity for a long time and is occasionally met as late as the 6th century (Volbach 1958: 348-352, Fig. 202).

VI. Utilitarian Decorated Small Objects

VI.a. Spoons

VI.a.1. Pear-shaped long-handled spoon (I)

Provenance: Sisak (Siscia)
Location: AMZ (1925)
Description: Silver; total length 22.9 cm. A spoon consisting of a pear-shaped bowl with fan-like ribs on the outside and a long, vertically-fluted tapering handle. The offset in the form of a solid round plate with two indentations on the inner edge bears on its outer surface a deep-cut equal-armed cross with expanded terminals.
Dating: 5th/6th centuries.
Literature: Simoni 1988; Katalog: 91, no. 75.
Commentary: This item can, on typological grounds be safely dated to after the 4th century (Johns - Potter 1985: 331-332). A chronology more precise than within the span of the 5th and 6th centuries is hardly possible; types of spoons with variously shaped bowls, handles and offsets were in use concurrently during the given time. The nature and use of these objects as well as their tentative ethnic affiliation have been broadly discussed (Milojčić 1970; Painter 1970; Johns - Potter 1985; Simoni 1988; Mawer 1995: 42-44), but to no particularly encouraging result. Such artefacts have been found in all kinds of contexts (domestic, funeral, religious, in hoards etc.) from the 4th century onwards and may in principle be considered as part of the autochthonous Roman heritage. The fact of their subsequent usage by the barbarian peoples does not in itself make them Gothic or Arian artefacts, as previously often suspected (see the above quoted literature; also Bierbrauer 1994: 211-213). Equally, more and more abandoned becomes a once very popular hypothesis of the specifically liturgical use of such objects, particularly when decorated with Christian devices. Only a sound context can resolve these uncertainties in each specific case, while no hard and fast overall rule appears to be sustainable. What matters in the present context in any event is the Christian appurtenance of the item from Sisak, attested by the device applied on the offset (for the cross cf. III.a.4.).

VI.a.2. Spoon-bowl (III)

Provenance: Sisak (Siscia); donated to AMZ in 1909.
Location: AMZ (6632)
Description: Pewter; 3.6 x 2.6 cm. A pear-shaped and completely flat bowl of a small spoon, handle missing. Within the beaded border of the upper surface, a hardly discernible motif of three fishes arranged head-to-tail is depicted in very low relief.
Dating: 2nd century.
Literature: Katalog: 91, no. 74.
Commentary: Despite its breaking through the general chronological scheme (the type was previously believed to be of the late Roman period, cf. Mawer 1995: 51-52) this object has been taken into consideration on account of possibly conveying a very early manifestation of Christian symbolism. The flatness and delicateness of the bowl should perhaps rule out its use for domestic/culinary purpose in favour of a cultic use; its putative symbolic meaning should relate to three fishes. It is true that one or two fish, rather than three, were preferably employd to convey Christian symbolic conceptions (Leclercq 1927; Cambi 1975: 64, Fig. 15, 16). However, instances, if rare, of the motif of three fishes were viewed as expressing the symbolism of baptism or the eucharist, depending for precise explanation on other elements of a scene as a whole (Garrucci 1873: 14, Tav. 8:5; Garrucci 1879: 130, Tav. 387:2; Garrucci 1880: 117, Tav. 478:2). The early Christian iconography of the Trinity is still a debatable issue and one liable to uncertainties; it was sometimes hypothesized, and with reason, that the basic features of the Trinity in both dogmatic and iconographic terms were drafted as early as the 2nd and 3rd centuries (see III.b.5.); in the 2nd century the symbolism of the Trinity was recorded in connection with the liturgy of baptism (Testini 1958: 5). Curiously enough, a spoon very similar in design and decoration to the one here was determined as a Christian liturgical item (Arthur et al. 1996: 210-211, Fig. 26). Its significance as a parallel is, however, considerably diminished by reason of the interval of several centuries (it was dated to the 10th/11th centuries).

VI.b. and VI.c. Lamps

Introduction

Christian conceptions attach to the flame of lamps the symbolism of eternal life (Forstner 1982: 381-386) rendering them, in addition to the practical purpose for lighting, highly symptomatic of early Christian sacred surroundings. Such a role would be conceived as most apposite when lamps are found in Christian graves. Yet although perhaps rather unexpectedly, early Christian lamps were on the whole more frequent finds in architectural settings, both churches and underground funerary structures, than in graves proper (Menzel 1969: 1-8; Février 1978: 258-263; Mainstone 1988: 125-126); this also holds true for the province of Pannonia (Vágó - Bóna 1976: 164). Equally, in view of the lack of contextual data on the lamps from northern Croatia, they can reasonably be conjectured as stemming in the main from architectural contexts, be they congregational churches or funerary chapels and mausoleums. Unfortunately there exists next to no usable data on the archaeological contexts of the huge Siscian collection of Roman lamps, now in AMZ and MS; they have mostly been dredged from the Kupa or have been discovered by chance during building or agricultural works (Vikić-Belančić 1971: 100). Typological clues for the local workmanship of many of them are nevertheless unquestionable (Koščević in: Koščević - Makjanić 1995: 14-15).

The majority of the lamps from northern Croatia belong to the so-called African or Mediterranean types, or their imitations (VI.c.1-11) (Menzel 1969: 90-95; Hayes 1972: 310-314; Coscarella 1983; Lyon-Caen - Hoff 1986: 90-121; Goethert 1993: 223-224); for the sake of convenience they are here labelled African (without quotation marks; if present, quotation marks denote apparent local imitations). Two of them are of the Syrian and Byzantine types respectively (VI.c.12, VI.c.13.) (Bagatti 1964; Menzel 1969: 101-102; Lyon-Caen - Hoff 1986: 130-145); another two are unindentifiable as only bases are extant (VI.c.14 and 15). The section on lamps was organized on the basis of first grouping together items of the same type or rather, sub-type; within these a sequence based on the differentiation according to the degree of evidence for Christianity was applied.

The chronology of these objects has been widely discussed, but the differentiation of types and groups still remains disputed; accordingly certain of them cannot be dated more precisely than to within the span of two centuries (Coscarella 1983: 155; Goethert 1993: 224). Despite these deficiences, it is exactly the chronology of items under discussion that is most interesting in terms of appreciating north-Croatian early Christianity. Dated mostly to the 5th and 6th centuries, these artefacts testify to a misconception about southern Pannonia as nearly deserted and bare of any substantial material evidence for Christianity after the end of the 4th century (cf. Barkóczi - Salamon 1971; Mócsy 1974, 351; Barkóczi 1980: 114; Fülep 1984: 285-301; Šašel 1992; Christie 1995: 305-310).

VI.b. Metal lamps and candlesticks

VI.b.1. 'Agnus Dei' lamp (I)

Provenance: Sisak (Siscia); found allegedly during building works in the 80s in the area of the northern Roman cemetery.
Location: MS (2464)
Description: Bronze; length 6.9 cm, width 4.8 cm, height 8.4 cm. A very neatly and skilfully executed (cast) lamp, designed in the form of lamb's body with a shafted Christogram attached to its head. The disc and shoulder sections are marked with three rows of superimposed oval bosses denoting the coat. The chi-rho is of a typical version with the serifed chi, unproportionately small in relation to the close rho, and crossing slightly over the shaft. The lamb's tail (lamp's nozzle really) has the shape of a hemispherical dish fluted on the outside with seven ribs, ending in seven corresponding lobes on the rim. The disc is provided with a large circular filling-hole. In place of a handle a lamb's head bent downwords is attached to the body of the lamp. There

was no need for a handle: the lamp was provided with a shaft attached to the underside of a circular moulded ring-base, supporting a cylindrical foot. The lamp was apparently intended for attaching to an appropriate surface and not for carrying by a handle or for hanging, as was occasionally the case. No sign of use is discernible.

Dating: 4th/5th centuries.
Literature: Katalog: 92, no. 76.

VI.b.2. 'Agnus Dei' lamp (I)

Provenance: Zagreb; building works in 1947 not far from the area of the actual town cemetery.
Location: AMZ (8884)
Description: Bronze; length 9.5 cm, width 3.5 cm, height 9.4 cm. Very similar to the previous item, with some different details and overall much more roughly and carelessly

executed. The foot is slightly higher, the lamb's head stretched forward and the nozzle rim bordered by seven triangular protrusions in a star-like arrangement; it was apparently not provided with a shaft. The chi-rho has been crooked and some damage is visible on the body; traces of use are visible.

Dating: 4th/5th centuries.

Literature: Vikić-Belančić 1978: 600-601, Fig. 19a,b; Katalog: 126, no. 179.

Commentary on VI.b.1. and 2.: Metal lamps are much rarer than those made of clay in all areas, Pannonia included (Pavan 1955: 441; Menzel 1969: 106-116). This probably comes not only as a consequence of antique metals being melted down for reuse in subsequent periods, but was also a reality of manufacture. Metal specimens were mainly provided with either shafts for standing or else chains for suspension (Voelkl 1951: 1629; Menzel 1969: 106-116; Bónis 1980: 367-368).

The Christian associations of the two lamps with the Lamb of God as a victim and the Redeemer are more than obvious, with stress layed on the latter role, as suggested by chi-rho and animal's standing posture (Leclercq 1924h: 879; Ferrua 1949: 462-463; see also II.1. and V.g.2.). Literary sources alluding to such a symbolism touch also on the chronology of these objects, but do not succeed in determining it securely. St John's Revelation is the prime literary source of the symbolic Agnus Dei, as it was as a whole a manifest glorification of the Lamb's triumphant victory over evil and death (see particularly 5:6 ff. and 14:1); the most convincing possible inspiration being the quotation 21:23, referring to the City of God, the New Jerusalem, as being in no need of the light of the sun or the moon: the Lamb was her light. The Apocalyptic symbolism can further be recognized in the prominence given the number seven (1:4; 12:3; 6; 8:1; 15:6) in the configuration of the lamp nozzle.

In regard to a hypothetical connection between the Revelation and its effect on the archaeological material of Pannonia, an outstanding ecclesiastical personality comes to mind as a possible indirect mediator - Victorinus, bishop of Poetovio († 304) and a distinguished theologian and writer, preoccupied in his work particularly by the Revelation

(Bratož 1986: 142, note 425, 301 ff.). Yet another source of artistic-iconographic inspiration, reflected in the decorative conception of the lamps' nozzles shaped like a seven-rayed device, can be observed: that of solar iconography and ultimately solar Christology (Thomas 1980: 133; Migotti 1995: 286-287, Fig. 15:2).

Drawing from the Scriptures and the solar cult could in terms of chronology possibly imply dating the Agnus Dei lamps earlier in the 4th century, which would also fit well with the chi-rho without an alfa and omega device (see III.d.1.). So designed, lamps might have given an impetus to the production of those rendered in the form of lamb with a cross, dated to the 5th century and later (see V.g.2.). This in turn would correspond with the first occurrences of the mentioned motif on sarcophagi from the late 4th century (Kaiser-Minn 1983: 330; Abb. 149). One of the four north-Pannonian specimens of the Agnus Dei series had a cross added to the body of the lamb at some later stage of repair, presumably in the 6th century (Thomas E B 1980: 117-118, Abb. 7).

A word should also be said about the presumed place of manufacture of these artefacts. As known, later Pannonian metal production and commerce are on the whole characterized by deteriorating standards and subsequent replacing of import with locally-produced wares (Pavan 1955: 449; Oliva 1962: 319-321); both these features would speak in favour of the local manufacture of the Agnus Dei lamps. Four items in all have been discovered to date in the territory of Pannonia (for the two from Hungary see Thomas E B 1980: 133; Tóth 1994: 254) with no parallels elsewhere. Except for the one from Sisak (VI.b.1.) the remainder are of quite modest artistic execution. On balance, the type was apparently unique to Pannonia and most probably manufactured at Siscia, a well-known centre of metalwork production in that part of the Roman Empire (Koščević in: Koščević - Makjanić 1995: 16-25).

VI.b.3. Votive plaque (I?)

Provenance: Sisak (Siscia)
Location: AMZ

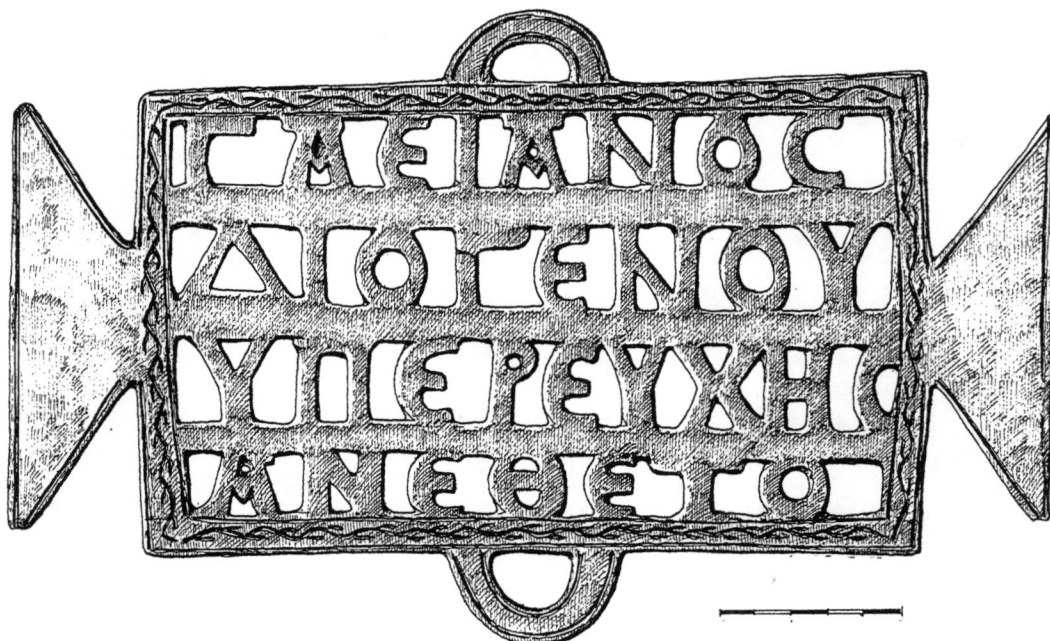

Description: Bronze; 17 x 29 cm, thickness 0.5 cm. A fairly massive cast openwork plaque in the form of rectangular *tabula ansata* with two solid *ansae* and an openwork inscription within the frame. The frame is all over decorated with a tiny schematized running tendril; its upper and lower borders bear each a semicircular suspension loop. Within the frame is an openwork inscription in capital Greek letters:

Γαειανος
Διογενου(ς)
υπερ ευχης
ανεθετο.

(Gaianos, son of Diogenos, had this made in fulfilment of a vow).

Dating: 4th century.
Literature: AIJ: 240, no. 525; Alföldi A 1942: 526, Taf. 40:1.
Commentary: The question mark by the classification number denotes a slight doubt about this object's Christian significance, resulting from its fragmentary state. A nearly identical plaque was found in the territory of Roman Dacia (modern Romania) containing an inscription of the same meaning, only in Latin script and language; this type of formula with occasional minor variations was very common among early Christian phrases (Engemann 1972: 157; Demandt 1986: 115; Mawer 1995: 87). A round openwork pendant in the form of a chi-rho was attached to the plaque from Romania (Alföldi A 1942: 255, Taf. 40:2, 4). It is accordingly a very plausible hypothesis (kindly pointed to me by Dr. Dragan Božić) that the specimen here had an identical pendant suspended from a chain attached to one of the loops. Such an interpretation is reinforced by a fair number of similar pendants with or without vestiges of chains, found throughout Pannonia and Noricum (Alföldi A 1942; Thomas E B 1982: 271, Abbs. 12, 13; Knific - Sagadin 1991: 106, nos. 1-3). Plaques like the one from Sisak were mostly parts of sumptuous lamps or candlesticks, donated usually to churches by the faithful in fulfilments of a vow, i.e. as payments to God for requests granted (Leclercq 1924d; Alföldi A 1942: 255-256; Gough 1973: 137, Fig. 126).

The inscription on the plaque from Sisak is the only secure early Christian Greek epigraphic testimony from northern Croatia; the three other here presented (I.b., V.e.7. and V.e.11.) are only hypothetically so. Neither of them is undisputably Christian and only two were inscribed in Greek letters (V.e.11 and VI.b.3.); the remaining two contain Greek words/names transliterated in Latin. Filiation on the inscription from Sisak belongs to common Christian formulae of this period (see III.c.6.). Despite the father's Greek name (Diogenes) and the son's Latin (Gaianos), which should point to a degree of Romanization, the inscription is still in Greek; also worth noting is a Greek form (ending in -os) of the Latin name Gaianus. The name Diogenes was widely spread all over Italy, particularly among freedmen, and except for a martyr so named (Delehaye 1912: 310) has no specific Christian overtones (Alföldi 1969: 188). Gaianos is common everywhere, frequent also among the Christians, who might have been attracted to the names Gaius or Gaianus by their reference to martyrs (Delehaye 1912: 180, 292; Kajanto 1965: 109, 172).

Neither the filiation formula nor the epigraphic features of the inscription, with chi-rho missing, are sufficient for a more precise dating within the 4th century.

VI.b.4. Chi-rho (I)

Provenance: Probably Osijek (Mursa) or its surroundings.
Location: AMZ (the Plavšić collection stemming from Osijek).
Description: Bronze; Chi-rho: 6.4 x 5 cm, length of chain: 21 cm. A solid chi-rho with expanding terminals and with at the circular intersection of the arms, eight shallow pits, one central and seven surrounding ones in the form of rosette; pits were probably intended for enamel or glass settings. The tip of the left-hand chi arm is provided with a hole and a hook on which a chain is suspended by means of a hook and loop device. Yet another hook is attached to the other end of the chain. Traces of soldering onto some surface are visible on the underside of the rho stem.
Dating: 4th century.
Literature: Katalog: 130, no. 193.
Commentary: Like the previous item, this one should have been part of either a sumptuous lamp or a candlestick. Although one of the four Agnus Dei lamps was provided with accessories for suspension in addition to its standing base (Thomas E B 1980: 133), the latter possibility seems more plausible. Among a number of Pannonian and Norican chi-rhos of the kind this is to my knowledge the only one with a central rosette-like decoration. The motif is otherwise a very common early Christian iconographic device, applied mostly to intersections of the arms of crosses, but familiar in other places, too (Garrucci 1873: Tav. 10:3; 46; 84; 86; 87:3; Ferrua 1958: 25-26). Given the regular number of dots - either seven or eight - the device should be perceived as not only decorative, but symbolic as well (for the relative numbers see Quacquarelli 1973: 261-262; Forstner 1982: 52-55; also VI.b.1.,2.). No secure indications for a more precise date are available.

VI.c. Clay lamps

VI.c.1. African lamp (I)

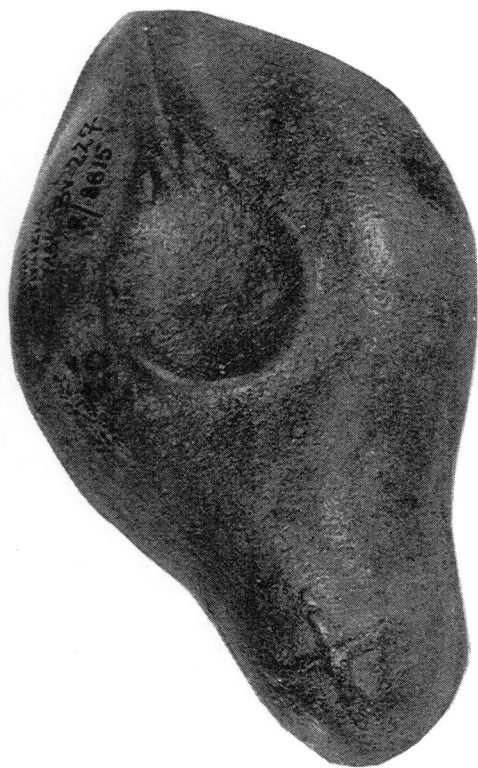

Provenance: Sisak (Siscia)
Location: AMZ (8615)
Description: Light red clay with reddish-brown coat; 12.4 x 7.8, height 3.2 cm. Between two vertical filling holes on the discus a worn-out relief motif of a running animal (a rabbit or a dog) is depicted. The broad sloping rim bears a pair of stylized spiny shapes, described conventionally as a herring bone or a palm branch motif. On the underside of the oval grooved nozzle a coarse equal-armed crosss was applied in low relief after the lamp had been moulded.
Dating: Beginning of the 4th century (Hayes type I B).
Literature: Vikić-Belančić 1971: 166, T. 17:1; Katalog: 92, no. 77b.
Commentary: By both its shape and decoration this item belongs to the early type covering the whole of the 4th century (Hayes 1972: 310-313; Lyon-Caen - Hoff 1986: 97-98, nos. 29-32; Goethert 1993: 215-217, 224, Abb. 44:1). As for the motif on the shoulders, termed in the literature as herring-bone or a palm branch respectively, the latter should be preferred in view of both its configuration and expected symbolism: African lamps are mostly decorated with overt or stylized Christian symbolic subjects. This, on the other hand, does not automatically denote the palm branch motif as a Christian device; the same is true of the dog and the rabbit (see III.b.1.). Decorative and symbolic motifs on African lamps were usually placed on the discus and shoulder area and not infrequently on the underside of bases, but are quite rare on the underside of nozzles (Bagatti 1964, Figs. 1-3; Menzel 1969: Abb. 80:1; 81:12; 82:1,3,10; Barnea 1977: 251, Fig. 101:2; Lyon-Caen - Hoff 1986: 95-109, 157-158, nos. 18, 21, 25, 29, 87 ff.;). The specimen from Sisak typifies apparently the last-mentioned instance; yet I know of no immediate parallels. As the cross was obviously not contained in the mould and was added to the surface before firing, it should be viewed as a kind of private expression of faith, be it a whim of the worker or a wish of the customer. The placement of the cross as not exposed to normal viewing should imply its date at the very beginning of the 4th century at the latest. It also testifies to the cross appearing quite early as a cryptic symbol; in the regular iconographic-chronological sequence it comes after the chi-rho (see III.a.4. and VI.d.34.).

VI.c.2. African lamp (I)

Provenance: Sisak (Siscia)
Location: MS (3119)
Description: Reddish clay; 10.9 x 7.2 cm, height 5 cm. Ovoid upper surface, slightly rounded, vertical stump-handle with deep central groove and short rounded nozzle provided with broad shallow chanel. Between two horizontal filling holes on the rounded discus is a relief motif of a chi-rho in a circular frame filled with parallel strokes, featuring a wreath. The chi-rho has expanded terminals and a dot in the middle. The broad rim bears an impressed motif of a pair of palm branches. On the much damaged underside of the base traces of an engraved chi-rho are identifiable, with the rho-loop barely visible.
Dating: mid 4th century/beginning of the 5th century (Hayes type I B).
Literature: Katalog: 93, no. 78 d.

VI.c.3. African lamp (I)

Provenance: Sisak (Siscia)
Location: AMZ (7774)
Description: Reddish clay; 9.1 x 6 cm, height 3.5 cm. Very similar to the previous item, only the chi-rho on the discus is less conspicuous and more roughly executed, while also lacking a wreath, and there is no device on the base.
Dating: mid 4th century - beginning of the 5th century (Hayes type I B).
Literature: Vikić-Belančić 1971: 170, no 304, T. 17:7; 24:17; Vikić-Belančić 1978: 600, Fig. 17; Katalog: 93, no. 78b.

VI.c.4. African lamp (I)

Provenance: Sisak (Siscia)
Location: AMZ (7774a)
Description: Reddish clay; 9.1 x. 6.5 cm, height 3 cm. Very similar to the previous item; discus and rims somewhat broader and nozzle's tip broken off.
Dating: Mid 4th century/beginning of the 5th century (Hayes type I B).
Literature: Vikić-Belančić 1971: 170, no. 305; Katalog: 93, no. 78c.

VI.c.5. African lamp (I)

Provenance: Sisak (Siscia)
Location: AMZ (8633)
Description: Reddish clay with dark flecks; 12.4 x 7.8 cm, height 3.2 cm. Ovoid upper surface, somewhat angular broad rim and damaged handle and long rounded nozzle with broad channel. On the discus provided with two horizontal filling holes is a motif of an elaborate relief chi-rho with expanded terminals ending each in a dotted-circle, with an additional circle in the middle. The chi-rho is enfolded by a wreath composed of a stylized branch and dotted circles. The broad rim bears a 'baroque' looping wreath intertwined with dotted circles.
Dating: End of the 4th century/beginning of the 5th century(?) (Hayes type I B).
Literature: Vikić-Belančić 1971: 170, no. 303, T. 17:6; 24:16; Vikić-Belančić 1978: 599, Fig. 15; Katalog: 93, no. 78a.

VI.c.6. African lamp (II)

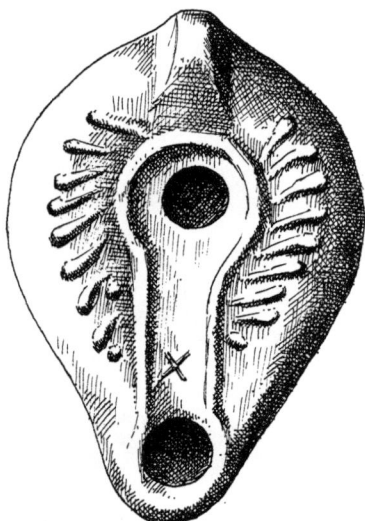

Provenance: Sisak (Siscia)
Location: AMZ (8238)
Description: Reddish clay; 10.1 x 7 cm, height 3.5 cm. Ovoid upper surface with stump handle and short near-triangular rounded nozzle. An inconspicuous discus with one filling hole is encircled by an irregular string stretching along the channel down to the nozzle. The fairly broad rim bears a motif of ovoid elongated shapes in low relief, some of them ending in rounded drops (very schematized palm branch motif?). Roughly in the middle of the channel is a clumsily executed low relief saltire cross.
Dating: 4th/5th centuries (a Hayes type I local derivation?).
Literature: Vikić-Belančić 1971: 170, no. 306, T. 25:1.

VI.c.7. African lamp (II)

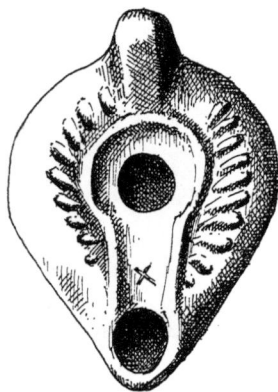

Provenance: Sisak (Siscia)
Location: AMZ (8238)
Description: 9.7 x 6 cm, height 2.8 cm. Very similar to the previous item, only smaller. The ovoid shapes of the rim decoration are somewhat better executed, as is the saltire on the channel.
Dating: 4th/5th centuries (a Hayes type I local derivation?)
Literature: Vikić-Belančić 1971: 171, no. 309, T. 25:2.
Commentary on VI.c.2.-7. Despite the item no. 5. being somewhat different from the remainder, they are all considered in conjunction on account of the chi-rho and branch motifs depicted consistently on their shoulders and disci. The palm branch motif on the rims of items 2., 3. and

4. is distinctive of Hayes type I, covering the whole of the 4th century (Hayes 1972: 310-311). The chi-rho is not to be expected much earlier than the mid century; it started to appear more frequently on coins and in other media from the time of Constantine's successors (Sutherland - Litt - Carson 1981: 36, passim). The type here apparently derived from lamps decorated with only palm branches and possibly some 'neutral' motifs (rosettes, running animals, etc.) on disci, dated to the first half of the 4th century (Goethert 1993: 149, Abb. 15). Such lamps are abundant everywhere, but seem to be typical of the northern provinces, Pannonia included (Noll 1954, Abb. 9; Kempt - Reusch 1965: 77-78, nos. 60, 62; Graziani Abbiani 1969: 121-123, Tav. 18:70; Menzel 1969, Abb. 79: 1-3; Hayes 1972: 310-311; Coscarella 1983: 160, no. 10:1; Goethert 1993: 226-229, Abb. 49:115; 50:124, 51:131).

Siscia is one of the Pannonian Roman sites with an immense quantity of clay lamps found and with local manufacture attested on stylistic grounds as well as by finds of clay moulds. Traces of workshops have been identified in various places, among others the north-eastern suburb in the area of the Roman cemetery (Fig. 5:4) (Vikić-Belančić 1971: 117-119; Koščević in: Koščević - Makjanić 1995: 14-15; Buzov 1996: 64). With this in mind, Siscia appears as the most probable manufacturing place of items 2, 3 and 4. All three are nearly identical in both their overall aspect and poor manufacture; the series is probably much more numerous (yet another item has shown up in the meantime in MS: Zdenko Burkowsky pers. comm.). The same should also be true of items nos. 6 and 7 (to be discussed further below). One (no. 3) of the four lamps nearly identical in style and execution (nos. 2-4) can be singled out for the chi-rho on the base, lacking in the remainder; such a superfluous accenting of Christian appurtenance is in principle familiar with African lamps (Graziani Abbiani 1969: 139, Tav. 22:86; Barnea 1977: 251, Fig. 101:2; Lyon-Caen - Hoff 1986: 109, 120, nos. 87, 144). The decoration of lamp no. 4. is slightly different from nos. 2. and 3. in showing a simple wreath around a chi-rho and introducing thereby a transition to the type represented by no. 5. Featuring a double wreath in a lavish 'baroque' manner, this lamp (no. 5.) is in terms of decoration the finest and most elaborate; I was able to trace only a near parallel within Hayes type IB (Lyon-Caen - Hoff 1986: 120, no. 145). As two types (I and II) of African lamps have as yet not generally been clearly differentiated by scholars (Hayes 1972: 310; Berti 1983: 148), a suggestion appears appropriate that lamps with elaborate wreaths like the one from Sisak (no. 5.) represent a transition between Hayes types I and II A. The rims on type II are decorated with various elaborate small geometric and floral motifs (square patterns, s-scrolls, palm-trees, quatrefoils, miniature animals and the like, see Hayes 1972: 312) instead of simple palm branches. A corresponding ambiguity about no. 5. is tentatively resolved here by placing it among type I and shifting its date towards the 5th century and slightly closer to type II A.

Lamps nos. 6 and 7 can be separated as a group representing a variation on Hayes type I. Their upper surfaces appear to be slightly more elongated, although not markedly so, the disci are more ar less inconspicuous and rim decoration features a high-rate stylization of type I palm branches. A vast quantity of rustic versions of this type of lamp is stored in AMZ; they all stem from Sisak, testifying to a probable Siscian manufacture. Lamps nos. 6 and 7 are presented here for reasons of the probable religious association of the motifs of saltire crosses (see S.3.). Interpreted as a local rustic version of 4th century type, they may reasonably be supposed to have continued well in the 5th century (Vikić-Belančić 1971: 120).

VI.c.8. African lamp (I)

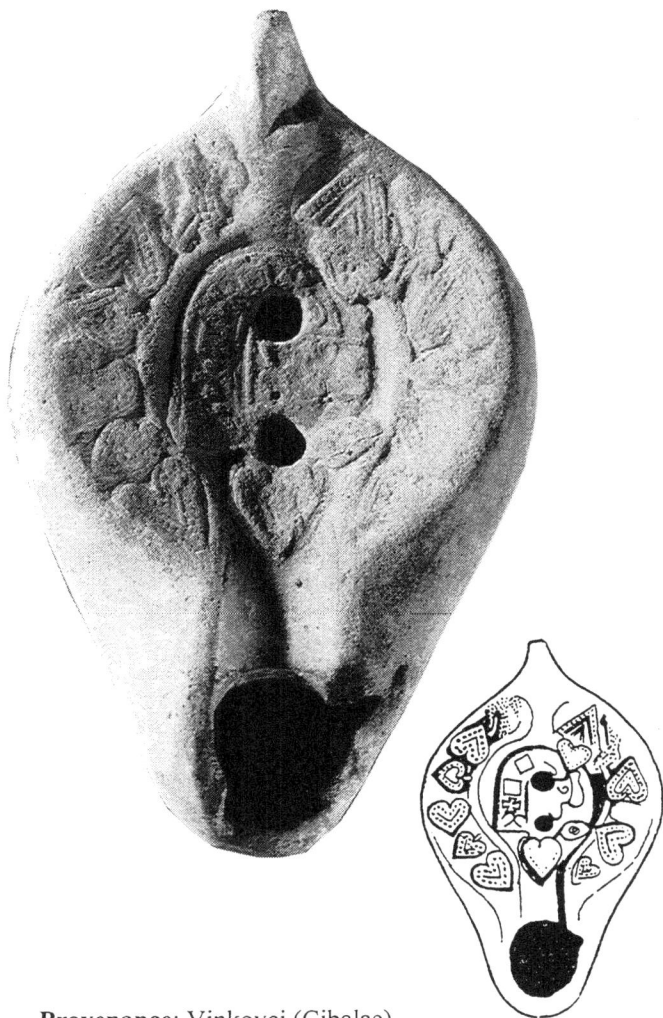

Provenance: Vinkovci (Cibalae)
Location: AMZ (8617)
Description: Red clay; 11.1 x 7 cm, height 3 cm. Oval shape and rounded upper surface with an indeterminate division between discus and rim. The rim is slightly sloping inward towards the discus so shaped as to accomodate a depiction of a helmet. A near-triangular and rounded nozzle is slightly damaged. The worn-out relief rim decoration conveys untidy crowded, heart-like and triangular shapes with variously scored, hatchured and dotted surfaces. Between two vertical filling holes on the discus a helmet or a helmeted head is depicted in profile to the right. Prominent among various indistinct shapes of the helmet's decoration is an equal-armed cross with extended terminals.
Dating: 5th century (Hayes II A).
Literature: Vikić-Belančić 1971: 169, no. 297, T. 24:13; Katalog: 102, no. 108.
Commentary: By its shape and rim decoration this item belongs to Hayes type II A (Hayes 1972: 312). Despite male and female busts occurring frequently on disci of this type, I

was not able to trace a parallel featuring a helmet. With Cibalae as one of the most outstanding Pannonian centres of clay manufacture in mind (Dimitrijević 1979: 222-223), the depiction on this lamp could tentatively be envisaged as a locally-contrived motif unparalleled elsewhere; the untidy crowded rim ornaments would also support this conjecture. A mention should be made of a lamp with a similar depiction in the Kunsthistorisches Museum in Bonn. A helmeted Constantine's head is depicted on it with a chi-rho on the helmet, but the artefact is assumed to be a forgery (Kantorowicz 1964: 189, note 50). While specific reasons to produce such a falsification were convincingly put forward for the lamp from Bonn, nothing of the kind is conceivable of the specimen from Vinkovci, which on all accounts should be genuine.

VI.c.9. African lamp (I)

Provenance: Sisak (Siscia)
Location: AMZ (8168)
Description: Light red clay; 14.3 x 6.3 cm, height 3 cm. Rounded upper surface, pointed stump handle, long nozzle rounded at tip. The worn-out relief decoration comprises a beading on the rim (six flattened bosses to each side of the rim) and a cross with a prolonged lower arm (Latin cross) and expanded terminals, placed between two filling holes on the discus. The cross is too worn-out for any reliable conjectures about its decoration, but a beading could be expected by analogy with a number of specimens of the type.
Dating: AD 450-460 (Hayes type II B).
Literature: Vikić-Belančić 1971: 169, no. 301, T. 17:5; Katalog: 94, no. 79.

Commentary: By its shape and decorative conception this item belongs to Hayes type II B, characterized by both the roughness of execution and subsequent wear (Hayes 1972: 312-313). Near-immediate analogies are numerous (Menzel 1969, Abb. 77:9, 78:1; Lyon-Caen - Hoff 1986: 112-113, nos. 109, 110, etc.; Goethert 1993, Abb. 45:13).

VI.c.10. African lamp (II)

Provenance: Osijek (Mursa); donated to AMZ in 1927.
Location: AMZ (8623)
Description: Red clay; 9.9 x 6.4 cm, height 4.3 cm. Rounded upper surface with pointed stump handle slightly damaged, long nozzle with tip broken off. The rim is decorated on each side with a row of eight fluted relief triangles. In the depression of the discus a relief motif of a 'rosette-cross' is spaced around a single filling hole; it is composed of four fluted and beaded rounded petals and four little three-leafed branches springing diagonally from the angles of the petals.
Dating: AD 420-500 (Hayes type II A).
Literature: Vikić-Belančić 1971: 169, no. 295, T. 24:11; Katalog: 108, no. 131.

VI.c.11. African lamp (II)

Provenance: Sisak (Siscia)
Location AMZ (8623, misplaced).
Description: Width 6.4 cm, height 3.4 cm. The omission of length in publishing (Vikić-Belančić 1971: 168)) is inexplicable; contrary to the previous item, this lamp was completely preserved (see photograph in Vikić-Belančić 1971, T. 17:3). The foregoing and some other uncertainties over the lamp cannot, however, be resolved as long as it is untraceable in AMZ. But for a slight difference in height it is completely identical with the previous item.
Dating: AD 420-500 (Hayes typ II A).

Literature: Vikić-Belančić 1971: 168, no. 294, T. 17:3.
Commentary on VI.c. 6 and 7: By their shape and rim decoration these two identical artefacts belong to Hayes type II A (Hayes 1972: 312). They even provoke a suspicion about the same mould (uncertainties over their lengths and possibly also heights might be explained away as mistakes in taking measurements). Should this be the case, there remains to explain the surprising sameness of two artefacts stemming from two quite distant sites, Siscia and Mursa. The diagnostic device on the disci is rendered as a double cruciform arrangement of two crosses, an upright and an oblique one, known as the Greek and the St Andrew's cross respectively. Instead of a classic iconographic conception, they are stylized in the guise of the blend of two different floral motifs; such an iconographical scheme for an emblem of the cross is verified time and again in the art of the early Christian and later periods. The lamps were nevertheless classified as only probably Christian to allow for a possibility of such 'everlasting' and common motifs being employed in a solely decorative role. The motif is on the whole quite familiar on late Roman lamps (Atlante I: 200, Tav. 160:7; Coscarella 1983: 161, no. 10:7).

VI.c.12. Syro-Palestinian lamp (I)

Provenance: Probably Sisak (Siscia).
Location: AMZ; collection Orlić (73) stemming from Sisak.
Description: Whitish-buff clay; 7.8 x 6 cm, height 4.1 cm. Very low (handle excluded) biconical almond-shaped body, vertical pointed stump handle and short triangular nozzle with rounded tip. A single large filling hole in place of discus is encircled by a deep groove extending into a broad channel and terminating in a hole on the nozzle. The broad outwards sloping rim holds a low relief motif of delicately stylized branches with oval thinly-spaced leaves. They are slightly different to those usally described as palm branches (so common on African lamps), looking more like olive branches In the middle of the channel an equal-armed cross is rendered by means of a cruciform arrangement of five pellets.

Dating: 5th/7th centuries.
Literature: Katalog: 92, no. 77a.
Commentary: The lamp belongs to one of the four variations on the Syro-Palestinian type. Given the complete lack of data on the context, any attempt at closer dating would remain futile; typological chronology of the type to enable differentiation between the four variants has not as yet been worked out satisfactorily (Bagatti 1964; Berti 1983: 149-150; Lyon-Caen - Hoff 1986: 133-141). No immediate parallels in terms of decoration are known to me; yet similarly stylized motifs occur frequently on this type.

The type of cross depicted on the channel is parallelled on various early Christian objects (see V.e.5.). Furthermore, it is here positioned exactly in the place intended for Christian devices on all types of late-Roman lamps (Bagatti 1964, Fig. 1: 5,6,11; Menzel 1969, Abb. 82:7; Lyon-Caen - Hoff 1986, nos. 114, 172, 181 etc.).

VI.c.13. Syro-Palestinian/Byzantine lamp I

Provenance: Probably Sisak (Siscia).
Location: AMZ; collection Orlić (72) stemming from Sisak.
Description: Dark buff clay with traces of brown coating; extremely course fabric; 10.4 x 5.7 cm, height 4.4 cm. Low, elongated boat-shaped body with upward slanting tongue-like broad handle and short oval nozzle. There is no demarcation line between the single large filling hole of the discus and the raking rim. The whole of the surface between these two elements is covered by an indistinct motif of a band composed of two strings, surrounding the filling hole. The handle bears the motif of a coarse Latin cross with three arms extended, and the lower one slightly tapering toward a roundel at its bottom (this element might as well be a knot of the band-like motif around the filling hole); it is rendered by means of double-contouring in low relief. The surface between the filling hole and the nozzle also has a roughly executed relief cross, but an equal-armed one.
Dating: 6th/7th centuries.
Literature: Katalog: 94, no. 80.
Commentary: This type is labelled variously Syro-Palestinian (Bagatti 1964, Fig. 2: 3-5; Lyon-Caen - Hoff 1986: 141-145) or Byzantine (Menzel 1969: 99, Abb. 54:12; Lyon-Caen - Hoff 1986: 126-128, no. 167). In terms of geographical and cultural background both these denominations amount ultimately to the same: the whole series is dated to the 6th and 7th centuries. Specimens with depictions of crosses on handles are familiar with this type (Lyon-Caen - Hoff 1986: 142-144, nos. 222-229). The rough execution and wear of the lamp from Sisak leaves it unclear whether the round shape under the larger of two crosses constitutes part of the band ornament or else represents the Cross on an orb motif (cf. Kaufmann 1913: 649, Fig. 273; Higgins 1987: 119, Fig. 43).

VI.c.14. Base-fragment of lamp (III)

Provenance: Osijek (Mursa); building works in 1895 (within town walls).
Location: MSO (312)
Description: Buff low-quality clay; 4.8 x 3.7 cm. A sherd from a lamp base of course workmanship. Within the roundel on the underside, composed of two irregular moulded bands and corresponding grooves, is a tiny plant motif in low relief intended most probably for a palm branch.
Dating: 4th/6th centuries.
Literature: Katalog: 108, no. 133.

VI.c.15. Base-fragment of lamp (III)

Provenance: Osijek (Mursa)
Location: MSO (262)
Description: 5.2 x. 5.1 cm. An item nearly identical with the previous one. The plant motif is rendered even more coarsely and can only be identified as a palm branch on analogy of no. 14.
Dating: 4th/6th centuries.
Literature: Katalog: 108, no. 132.
Commentary on nos. VI.c. 14. and 15.: Bases solely are apparently not sufficient for the identification of the type of these lamps; several series, dating from the 3rd/7th centuries, have a palm branch on the undersides of bodies. Such motifs have been found on lamps of indistinct types (Menzel 1969, Abb. 75:3; 82:3; Lyon-Caen - Hoff 1986: 151, no. 258), as well as on African (Goethert 1993: 223, Abb. 48:3b) and Syrian lamps (Bagatti 1964, Fig. 1:30). On account of their similarity and their courseness, the two sherds from Osijek should tentatively be ascribed to a local workshop, clay production having been attested for Mursa (Bulat 1989a: 25). A palm branch or a palm tree on late antique lamps has mostly been attested in Judaic and Christian surroundings (Voelkl 1951: 1630). The Jews and the Christians alike accepted the basic pagan religious association of the palm as an emblem of victory, only the Christians enriched it with the meaning of victory over sin and death. Accordingly it became (very often in tandem with the wreath conveying similar symbolic connotations) one of the most widespread motifs of early Christian art, particularly funerary (Leclercq 1937; Kaufmann 1917: 205-206; Testini 1958: 361; Daniélou 1969: 262; Forstner 1982: 169-170). Despite these facts, the palm in itself cannot be ascribed more than a possibility of Christian meaning (cf. Mawer 1995: 6, passim). Such a possibility here is reinforced by the fact of the palm being employed as the sole motif on a symbolically significant surface.

VI.d. Pottery vessels

VI.d.1. Base fragment of bowl (African sigillata) I

Provenance: Sisak (Siscia)
Location: AMZ (7988)
Description: Orange clay with dark orange slip; 6.7 x 6.3 cm. A relief composition is applied of two female figures clothed in particular garments covering their lower bodies and breasts. The left one is tied to a pole and is being attacked by a bear. Two animals, one of them possibly a lion, are grasping at the other figure.
Dating: 2nd half of the 4th century/beginning of the 5th century.
Literature: Katalog: 95, no. 85; Makjanić in: Makjanić - Koščević 1995: 71-72, Pl. 72:301.
Commentary: The fragment apparently has a scene of a Christian martyrdom (*datio ad bestias*). This particular instance represents a rare variation on the theme which in itself is not particularly frequent either on pottery or in other media (Leclercq 1924e; Makjanić in: Koščević - Makjanić 1995: 72). Such a scene on an object of daily use in a city which at the beginning of the 4th century produced a world-famous martyr in St Quirinus (Jarak 1994: 161 ff.) would certainly have provoked significant memories even in the 5th century. It should also be borne in mind that in all probability Siscia not only cherished the memory of Quirinus but became possibly a pilgrimage centre (see V.f.2.).

VI.d.2. Dish ('African sigillata') (I)

Provenance: Osijek (Mursa); rescue excavation in 1961 immediately outside the north town wall (Fig. 1: 3).
Location: MSO (7437)
Description: Red-brownish fabric and slip, coarse execution (probably a local imitation of African ware); rim diam. 24.5 cm, height 6.5 cm. A large rounded dish (restored and partly reconstructed on the basis of a few reassembled fragments) with thickened rim and flat bottom and with a foot-ring. On the innerside of the base an elaborate geometrically stylized cruciform composition is impressed, rendered by means of

double parallel short strokes and concentric circles in the form of an equal-armed cross with diagonal saltire-shaped lines between the cross's arms.

the overall monogrammatic scheme, popular in Christian iconography of the 5th and 6th centuries (see S.5.), and the central motif of the Greek cross.

Dating: 4th/5th centuries.
Literature: Bulat 1987: 56, no. 2, Fig. 11:7; Katalog: 109, no. 134.
Commentary: Taken as a whole the motif represents a radial monogrammatic device composed of the Greek and St Andrew's crosses. Decorative schemes on 4th and 5th centuries African red slip wares (terra sigillata) are on the whole dominated by floral and geometric star-like patterns based on radiating palm-branch motifs and sets of concentric circles. In the course of the 5th and 6th centuries the basic radial scheme became enriched with various additional motifs, including combinations of Christian devices, primarily chi-rhos and crosses (Hayes 1972: 217-220; Rigoir - Rigoir - Meffre 1973, Pl. 25:2183, 2527 etc.).

The decorative conception of the dish from Osijek fits loosely in the outlined general scheme but is otherwise unique, particularly as concerns the motif of the central Greek cross. On account of its poor quality and a rather singular symbolic-decorative device, and with attested ceramic production at Mursa in mind (Bulat 1989a: 25), this object should tentatively be ascribed to a local workshop. This would accord well with the single near (although not quite close) analogy I could trace for it - a fragment of a plate stemming from the Ravenna area (Maioli 1983: 96-97, no. 4.8); prompted by the lack of immediate parallels, the commentator interpreted the vessel as belonging to a local production.

There should be no doubts about the Christian meaning of the device on the dish from Mursa. It is ascertained by both

VI.d.3. Base fragment of bowl (African sigillata) (II)

Provenance: Sisak (Siscia); dredging of the river Kupa in 1912.
Location AMZ (7957)
Description: Orange fabric and slip; 2.7 x 2.7 cm. Impressed on the innerside of the bottom is a motif conveying a central concentric roundel and radially disposed geometrical trefoils composed of triple concentric circles.
Dating: Beginning of the 5th century.

Literature: Katalog: 95, no. 86; Makjanić in: Koščević - Makjanić 1995: 71-72, Pl. 72:302.

Commentary: It may reasonably be hypothesized that the radial scheme of the motif was based on a iota-chi monogrammatic device; it should be ascribed a probable Christian meaning, similar to the one advanced for VI.d.2. (see also S.5.). Curiously enough, individual components of this composition are frequent on African sigillata, but not so the motif as a whole (Makjanić in: Koščević - Makjanić 1995: 72).

VI.d.4. Base fragment (II)

Provenance: Vinkovci (Cibalae); found during building works in 1993 within town walls roughly in the position marked on Fig. 4:1; recovered from a 3rd century layer.

Location: GMV (A-3120)

Description: Coarse reddish fabric with dull red slip (imitation of terra sigillata); 6.8 x 6.2 cm. A flat base fragment of a vessel of unidentified shape. A graffito in the form of two crossed lines is intended probably for an upright equal-armed cross, but with right arm slightly overextended, is roughly incised. The graffito was clearly scratched after firing.

Dating: 3rd century.

Literature: Katalog: 102, no. 109.

Commentary: In late Roman and mediaeval times manufacturers' marks were as a rule applied (either impressed or molded in relief) on the undersides of the bottoms of pottery vessels. While their primary role was functional, a number of them were designed so as to display unquestionable religious and apotropaic symbolism. A similar, although perhaps rarer feature is graffiti variously incised after firing on the outer or the inner walls of vessels, featuring occasionally clearly distinguishable names or signs and at other times indistinct shapes (Gabler 1968; Tovornik 1986: 209, Abb. 9, 10; Fiedler 1992: 164-170; Mawer 1995: 34-41). A variety of possibilities (other than religious associations) have been presumed for graffiti designed in forms close to or identical with Christian devices: marks of numeration or possession or identification (Mawer 1995: 34-41). With due respect for such a justifiable line of reasoning, the possibility of cross-like motifs represent Christian devices remains strong, if liable to verification in every instance. Christian symbols in the guise of graffiti are attested on various objects and in different media during the whole of the early Christian period (Testini 1958: 269, Fig. 106; Kempt - Reusch 1965: 83, no. 65; Sági 1968; Török 1974: 371-372; Barnea 1977: 257, Fig. 105:2; Mawer 1995: 37, C8.Po.10, 12).

The case for a personal expression of Christian feelings on this sherd might further be substantiated by two arguments. First, it dates from the period when a see was already established at Cibalae (Jarak 1994: 169-170), and second, it was discovered in an area of a hypothesized Christian surroundings (see I.a.2., III.c.4. and Fig. 4:1). The idea of so expressing religious affinities in times unfavourable to Christians is akin to a similar feature observed in relation to no. VI.c.1.

VI.d.5. Base of vessel (II)

Provenance: Ozalj, a mediaeval castle; excavation in 1992; found on the site of the Romanesqe and a putative early Christian church in a 6th century layer.

Location: ZMO

Description: Coarse brownish clay; base diam. 7.3 cm. A flat round base and small side section of a vessel with conical walls. Impressed or, rather, deeply engraved on the outer side of the base is a saltire or maybe an equal-armed cross.

Dating: 6th century.

Literature: Katalog: 114: no. 148.

Commentary: Contrary to the previous item, a putative Christian device was applied to this vessel before firing. It was situated in a place reserved for various types of signs on late Roman and mediaeval vessels, denoting primarily their manufacturers (see VI.d.4). Cross- and x-shaped signs have in such contexts at times been interpreted as traces of either cruciform struts inserted into the base to enhance strength and solidity or else a technical device for establishing the centre of the base, necerrary to the manufacturing procedure (Tovornik 1986: 209; Mawer 1995: 35). With undisputably Christian devices on some late-Roman and particularly mediaeval pottery in mind (Tovornik 1986, Abb. 9, 10; Fiedler 1992, Abb. 37), suspicion of the symbolic meaning of any cross in a significant place on a vessel cannot be completely discarded. In this particular example the possibility is further substantiated by the context.

VI.d.6. Rim fragment of bowl (African sigillata) (III)

Provenance: Sisak (Siscia); dredging of the river Kupa in 1912.

Location: AMZ (7957)

Description: Orange fabric and slip; 3.3 x 4.2 cm. On the innerside is applied a relief head of the god Ocean (personification of the ocean) with flashy cheeks and rich curls of hair and beard and a benign expression on his face.

Dating: 4th century.

Literature: Katalog: 94, no. 82; Makjanić in: Koščević - Makjanić 1995: 71-72, Pl. 72: 294.

V.i.d.7. Rim fragment of bowl (African sigillata) (III)

Provenance: Sisak (Siscia); dredging of the river Kupa in 1912.

Location: AMZ (7957)

Description: Orange fabric and slip; 7 x 2.5 cm. On the innerside is applied the relief figure of a fish swimming to the right, with neatly executed details of the body.

Dating: End of the 4th century/beginning of the 5th century.

Literature: Katalog: 95, no. 83; Makjanić in: Koščević - Makjanić 1995: 71-72, Pl. 72:297.

Commentary on nos. VI.d. 6. and 7.: Both motifs are in theory pagan as well as Christian, a differentiation depending exclusively on context. Within the framework of Christian cosmology (with all creatures assigned the power and holiness of God's emanations, see Grabar 1968: 53; Craveri 1969: 84; Forstner 1982: 17) water scenes and water things figure prominently (Brandenburg 1983; Provoost 1986: 52-53). Among numerous marine creatures particularly significant in terms of Christian symbolism is apparently the fish (see III.b.3.); less markedly so is Ocean, yet occurrences of his image in early Christian art are quite frequent (Garrucci 1873: 18, Tav. 14; Velmans 1969: 34-35, Fig. 8; Forstner 1982: 17, note 7).

With no contextual data available, two additional arguments can tentatively be put forward in support of possible Christian meaning of these two fragments. First, it is their dating in the period of the Empire as officially Christianized, and second, it is their African provenance, Africa being one of the earliest and most thoroughly Christianized areas of the Roman world.

VI.d.8. Base fragment of bowl (African sigillata) (III)

Provenance: Sisak (Siscia); dredging of the Kupa river in 1913.
Location: AMZ (7957)
Description: Light red fabric with red-brown slip; 4.6 x 5.2 cm. On the innerside of base a relief hunt scene (*venatio*) is depicted containing three men, one of them holding a boar.
Dating: End of the 4th century/beginning of the 5th century.
Literature: Katalog: 95, no. 84; Makjanić in: Koščević - Makjanić 1995: 71-72, Pl. 72:300.
Commentary: The *venatio* motif is quite frequently employed in early Christian art. As attested by documentary sources, in Christian settings this scene naturally assumes the meaning of victory over evil and sin and death (Marucchi 1903: 192; Testini 1958: 254; Briesenick 1964: 95-96; Grabar 1968: 16, 53; Engemann 1972: 155; Huskinson 1974: 74; Thomas E B 1980a: 198); its popularity might additionally have been provoked by association with Christian martyrdoms staged most usually in arenas (*datio ad bestias*); it was this fact that in time nourished with martial terms a great deal of martyrological literature (Leclercq 1924e; Gagé 1969: 168). With a complete lack of contextual data, no additional arguments to those noted in relation to nos. VI.d.6 and 7. can be put forward in support of a possible Christian appurtenance of this artefact.

VI.d.9. Terra sigillata bowl (III)

Provenance: Novačka, site of Gradina; a cremation burial in a tumulus excavated in 1980; found among rich gravegoods of mostly glass and pottery vessels. Brooch (V.a.16) also stems from this context.
Location: MGK (2843)
Description: A terra sigillata bowl stamped by Cerialis (restored from extant fragments and partly reconstructed); rim diam. 17.6 cm, height 8.5 cm. The outer walls are completely covered with a relief motif of alternating rosettes and trees under the ovolo frieze. Rosettes containing six petals are encircled within frames filled with parallel strokes, featuring stylized wreaths; free-standing trees are rendered more naturalistically with flaring branches and an abundance of leaves.
Dating: 2nd half of the 2nd century/beginning of the 3rd century.
Literature: Šarić 1981, T. 56: 4; Katalog: 76, no. 15a.
Commentary: For an explanation of includng an object of such an early date see V.a.16. The grave find in question is not only quite early, but it also contained a cremated burial, which for the majority of scholars would constitute a sufficient reason for ruling it out of the evidence for early Christianity. However, the issue of the essential nature of Christian burial in terms of the ambiguity between cremation and inhumation was exactly the reason for considering two finds from Novačka (V.a.16 and Vi.d.9.). A generally accepted axiom of classical and early Christian archaeology postulates that cremation, by its intrinsic nature a pagan funeral procedure, leaves inhumation as the exclusive characteristic and stipulation of Christian burial (Sági 1868: 394; Kaiser-Minn 1983: 318; Plesničar-Gec et al. 1983: 48);). While true in a considerable measure, this fact cannot be taken for granted and needs reconsideration. That Christian burials are nearly all skeletal is not to be questioned at all; yet it should be borne in mind that a search for Christian burials prior to the 4th century is a torturing and unrewarding task (for obvious historical reasons) in the first place (Thomas E B 1974: 46). Worthy of note in this context is also the fact that Christians' choice of inhumation came less as a consequence of an obligation towards Christian religious convictions, and more under the influence of general spiritual attitudes of the 2nd and 3rd centuries. The issue of the physical integrity of the body as the inevitable condition to achieve resurrection and life eternal was raised in early Christian exegesis by various writers; those supporting the idea of the physical integrity (overlooking apparently the process of decay) were, however, in the minority. The remainder considered it as recommendable but not unconditional, holding that Providence took care of such things. If not, what would have become of a number of Christian martyrs burned at the stake? Consequently, skeletal burial as imposed by the law was not the official attitude of the early Church; this transpires unquestionably from the first regulation of this issue occurring as late as the 8th century

and imposed not by Church authorities, but Charlemagne (Leclercq 1948d; van Doorselaer 1967: 44-50). In brief, early Christian burial is almost certainly likely to be skeletal, but the reverse is not inconceivable.

It is in the light of the above-mentioned facts that the burial from Novačka should be reconsidered. As for the bowl, its decorative scheme reveals a combination of elements that are either individually, or in nearly identical arrangements, frequently found in early Christian art (Kempt - Reusch 1965: 46-47, no. 38). Solitary trees might well have been meant to represent the Christian tree of life (Briesenick 1964: 121-122; Forstner 1982: 149-154), and the six- or the four-petalled rosette is a well-known emblem of the cross (Garrucci 1873, Tav. 192:6; Garrucci 1879, Tav. 300:4; Kaufmann 1917: 63-67; Salin 1952: 159, Figs. 95, 96; Briesenick 1964: 107; Schulze-Dörrlamm 1990: 171, Taf. 22:6).

In raising the issue of the possible Christian association of the finds from Novačka (V.a.16. and VI.d.9.) a fact should be borne in mind that this possibility concerns both the surroundings where objects were used (*Pannonia Savia*) and that of their manufacture - *Germania Superior*, bordering on *Gallia* (cf. Böhme A 1972; Makjanić in: Makjanić - Koščević 1995: 68-70). It is important to note that 2nd century Christian martyrs from Lugdunum (Mediterranean portion of *Gallia*) originated from the circle of immigrant Greek manufacturers and traders; they are known to have reached more distant inland Gallic and Germanic areas by means of both selling their products and influencing local manufacture (Frend 1964: 126-127), which was inevitably accompanied by the spreading of ideas and religious affinities. And this is exactly a possible explanation for the occurrence of objects bearing cryptic Christian images at this early period and in an area not yet considerably Christianized. The display of religious symbolism on pottery is a well-known fact throughout history, as is a close relationship in imperial times of priest families and pottery manufacturers in *Gallia* and *Pannonia* (Bónis 1980: 360). A like situation can accordingly also be hypothesized for early Christian milieus.

VII. Instruments

VII.1. Key (II)

Provenance: Sveti Martin na Muri (Halicanum?); excavation in 1978; Roman settlement.
Location: MMČ
Description: Bronze; length 6.8 cm. Key in the form of an elongated rectangle with rhomboid handle section pierced in the middle and a saltire cross incised neatly in the field of the opposite end.
Dating: 3rd/4th centuries.
Literature: Katalog: 127, no. 185.
Commentary: The type is typically late Roman (Gáspár 1986: 75-76, Taf. 252:7). Despite its emphasized utilitarian purpose, the key in Christian thinking has also strong symbolic associations, based on biblical quotations (eg. Mathew 16: 19; Rev 1: 18). Mediaeval and later keys are very often decorated with manifest Christian devices and the same can reasonably be hypothesized, and in several instances indeed verified, for the early Christian period (Garrucci 1880: 35, Tav. 429: 4-6; Forstner 1982: 402-403; Johnson 1982: 168; Gáspár 1986: 53, no. 165, Taf. 19: 46; Provoost 1986: 153). With this in mind, the saltire cross here should probably be assigned Christian religious associations (see S.3.) in addition to inevitable apotropaic overtones.

VII.2. Dividers (III)

Provenance: Sisak (Siscia); dredging of the river Kupa in 1912.
Location: AMZ (6697)

Description: Bronze; length 20 cm. A pair of dividers in an excellent state of preservation. The nail-shaped securing device and the outer surface of arms bear engraved geometrical decoration composed of groovings, hatchurings and notchings. On the innerside of left arm incised is the inscription between two leaf-stops: *QVINTIANE VIVAS*.
Dating: 3rd/4th centuries.
Literature: Centuries...,1996: 19 (no illustration).
Commentary: Dividers and compasses with or without Christian devices are known from early Christian contexts (Kaufmann 1917: 15, B. 3; Burger 1966: 231, Fig. 124: 280; Mawer 1995: 99, F4.Br1.). These objects are characterized by stationary and therefore chronologically irrelevant shapes and can best be dated on other grounds; the item here has been tentatively dated on the basis of its decoration and particularly the inscription, composed of a name and the formula *vivas* (the formula bearing fairly strong Christian associations - see V.e.11.). The name Quintianus - a derivative of the earlier form Quintus - was widespread everywhere and also attested frequently among Christians (Kajanto 1965: 113, 153; Alföldi 1969: 297), possibly in memory of martyrs of that name (Delehaye 1912: 322, 411, passim)

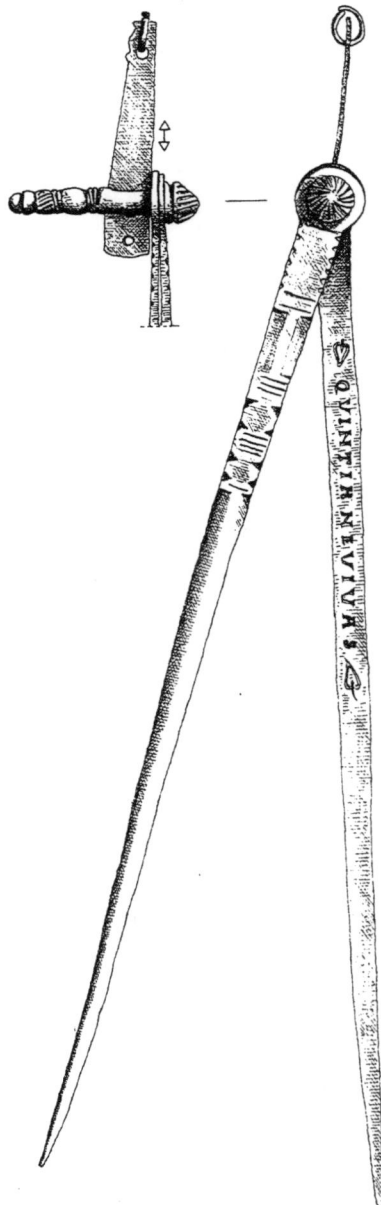

92

VIII. Coins

VIII.1. Vetranio (I)

Location: AMZ (20797)
Description: Bronze follis; reverse: emperor with spear and labarum crowned by Victory and encircled by the inscription spaced around the rim: *HOC SIGNO VICTOR ERIS*.
Dating: AD 350 (Siscian mint).
Literature: RIC 275

VIII.2. Constantine the Great (II)

Location: AMZ (15295)
Description: Bronze follis; obverse: Constantine's helmeted bust in profile to the left. The helmet is decorated with two six-pointed stars in the guise of a iota-chi device.
Date: AD 318-319 (Siscian mint).
Literature: RIC 55
Commentary on VIII.1 and 2.: These two coins bear either unquestionable (no. 1.) or probable (no. 2.) Christian devices, which, however, would not in itself suffice for counting them among the evidence for Christianity in Roman northern Croatia. They have not been included on the basis of their find spots either: hundreds of coins with Christian symbols derive from the area. It is the combination of their bearing Christian emblems and being struck in the Siscian mint that qualifies them as evidence. At the same time the two coins are used as an opportunity to discuss a few aspects of the meaning of coinage for early Christian archaeology. It is naturally understandable that the presence of coins bearing Christian devices, except when specifically arranged, does not by itself testify to a Christian context of a find (Salin 1959: 376; Mawer 1995: 92). It is a commonly held opinion that coins were not put in early Christian graves; their occasional appearance there is axiomatically explained in terms of residual pagan features within Christianity (Burger 1966: 158; Lányi 1972: 140-141; Thomas 1982: 279; Garraffo 1981: 322; Fülep 1984: 154). While not totally wrong, such a reasoning needs scrutiny in each instance.

Coinage, as a special category of the archaeological material with inherent political, economic, artistic-stylistic and religious significance, also has an important position in the early Christian period: coins have been abundantly found on early Christian sites comprising both buildings and cemeteries. This fact is often overlooked unfortunately, and the relationship of Christianity to coinage is interpreted in a prejudicial manner. However, the late Roman and early Christian moralistic and religious attitude towards money was even more accented and singular than that of previous periods. Money was referred to in early Christian documentary sources in a phraseology of symbols and metaphors. Thus, for instance, religious doctrines as the words of God were compared to a spiritual coinage, with which one earns heaven. In a word, a religious-apotropaic attitude towards money has been present in Christian thinking, if imbued with touches of pagan syncretism, from its very beginnings down to the present day (Dölger 1960: 12-13; Kyll 1966: 80-81; van Doorselaer 1967: 138; Jeločnik 1973: 102; Barton 1975: 60; Bogaert 1976; Garraffo 1981: 286-322; Nikolajević 1984: 535; Provoost 1986: 167). A most telling example of such a Christian attitude towards coinage is the burial of 3rd century pope Gaius: the only objects placed in the grave with him in the sense of gravegoods were three Diocletianic coins with apparently no Christian signs on them (Leclercq 1924a: 2185, note 5). It follows therefore that late Roman graves cannot be established as Christian or pagan solely on the account of the presence or absence of coins in them.

Coinage is primarily a material and trade category and only secondarily religious and cultic, and not everyone who held a coin would consider its religious meaning. Despite this, the circulation of coinage was probably the simplest and most effective vehicle for the universal spreading of imperial propaganda in terms of Christian religious policy (Sutherland - Litt - Carson 1966: 45-46; Sutherland - Litt - Carson 1981: 8 ff.).

Numismatic iconography was always planned, designed and supervised from the central authorities attached to the circle of the emperor himself, which also holds true for the period of Christian rulers. Accordingly, when a possibility arises of detecting specific Christian attitudes within a single mint, question of the degree of its independence from the official iconographical standards should be examined (Koepp 1958: 101; Sutherland - Litt - Carson 1966: 13-27; Jeločnik 1973: 109-110). In other words, there was always an outlet for an individual graver's or a lower official's religious whims to be smuggled onto coins struck in local mints. It should also be noted that urban Christians in the 4th century originated mostly from the lower and middle classes, among whom mint workers were particularly important (Jones 1963: 21-22).

After AD 315 a silver medallion was minted at Ticinum with the image of a helmeted Constantine's head and a chi-rho depicted on the helmet. This was the first appearance of the chi-rho (to become so widespread in time) on coinage (Sutherland - Litt - Carson 1964: 62). The mint at Siscia was set up in the mid 3rd century and operated with periodical interruptions up to the middle of the 5th century (Bíró-Sey 1980: 344-346; Sutherland - Litt - Carson 1981: 339-347); between AD 318 and 319 it was the first to apply the chi-rho on coins (Kantorowicz 1964: 187-188; Sutherland - Litt - Carson 1966: 61-64, 75; Mawer 1995: 92). As unfortunately museums in Croatia possess no single example of the type, it could not be presented in the material. Instead, the nearest parallel was chosen - a coin featuring two star-like shapes (no. 2.) each intended most probably as an iota-chi (cf. Kaufmann 1913: 638 ff.; Sutherland - Litt - Carson 1966: 61-64). The best way perhaps of viewing the symbolic background of these 'stars', when it comes to Constantine, is to accord them a syncretistic solar-Christian meaning. At one time the opinion was advanced that Christian devices on Constantine's coinage were a consequence of the attitudes of individual workers in local mints, rather than an official issue (Koepp 1958: 101; Sutherland - Litt - Carson 1966: 62). With Constantine's well-known religious uncertainties in mind (Vogt 1957; Winkelmann 1961), this hypothesis gains much in persuasion. It should also be noted that the Siscian mint introduced coins with star-like devices, employed either as a decoration on Constantine's helmet or else as a mark on the reverse, in AD 319-320 - simultaneously or even a little prior to other mints (Kaufmann 1913: 643; Sutherland - Litt - Carson 1966: 20, 61-62). The Siscian priority in minting the 'chi-rho on the helmet' series raises the case for a possible local Siscian, rather than any other initiative also for the type with star-like devices.

A similar line of reasoning is applicable to the other specimen (no. 2.). This type was struck in AD 350 for Constantius II and Vetranio solely in the mints at Siscia and Salonica (Sutherland - Litt - Carson 1981: 367-369, 416, nos. 146, 283 and 284). It is significant primarily for its formula as reminiscent of Constantian religious policy and cherished subsequently not only by his sons, but also by the usurper Vetranio. It testifies further to an impetus at the Siscian mint for issuing fresh types with Christian symbols during the whole period of the House of Constantine. There are sound reasons to ascribe such a line of operating not only to imperial policy, but to the religious atmosphere among workers in both the Siscian mint and the town itself.

IX. Objects of Uncertain Use

IX.1. Liturgical(?) staff (II)

Provenance: Sisak (Siscia)
Location: AMZ (1929)
Description: Bronze; height 17.8 cm. A shaft with a collar-like moulding at the middle of its height, topped by a solid cast sitting bird (dove?) and ending in a ring handle.
Dating: 5th/6th centuries.
Literature: Simoni 1989: 118-119, no. 71, T. 8:1; Katalog: 87, no. 58.
Commentary: In terms of religious symbolism this object belongs to the series of personal ornament decorated with images of birds, presumably doves (see V.a.8-11. and V.d.1-3). It has been interpreted as a Germanic cultic object (Simoni), while for its immediate parallels from Dacia early Christian liturgical function has been envisaged (Gamzigrad 1983: 135); its usage in a church ritual as a kind of ceremonial rod is indeed substantiated by three nearly identical items rcovered from the site of the late Roman and Byzantine fortified settlement Romuliana in the province of *Dacia Ripensis* (present-day Gamzigrad in Serbia) (Gamzigrad 1983: 135-136, nos 186-188). Concieved as a palatial villa of the emperor Galerius (293-311), it developed in subsequent centuries into a settlement with urban characteristics, sheltering a couple of Christian churches among other buildings.

IX.2. Inscribed tile (III)

Provenance: Site Plandište on a plateau at the Village of Cerić near Vinkovci (Cibalae); found during an amateur surface survey in 1966 in conjunction with remains of construction material and small finds from the prehistoric and Roman periods.
Location: Private possession (inaccessible).
Description: 41 x 30 x 6 cm. On the surface of a tile an inscription was engraved with a dull instrument before firing. It was rendered in single stroke letters and runs as follows: *FINCTOR VIVE DOMINIS TVIS.* Although the strokes are of uneven thickness and depth and the letters are of different height, the inscription was on the whole executed in a fairly good *capitala actuaria*.
Dating: 3rd/4th centuries.
Literature: Virc 1969.
Commentary: Contextual data are quite insufficient for a more secure determination of the nature of this graffito. There is a fair possibility of the *vivas* formula implying Christian connotations (see V.e.11.), enhanced possibly by also the words *dominis tuis*. This syntagm is parallelled in early Christian hagiographical literature in a letter to a Christian prisoner, where those who had already suffered martyrdom were referred to in the following context: '...*eos dominos meos qui coronati fuerint...*' (Delehaye 1912: 17, note 3). Athough there are various meanings to the term *dominus*, temporal as well as sacral (see III.b.2), a Christian sense would not be inappropriate in this context: the area of Cibalae has a tradition of Christian martyrdom reaching down to the mid 3rd century (Jarak 1994: 161).

Graffito inscriptions on tiles, covering various subject matters, were quite common in late Roman Pannonia as in other provinces; more often than not they were related to Christian surroundings (see III.d.1.).

The name Finctor is unattested elsewhere. It was tentatively perceived as a corrupted version of Fictor (Virc 1969: 139), a name derived from and related to the meaning of the verb *fingo (finxi, finctum).* Fictor would then be a name construed from a profession and would imply various meanings, such as the priest's servant, craftsman, actor or pretendor etc. (Kajanto 1965: 21, 82). Whoever and whatever he was, the author of this inscription was a thoroughly literate person, as transpires from the text, free of usual errors (transpositions and confusions of letters typical of graffiti), save for a possible addition of a superfluous letter *n* to the name Fi(n)ctor. Furthermore it was not written in cursive symptomatic of graffiti, but was rendered in *capitala actuaria*, more appropriate in principle to inscriptions on stone (Testini 1958: 345-349).

Concluding Discussion

All forms of material evidence for Christianity in northern Croatia have been included in this catalogue: small items in addition to structural and non-portable materials. In theory such an approach should enable a sound, well-substantiated and in a large measure final assessment of all material aspects of Christianity. The real situation, however, is quite different: the evidence, if variegated, has turned to be fairly inadequate in terms of both the quantity and contextual data. It is mostly either based on chance and stray finds, often very old, or has been obtained by means of small scale rescue excavations, limited soundings or surface surveys; planned systematic excavations remaining a rarity. Accordingly, conclusions in terms of the distribution, nature and chronology of Christianity in the given territory can not at this stage of research rest on analyses based on rigorous statistics: the sample would prove too small and random. What results could be obtained under such circumstances are provisory and of a limited value and liable to alterations and corrections; they should be taken as general indications rather than anything in the nature of final conclusions. The structural organization of the study has been adapted to the given deficiencies by means of discussing the majority of important issues (more suitable in principle for a conclusive synthesis) in the commentaries to individual catalogue entries or groups of them. Some more general issues, related mainly to common characteristics of various forms of materials, and therefore inappropriate for individual commentaries, have been left for the Concluding Discussion. They cover distributional and chronological patterns and the nature of the material evidence, touching occasionally also on spiritual matters. Although the possibility was open of choosing between a much reduced database (including only the unquestionable or at best probable evidence) and one expanded with the possible items but in turn open to misconceptions and ambiguities, it was decided to base the foregoing discussion on all three categories of the material evidence. Despite the risk of reaching unsubstantiated or even distorted conclusions, the latter has been chosen. In so doing, it was considered that more data, if selected with some measure of scholarly criteria, should be able to compensate for possible mistakes and distortions, particularly if these are anticipated and accounted for.

1. Types of sites and distribution of evidence (Map 2)

Note: As there was no ready model to lean on, a somewhat arbitrary system was devised and adapted for the needs of this stage of work, which allows for inclusion of all 18 secure or putative early Christian sites in the territory of northern Croatia. Cemeteries pertaining to major towns were not considered as separate sites, but were treated in conjunction with these towns.

Coloniae (all confirmed also as episcopal sees): Ludbreg (Iovia?), Osijek (Mursa), Sisak (Siscia), Vinkovci (Cibalae);

Municipia: Daruvar (Aquae Balissae), Sotin (Cornacum), Sveti Martin na Muri (Halicanum?);

Settlements with no municipal status confirmed: Štrbinci (Certissa?), Vara`dinske Toplice (Aquae Iasae);

Upland settlements: Čečavac (Rudina), Donja Glavnica (Kuzelin), Ozalj (Stari Grad);

Cemeteries: Novačka (Gradina);

Individual grave finds: Samobor, Veliki Bastaji;

Cave dwellings: Kamanje (Vrlovka);

Unestablished contexts: Samobor, Zagreb.

Question marks by the sites Štrbinci and Sveti Martin na Muri denote their hypothetical identification with Roman Certissa (Raunig 1980: 168) and Halicanum (Demo 1986: 46) respectively. Other *municipia* listed here are less problematic in terms of their Roman names and status (Mócsy 1962: 596-612; Mócsy 1968; Pavan 1991: 479 ff.; Póczy 1980). The most complex and complicated question attaches to Roman Iovia (Ludbreg) which was definitely not a *colonia* in the sense of the imperial administrative classification; yet it was a late Roman *civitas* which ultimately amounts to the same. Particularly problematic, however, is its identification with the see of Iovia (see I.a.4.).

Table 1: Distribution of finds (categories I-III marked) according to sites:

1. Cerić (Plandište)	III: IX.2.
2. Čečavac (Rudina)	II: III.b.5.
3. Daruvar	III: II.2; II.3.
4. Donja Glavnica (Kuzelin)	II: V.e.8.
5. Kamanje (Vrlovka)	II: V.e.9.
6. Ludbreg	II: V.d.3.
7. Novačka (Gradina)	III: V.a.16.; VI.d.9.
8. Osijek	I: V.a.1.2.; VI.b.4.; VI.d.2. II: IV.2.; V.e.7.; V.g.2.; VI.c.10 III: V.b.7.; V.e.12.; VI.c.14.,15.
9. Ozalj (Stari Grad)	I: V.a.3. II: VI.d.5.
10. Samobor	I(?): II.a.4. II: V.e.10.
11. Sisak	I: III.b.1.; V.a.4.,5.,6.,7.; V.b.1.; V.e.1.,5.; V.f.1.,2.,3.; V.g.1.; VI.a.1.; VI.b.1.; VI.c.1.,2.,3.,4.,5.,9.,12.,1 3.; VI.d.1.; VIII.1. I(?): III.b.2.; VI.b.3. II: III.c.4.,8.; V.a.8.,9.,10.,11.,1,2.,13.;

V.b.3.,5.,6.; V.d.1.,2.;
V.e.2.,3.,4.,6.;
VI.c.6.,7.,11.; VI.d.3.;
VIII.2.; IX.1.
III: II.4.; III.c.9.; V.a.14.;
V.b.8; V.c.1.; V.d.4.;
V.g.3.; VI.a.2.;
VI.d.6.,7.,8.; VII.2.

12. Sotin	I(?): V.b.2.
	III: V.a.15.
13. Sveti Martin na Muri	II: VII.1.
14. Štrbinci	I: II.1.; III.a.1.; III.c.2.;
	III.d.1.
	I(?): III.a.2.,3.
	II: III.c.5.; V.b.4.
15. Varaždinske Toplice	I: II.8.; II.9.
	II: IV.1.
16. Veliki Bastaji	I: III.c.
	I(?): III.b.4.
17. Vinkovci	I: III.c.1.,6.; VI.c.8.
	II: II.5.,6(a-c).,7(a-f).;
	III.b.3.; III.c.7(a-d).;
	VI.d.4.
	III: V.e.11.
18. Zagreb	I: VI.b.2.

Notes

V.e.1. (Sisak) may have belonged to only the possible Christian finds; VIII.1. and 2. (Sisak) were not found at Sisak, but were struck there. Entries V.a.7 and VI.b.4. only hypothetically stem from Sisak and Osijek respectively; II.6. and 7. (Vinkovci) were not itemized in counting, as they constitute parts of single wholes.

As a result of the low rate of research into the early Christian period in northern Croatia, a classification of sites according to type is inevitably somewhat ambiguous and incomplete; some of the sites might equally have been classified differently. Štrbinci, for instance, was included among sites without municipalities, based on its probable identification with Roman Certissa. It could have, however, been equally well designated as a cemetery on account of all of its finds stemming from funerary contexts. Veliki Bastaji was classified as a single grave find, although various data on this very important, but as yet completely unresearched site, point to a luxury villa settlement. In the face of these obstacles an attempt can still be made at the distributional pattern of evidence by site type. It follows that the sites by far most likely to produce Christian artefacts are large towns (*coloniae, municipii*) with smaller urban settlements following at a considerable distance. The only site type attested other than towns is upland settlements (hillforts), but they are as yet insufficiently researched and not securely substantiated in the first place. This type should otherwise naturally be expected in an area exposed to considerable barbarian attacks over a long period (4th to 7th centuries). Such expectations are further reinforced by the manifest

mention in the sources of fortresses donated by the emperor Justinian to the Longobards in southern Pannonia (Šašel 1992; Christie 1995: 309).

Yet to be compiled is a map of the territory of northern Croatia with all Roman settlements recorded (compiled on the basis of the documentary sources and the material evidence) and with both the secure and putative identifications of sites and the correlation between archaeological sites and Roman names. Such a product would be invaluable for the understanding of the rate of the earlier imperial Romanization/urbanization and the corresponding situation in the late Roman period. In other words, it would be most interesting to compare the distribution of early Christian finds with the locations of Roman settlements. However, even if this condition be fulfilled, it would at this stage still be impossible to produce a complete and well-documented picture of the spread of Christianity as viewed against the Roman background. This is mostly due to the fact that the majority of finds are concentrated in three large towns, or, rather, Siscia alone, this being also the reason for a considerably reduced significance of the attempted classification by site types. Of the total of 113 items (with all forms of material evidence included save for the church buildings) distributed at 18 sites, 61 (53,9%) is attributable to Sisak, 13 to Vinkovci, 12 to Osijek and 8 to Štrbinci: 94 of the total of 113 finds (83,1%) are distributed among four sites. Moreover, only one of the remaining 14 sites has produced as many as three artefacts (Varaždinske Toplice), while at each of the remainder only one or two objects were found, rendering them insignificant in terms of locational evidence. Equally surprising and as yet unexplained remains the fact that Varaždinske Toplice, the single site with secure early Christian building remains in northern Croatia and a systematically researched one, has failed to produce the evidence of small finds in any measure.

The question arises of whether the distributional pattern by site type as it appears at this stage reflects a true picture of Roman Christianity in northern Croatia: probably only in a measure. While the concentration of finds in major towns, particularly given that all of them were early Christian sees, is not exactly unexpected, two features appear totally surprising. First is the number of finds from Siscia. It is, however, neither the number alone nor the fact of its prevalence among other sites that surprises so much, but an unusually high ratio of the finds from Siscia to other places. If real, such a disproportion would virtually reduce all other places, the three sees included, to a level of nearly negligible sites. To add to the confusion, this situation should be viewed against the background of a very low rate of research at Sisak, while both Osijek and Vinkovci have experienced fairly abundant rescue excavations. The 'rivalry' sees of Iovia, Mursa and Cibalae should be expected to produce more material evidence and figure prominently among early Christian places in southern Pannonia for yet another reason: their placement along the route of the *Itinerarium Hierosolymitanum (Burdigalense)*. During the 4th century this much frequented traffic-line carried pilgrims from the West to the sacred sites in the Holy Land (Salin 1950: 151; Soproni 1980: 213). To sum up, only systematic excavation can possibly resolve the ambiguity of the material evidence stemming from the majority of sites, very slight as compared with the vast amount of the material from Sisak.

A further unexpected aspect to the distribution of early Christianity in northern Croatia is the entire lack of Christian finds from villa settlements in rural areas. While not lacking in towns and fortifications, the most typical feature of Pannonia's rural landscape and its urbanization in broad terms was always the villa settlement. Furthermore, in later periods a number of villae assumed, as attested for the northern sections of the province, the role of Christian centres (Thomas 1987: 285; Christie 1995: 304-305). The single site pointing possibly to such a type of settlement in southern Croatia is that of Veliki Bastaji near Daruvar, where a burial of a high dignitary was hypothesized within the premises of his luxury estate (Migotti 1986: 150-151). A church within such an architectural setting would not be inappropriate, but can at this stage only be speculated upon. To answer the question of whether Christianity was prevalently concentrated in towns, particularly Siscia, or whether the lack of evidence for rural areas is only accidental, should be one of prime desiderata of north-Croatian early Christian archaeology. Systematic investigation would improve the present understanding of the situation in the rural areas, and quite probably that in towns as well.

The ecclesiastical administrative organization followed in broad outline that of the previous civil division resulting in general, although not automatically, the establishment of bishoprics in *coloniae* and *municipii*. In principle this means that in provinces where the Church was relatively weak, one see could be expected to cover the area of two or more *civitates* or corresponding units (Krautheimer 1963: 17; Menis 1973: 277; Mócsy 1974: 329; Barton 1975: 31; Johnson 1982: 129; Salway 1993: 517). It could nevertheless be assumed that at least the majority, if not all of the *civitates* in Pannonia, held a see by the second half of the 4th century. The spread of sees in the territory of northern Croatia confirms the foregoing axiom only up to a point, and is substantiated primarily in the documentary sources, while more bishoprics are likely to be discovered whose interpretation is based on archaeological evidence. Two sees in the easternmost section of the province - Mursa and Cibalae, at a small distance from each other - testify possibly to two features: first - a hypothetical more advanced Christianization of the eastern section of south Pannonia with corresponding greater number of sees. This is partly contested by the situation at Siscia, but, as already observed, Siscia might eventually prove an exception to all kinds of rules. Another possibility allows for more sees (unremarked in the documentary sources) in the entire area. Of the two early Christian sites (other than Mursa and Cibalae) in the easternmost parts the first one – Sotin (Cornacum) - should have belonged to Cibalae, a hypothesis attested by the previous relationship between the two settlements (Mócsy 1962: 605). The other one - Štrbinci, putative Certissa - does not immediately reveal its ecclesiastical appurtenance: it was roughly midway between Cibalae and Mursa. This place should otherwise be singled out as one of the most promising early Christian sites in the territory of northern Croatia (Migotti 1997: 213).

The situation in the westernmost section (*Pannonia Savia*) is different in that its two sees - Siscia and Iovia (the latter not yet finally proved to be identified with Ludbreg) - are placed at a greater distance from each other than Mursa and Cibalae, thus possibly implying a more dispersed arrangement of sees in that section of the province. The see of Iovia, on a combination of literary and epigraphic sources, is by Hungarian scholars preferably identified with Heténypuszta in the territory of *Pannonia Valeria* (Hungary); a unanimous general opinion on this issue has not yet been reached. It transpired in earlier literature that among three Pannonian settlements named Iovia - all of them known from the sources - it was Ludbreg, the Croatian town on the river Drava that was favoured among the commentators in terms of the identification of the see of Iovia. This is an opinion still held by many, but one that has yet to be finally proved (Barton 1975: 101; Tóth 1988: 61; Jarak 1994: 175; Tóth 1994: 252-252; Gáspár 1995: 117; Bratož 1996: 329). If in fact the see of Iovia is to be identified with Ludbreg, this town's late Roman status as a *civitas* should be related to its role as a bishopric. Iovia had been mentioned in earlier sources as lacking any civic status; it was first recorded as a *civitas* in the *Itinerarium Hierosolymitanum*, dated to the first half of the 4th century (Salin 1950: 151; Sóproni 1980: 213:215). The situation then of Iovia on the route of the Jerusalem itinerary should be taken as an additional argument for a south-Pannonian (Croatian) see of Iovia.

No data in the documentary sources exist to improve understanding of the territorial extents and boundary between the sees of Siscia and Iovia. A difficulty in resolving this issue is caused, among other things, by the presence of the *municipium* Andautonia midway between Siscia and Iovia, rather nearer to the former (Mócsy 1962; Pavan 1991: 419-421). Despite systematic excavations carried on the site of Andautonia (Sćitarjevo south-east of Zagreb), no Christian remains have appeared. Based on geographical characteristics of the area and distances between settlements, the sites south of the river Sava (Kamanje, Ozalj and Samobor) should be envisaged as belonging to the see of Siscia, while those north of the river (Sveti Martin na Muri and Varaždinske Toplice) were probably under the jurisdiction of the see of Iovia. Most problematic in terms of territorial appurtenance remains the site of Zagreb.

Surprisingly enough, there is no single early Christian site in the territory between Sisak and Daruvar; this area should have been in the diocese of Siscia, as based on its previous status as part of the Siscian *territorium*. The lack of Christian finds there is at least partly a result of the area being one of the least archaeologically explored in the whole of northern Croatia. The eastern boundary of Siscian territory borders on the dividing line between eastern and western sections of the province of Pannonia - *Pannonia Savia* and *Secunda* (Pavan 1955: 419-420). This is probably where a boundary between Siscia and another see (a putative one lying to the east of Siscia) should be looked for; it has so far been attested neither in documentary sources nor through archaeological evidence. The existence of a see should nevertheless be envisaged in the territory of central northern Croatia; such a fairly vast territory was not likely to have remained bare of a bishopric. Two settlements with attributes necessary for a see figure in the given area. The first one is Daruvar, the Roman *municipium* of Aquae Balissae, rich in Roman finds despite lack of exploration (Szabó 1934; Migotti 1994: 195-196). Another possible see can be hypothesized in the valley of

Požega east of Daruvar. Roman Incerum has been located in the area, which itself in recent years has been researched better than other sections of northern Croatia, yielding consequently a variety of imperial and late Roman finds (Sokač-Štimac 1984; Katalog: nos. 164-171; Migotti 1994: 195-202). To the putative bishopric in central northern Croatia the sites of Čečavac, Daruvar and Veliki Bastaji would then have been subject.

2. Devices

Of the total of 113 artefacts (sections S. and G. are obviously excluded) 96 bear some kind of decorative device; they are considered in separate groups of signs, formulae, figural motifs and figural compositions. As usual with such classifications, the ones devised here are not clear-cut in all their elements and there are certain overlaps between the groups of figural motifs and compositions (to be dealt with later in the text). It is important to bear in mind that a category mark attached to a device relates to the artefact as a whole, and not to its individual artistic attributes. For instance, a hare and a dog (III.b.1.) as well as bucolic motifs (III.b.1.; II.b.4.) were classified as secure Christian devices, based on their appearance on unquestionable Christian sarcophagi, although probably no such meaning was intended for them individually, at least not at the time of their manufacture. Similarly, a six-pointed star (III.a.1.) and a saltire (II.9.; V.f.3.) were classified as a iota-chi and a St Andrew's cross respectively. This was on the basis of their occurrence on undeniably Christian objects, while they might equally have been only metaphors for the heavenly bodies (III.a.1.; V.f.3.) or even only a technical device (II.9.). The same is true of the mask (V.b.1.) and floral crosses and rosettes (V.a.1.). In short, devices which individually or without context would figure differently, are attached a higher rate as evidence for Christianity than basically inherent to them. Such a course might appear somewhat confusing and even distorting; it would, however, be virtually impossible to separate individual components on a single object and attach to them differential classifications. The choice was made to discuss them as problematic occurrences instead.

a. Signs (various types of monogrammatic devices and crosses)

Saltire
I: II.9.; V.f.3.
II: V.b.6.; V.e.2.,3.; VI.c.6.,7.; VI.d.5.; VII.1.

Saltire with four letters in the interstices
I(?): III.b.2.

Greek cross
I: V.a.2.,3.,4.,5.; V.b.1.; V.e.5.; V.f.1.; V.g.1.; VI.a.1; VI.c.1.,8.,12.,13.; VI.d.2.
II: V.b.5.; V.e.4.,6.; VI.d.4.
III: V.c.1.

Latin cross
I: VI.c.9.,13.
I(?): III.a.2.,3.,4.

Cross of Jerusalem
I(?): V.b.2.

Swastika
III: V.a.14.,15.; V.d.4.

Duplex knot (the cross of Solomon)
III: V.b.7.

Cross stylized as floral/geometrical shape
I: V.a.1.
II.: V.b.3.,4.; VI.c.10.,11.

Iota-chi (six-pointed star)
I: II.a.1.
II: V.e.3.; VI.d.3.; VIII.2.

Greek cross and chi (eight-pointed star)
I: VI.d.2.
II: V.e.9.

Chi-rho ('Constantinian Christogram')
I: II.1.; III.a.1.; III.b.1.; III.c.2.; V.a.1.; V.f.3.; VI.b.1.,2.,4.; VI.c.2.,3.,4.,5.; VIII.1.
I(?): VI.b.3.

Chi-rho with alpha and omega
I: III.d.1.

Chi-rho and Greek cross with alpha and omega
I: III.c.1.

Chi-rho with two stars
I: V.a.6.7.

Oblique rho-cross
I: V.e.1.
I(?): III.b.2.

Notes: V.e.1. was tentatively placed among rho-crosses, while it might have been only a saltire. The chi-rho on III.c.2. might have been provided with an alfa and omega. It is difficult to establish whether the device on V.e.9. was intended for a chi-rho with a superfluous stroke attached, or whether it was a blundered Greek cross and iota-chi.

It is clear at first glance that signs, amounting to 70 of the total of 96 decorated items, constitute the most widespread means of attaching Christian significance to various material objects. This in turn should mark the material in question as relatively dull and unimaginative in terms of decoration, which, however, is true only up to a point. A certain vivacity in this decorative group is provided by a significant number of variations (12) on the three primary shapes of the cross and the chi-rho, as well as through peculiar amalgamations of them.

Particularly problematic among the signs are various florally and geometrically stylized cruciform shapes. Symbolically ambiguous on account of their undeniable ornamental role, this group of pictorial signs is most often unjustifiably overlooked by commentators; various cruciform stylizations are as a rule considered to be a pure decoration, and no symbolic significance, which they at times must have encompassed, is claimed for them. However, a blend of symbolism and decoration at least should be occasionally considered for this type of device.

Next among ambiguous signs - the saltire or the St Andrew's cross - appears with a considerable frequency. Its occurrence in the first category on II.9. and V.f.3. is, unfortunately, not indisputable for reasons stated above; it was probably employed there to depict crossed rails of a fence (II.9.) and stars (V.f.3.). The symbolism of crosses might have, however, lingered as an afterthought in such artistic schemes and the saltire should by no means be generally excluded from the symbolic repertoire of early Christian art (see S.3.). Particularly curious in this regard is the occurrence of the saltire accompanied by the apocalyptic letters and two colateral signs, pointing possibly to a gnostic context (II.b.2.). For reasons of doubts and ambiguities in regard to their employment as early Christian signs at all, important is the appearance of a six- and an eight-pointed star on indisputably Christian items (III.a.1. and VI.d.2. respectively). While in the latter instance the first category is convincing enough, in the former it is unfortunately much diminished by probable stellar, rather than monogrammatic associations. Well-known uncertainties concerning the putative Christian connotations of the swastika and the cross of Solomon are further confirmed in the material from Croatia. Most curious and unclear appears, however, to be the cross of Jerusalem (V.b.2.).

Much scholarly discussion has been provoked by the issue of the possible symbolic meanings of signs surrounded with circles. While circles may at times be purely decorative, crosses or other Christian devices placed within circles should almost certainly bear the meaning of either a symbolic wreath or of solar symbolism (see chapter 4. within this section). Enveloped with circles or wreaths are mostly chi-rhos and their equivalents (III.a.1.; III.c.1.; III.d.1.; V.a.6.,7.; V.e.9.; V.f.3.; VI.b.4.; VI.c.2.,5.; VI.d.2.) and Greek crosses (V.a.2.; V.e.5.; V.f.1.; VI.d.2.). Quite interesting and possibly significant in this context is the ratio of the Greek and Latin crosses (19:5), as possibly indicative of the strong influence of the solar cult on Roman Christianity in Pannonia. Even crosses in the form of floral and geometrical stylizations stick to the Greek version. The Latin cross is essentially the cross of sufferings and triumph, while the Greek cross is the metaphor for Christ as Sun and Lord of the Universe (see Forstner 1982: 19-20; Migotti 1995). This feature merits further investigation.

b. Formulae (formulas, words and their contractions)

Arca	I: II.b.1.
Benedictus, -a, (benedicte)	II: III.c.4.
(De)positus	I: III.c.1 II: III.c.6.
Deus	I: III.c.3. I(?): III.b.2.
Dominus	I: III.c.3.

	III: IX.2.
Domus aeterna	III: III.c.9.
Eusebei	II: V.e.7.
Famula Christi	I: III.b.1.
Fedelis	I: III.c.2.
Υπερ ευχης	I(?): VI.b.3.
Hoc signo victor eris	I: VIII.1.
IH (meaning IE)	II: V.e.8.
Innocentes	I: III.c.1.
In pace	II: III.c.5.
Plus minus (vixit)	III: III.c.8.
S	III: V.a.16.
Spes in Deo	I: V.f.2.
Vivas (ζεσαις)	III: V.e.11.; VII.2.; IX.2.

Notes: The name Eusebius was possibly intened on V.e.7. instead of the verb.

With the scarcity and the fragmentary state of the epigraphic material in mind, the formulaic evidence appears diversified enough, though not particularly imaginative or sophisticated. This is the more so if it is remembered that late Roman epigraphic material pertaining to a single area is as a rule quite stylised. The occurrence of the *vivas* formula on objects with only possible Christian significance testify to its generally dubious Christian meaning.

c. Figural motifs (individual motifs and figural groups)

Anchor	III: V.a.16.
'Architectural' form	II: V.e.10.
Bird (unspecified)	I: III.b.1. II: V.c.1.
Butterfly	I: V.f.3.
Dog	I: III.b.1.
Dolphins by a trident	III: V.g.3.
Dove	II: V.a.8.,9.; V.d.1.,2.,3.; IX.1. III: II.2.
Eagle	II: V.a.12.,13.
Fence of paradise	I: II.9; III.a.1.
Fish (unspecified)	II: III.b.3.,5. III: III.b.8.; VI.a.2.; VI.d.7.

Good Shepherd	III: V.e.12.
Heavenly bodies (sun-, star- and moon-like shapes)	I: III.a.1.; V.f.3.
Helmet with Christian device	I: VI.c.8. II: VIII.2.
Horse	III: V.a.15.
Lamb	II: V.g.2.
Masque	I: V.b.1.
Ocean	III: VI.d.6.
Palm branch	I: VI.c.2.,3.,4.,12. II: V.e.2.; VI.c.6.,7. III: VI.c.14.,15.
Panthers by a vase	I(?): III.b.4.
Peacock	I: III.a.1. II: V.a.10.,11. III: II.2.
Rabbit	I: III.b.1. III: II.2.
Rosette	I: V.a.1. II: III.b.3. III: VI.d.9.
Saint	I: II.8.
Tree of life	I(?): III.b.4. III: II.2.; VI.d.9
Trefoil	II: III.b.5. III: II.2.
Vase	I: III.a.1.; III.b.1. I(?): III.b.4. III: II.2.
Vines and grapes	I: III.b.1. I(?): III.b.4.
Wheat ears	I: III.b.1.
Wreath	I: III.d.1.; V.f.2; VI.c.2.,5.

d. Figural compositions

Bucolic scene	I: III.a.1.; III.b.1. I(?): III.b.4.
Datio ad bestias	I: VI.d.1.
Hunt	III: VI.d.8.

Groups of figural motifs and compositions are discussed in conjunction to reveal their apparent similarities and interrelatedness. At first examination these two groups appear to be relatively abundant, which, however, is a considerably distorted picture. Figural compositions are in fact a rarity, and many of the figural motifs occur only once or/and in the category of only possible Christian artefacts. In short, the decorative vocabulary is not so rich as might appear from the overall picture composed of the conjoined items of secure, probable and possible Christian significance.

As already noted, some inconsistencies and overlaps in the organization of these two groups are inevitable. For instance, in spite of the Good Shepherd belonging generally to bucolic scenes, it has been here chosen to view it as a single motif in its essential symbolic sense. Similarly, the 'dog chasing a rabbit' motif is not separated from its bucolic surroundings on III.b.1., while the rabbit is in addition treated separately for its double occurrence in the material. Panthers and dolphins are not treated individually: both appear solely in a heraldic stance with an object (a vase and a trident respectively) between them. Contrarily, the peacock, the rabbit, the vase and the tree of life are considered individually, based on their appearance not only in confronted groups and bucolic scenes, but also separately. One of the most complex symbolic scenes is represented on III.a.1: a highly stylized, though not less sophisticated, bucolic composition representing the universe in the guise of paradise. Its individual components are, however, further considered as separate figural motifs. This has been done not only for the sake of convenience but also in order to produce a more thorough picture of figural decorative systems as they appear on the material. Finally, it should be remembered that more subtle meanings of the presented motifs and compositions are not touched upon in this section; they have been discussed in the commentaries on individual entries within the catalogue.

Most of the motifs and compositions appear once or twice, effecting thus a skewed picture of the richness of decoration, and impeding at the same time its systematization. Greater frequency of the dove, the peacock, the fish, the vase, the palm branch and the wreath reveals these as the most typical figural motifs. The symbolic meaning of the palm branch was probably merged with the decorative one, as revealed by its appearance solely on lamp rims. Among the remainder only the tree of life and the rosette appear more than twice, which might suggest their effective prominence. The almost total omission of otherwise so typical motifs as the vine and grapes and the Good Shepherd comes as a surprise. Contrarily, the motif of a helmet with a cross, a rare instance of early Christian iconography, appears on a clay lamp from Vinkovci (VI.c.8). It might therefore be envisaged as a possible local imitation of the similar motif on a Constantinian coin, only minted in the Siscian mint (see VIII.1.,2.).

On the basis of all four groups of the material diagnostic of the vocabulary and artistic devices of early Christianity in southern Pannonia, a picture can be drawn of an environment, not very sophisticated, yet rather rich and diversified in expression.

3. Chronology

With accurate dating based on archaeological context a rarity, the majority of finds from northern Croatia have been dated on artistic or typological grounds. This in turn implies dating of many of them as widely as the span of two or even three centuries. Such a serious shortcoming is mitigated in a measure by the fact that the 6th century evidence (cross-like ornaments and some of the clay lamps), as apparently particularly important in this context, is fairly accurately and precisely dated on basis of well-worked typologies. Contrarily, the 4th/5th centuries material constitutes the weakest chronological point in that the majority of the finds so dated belong in terms of typology to the 4th century, with possible, but contextually unattested, extension into the 5th. This is particularly true of the epigraphic evidence: it is by no means safe to rely on the epigraphical axiom that the later material the worse the execution, unless substantiated on other grounds. Accordingly, some singular features of lettering, while basically resting on typological-chronological grounds, bear also on local (concerning the workshop) or even personal (concerning the cutter) competencies and choices (Kaufmann 1917: 25, 80, Bild. 47-56; Testini 1958: 345, note 1.; Kempt - Reusch 1965: 35, no. 25; Oliva 1962: 23-24; Thomas E B 1980: 121; Ševšenko 1992: 39-40; Sartori 1994: 15). Three inscriptions from northern Croatia, dated securely to the 4th century (III.c.3.; IV.1.,2.), are a good case in point. While all the three of them are executed in a manner absolutely superior to the remainder of the epigraphic material, this should rather be perceived as the consequence of the high social status of those who ordered them, than their early date.

Thus, while no overall precise chronological analyses of the material can be attempted, such dates as available still constitute a background sufficient to reach the prime objective of this section: to prove that finds later than the end of the 4th century are not a rarity in the area. Items dated earlier than the 3rd/4th centuries accordingly have not been considered in this context.

3rd/4th centuries
I: II.8.,9.; III.a.1.,3; III.b.1.; III.c.2.,3.; V.a.1.,6.,7.; V.e.1.,5.; V.f.2.,3.; VI.b.4.; VI.c.1.; VIII.1.
I(?): III.a.2.,4.; III.b.4.; VI.b.3.
II: III.b.3.,5.; IV.1.,2.; V.b.4.; V.e.2.,3.,4.,6.7.,8.,9; V.g.2.; VI.d.4.; VII.1.; VIII.2.
III: III.c.9.; V.a.15.; V.b.8.; V.e.11.,12.; VI.d.6.; VII.2.; IX.2.

4th/5th centuries
I: II.1.; III.c.1.; III.d.1.; VI.b.1.,2.; VI.c.2.,3.,4.,5.; VI.d.1.,2.
I(?): III.a.4.; III.b.2.
II: II.5.,6.,7.; III.c.4.,5.,6.7(a-d).; V.d.1.,2.,3.; VI.c.6.,7.; VI.d.3.
III: III.c.8; VI.d.7.,8.

4th or 5th/7th centuries
II: V.a.8.,9.,10.,11.
III: II.4.

5th/7th centuries
I: V.a.2.,3.,4.,5.; V.b.1.; V.f.1.; V.g.1.; VI.a.1.; VI.c.8.,9.,12.,13.
I(?): V.b.2.

II: V.a.12.,13.; V.b.3.,6.; V.e.10.; VI.c.10.,11.; VI.d.5.; IX.1.
III: II.2.,3.; V.a.14.; V.b.7.; V.c.1.; VI.c.14.,15.

Much scholarly effort has been invested during the last twenty years or so in arguing against the previously common opinion that Roman civilization in Pannonia was nearly extinguished by the beginning of the 5th century. It has transpired in the meantime that the picture of 4th century decline had been overstated and that it is difficult to sustain the older view of the universal stagnation in the civil life of southern Pannonia from the end of the 4th century. With the Byzantine empire so eager to maintain its sovereignty, if partial, over Pannonia, it could hardly have been so (Harmatta 1970; Barkóczi - Salamon 1971: Mócsy 1974: 351; Dimitrijević 1979: 216-217, 258; Salamon - Sós 1980; Salamon - Barkóczi 1982; Fülep 1984: 285-301; Bálint 1985; Thomas E B 1987; Šašel 1992; Šašel 1992a; Christie 1995: 306-307). Confronted opinions on this issue were to a great measure caused by insufficient archaeological exploration on one hand, and occasional misapprehensions of often contradictory literary sources about 4th century Pannonia on the other: reports in the sources sometimes represented catastrophy and at other times pictured Pannonia as a prosperous province (Mócsy 1974:299, 307, 342, 351).

The early Christian finds from northern Croatia as listed above do not support the theory of the area deserted and impoverished in the archaeological sense at the end of the 4th century. When assembled, the finds from the 4th/7th centuries appear far more numerous then those from the 3rd/4th centuries. Of the total of 106 objects (excluded are those dated loosely to the 4th/7th centuries) 45 are dated to the 3rd/4th centuries, and the remaining 61 to the 4th/5th and 5th/7th centuries. True, the veracity of such a calculation is weakened by loose dating in the category of the 4th/5th centuries. On the other hand, a number of finds from the 5th and 6th centuries alone is sufficient to militate persuasively against the theory of 'Pannonia abandoned'. The chronologically relevant issue of the ratio of the finds from Siscia to other sites remains, however, still unclarified; it even generates a possibility that would invalidate the hypothesis of the continuation of life in the whole of southern Pannonia during the 5th-6th centuries. In theory, namely, it could have been Siscia alone of all settlements that stood out at this late period, while life in the remainder was either extinguished or very much reduced. Rural areas of northern Pannonia, known to have flourished from the end of the 4th century onwards (Mócsy 1974: 299-308; Thomas E B 1987: 285; Christie 1995: 304-305), the abandonment of the southern part of the province is not very likely.

4. Spiritual and social aspects of early Christianity as based on material evidence

a. Pagan-Christian syncretism

Gnostic sects in Pannonia are never mentioned in documentary sources (Šeper 1942: 41). On the other hand, magical, apotropaic and superstitious practices, essential to various gnostic doctrines, are amply documented for the Roman civilization of the area. Magicians from *Pannonia* - the famous *Pannoniciani augures* - were recorded earlier in the literary sources (Alföldi 1960), and burial rites in the 4th century were imbued with magic-apotropaic procedures (Lányi 1972: 134; Nikolajević 1984: 535). The flourishing of gnostic doctrines in the 2nd and 3rd centuries was also fostered by already well-established oriental mistery cults with their profound leaning on astrological practices (Alföldi 1960; Thomas E B 1980a: 185-193). The material and artistic evidence for gnosis in the whole of Pannonia is nevertheless insufficiently explored, making it as yet unsafe to speculate on the role of gnostic sects as an essential component of nascent Christianity of southern Pannonia. Some significant features, however, transpire from a number of certain or putative gnostic objects, recognized lately among the archaeological material of the 3rd/4th centuries from northern Croatia (Migotti 1994: 189-190). Even two well-known sects - the Basilidians and the Ophites - can tentatively be identified (see G.1.3.5.). The latter is particularly important in the light of the fact that its doctrine might have been implied in some mysterious expressions from the liturgical hymn inscribed on the stone slab from Veliki Bastaji (III.c.3.). Found in tandem with a marble sarcophagus (III.b.4.), the slab is one of the most spectacular late Roman finds in the whole of Pannonia to date. It has been defined as essentially Christian on the basis of the subject matter of its versed inscription - the dogma of original sin and redemption. The text has not yet been sufficiently studied and clarified, but certain traces of gnostico-heretical overtones transpire from its verses immediately. In so assuming it is important to remember that certain gnostic doctrines were also based on the dogma of redemption through Christ's sufferings (Šeper 1942: 31, note 137; Stutzinger 1983: 89-91). Accordingly, doctrinal elements pointing to the cosmogony of the Ophites can tentatively be recognized in some of verses of the foregoing hymn, particularly those describing perishing in the abyss and rescue from it, Adam's progeny and the redemption of mankind. Yet another seemingly authentic Christian piece - the lost sarcophagus from Sisak (III.b.2.) - displays putative gnostical elements, such as curiously devised saltire-based monogrammatical signs. Any further assumptions in terms of tracing gnostic artistic elements in the available material remain at this stage in the realm of pure speculation. This issue is on the whole much complicated also by the fact that orthodox Christian doctrines were basically gnostic derivations and that in time many 'heretical' notions were accepted and sanctioned by the Church (Grant 1969: 318; Johnson 1982: 43-45).

Syncretism, essential to gnosis in terms of spiritual and artistic expression, also plays a prominent role in the early Christianity of southern Pannonia; this is first reflected on objects containing elements of the solar cult and consequently solar Christology. Most prominent among them

is the fresco from Štrbinci (III.a.1.) with its curious blend of metaphors for universal eternity and Christian resurrection. Next in line are motifs of encircled crosses and kindred signs, as well as circular devices within crosses (III.c.1.; III.d.1.; V.a.2.,6.,7.; V.b.1.; V.e.5.,9.; V.f.3.; VI.b.4; VI.d.2.). Omitted from this list are clay lamps featuring chi-rhos in a circle (VI.c.2.,5.); in these instances the circle was intended as the wreath, the symbol of victory (V.f.2.), rather than the sun-disc. Solar-Christian syncretistic symbolism should be interpreted for artefacts decorated with concentric circles (V.a.3.,4.,5.,12.,13.; V.b.4.), as well as those shaped like the swastika (V.a.15.; V.d.4.), the eagle (V.a.12.,13.) and the horse (V.a.15.). Conceptions reflecting solar Christology are evidently also inherent to Agnus Dei lamps (VI.b.1.,2.).

Bucolic scenes figure prominently in early Christian iconography, conveying the originally pagan idea of a peaceful happiness enriched with Christian overtones of the eternal peace in Paradise (III.b.1.). While in theory it is virtually impossible to tell pagan bucolic scenes from those Christian when rendered in a syncretistic manner, the latter nevertheless seem to be recognizable in depictions on sarcophagi from Sisak and Veliki Bastaji (III.b.1.,4.). The Christian identity of the former is attested by (subsequently added?) chi-rhos squeezed within two ansae by the inscription field. The latter, bare of any specific Christian devices, was confirmed as Christian by context. Bucolic contents with syncretistic overtones are probably present also in the motifs of Ocean (VI.d.6), hunt (VI.d.8), rosette, tree-of-life (VI.d.9.) and Good Shepherd (V.e.12.). The fish's syncretistic symbolism (possibly on VI.d.7) is hardly separable from its more specific overt Christian meanings (possibly on VI.a.2.; V.b.8. and probably on III.b.3.5.), unless based on a diagnostic context.

Other than pictorially, syncretistic ideas were conveyed formulaically, as presumably in the instance of the expression *domus aeterna* (II.c.9). From the formal point of view this syntagm appears to be manifestly pagan, while it really conveys a meaning much closer to the Christian and Jewish line of thinking, than pagan. *Domus aeterna* should better be understood in the sense of spiritual eternity, than literally.

A kind of practical, as opposed to spiritual syncretism transpires related to two graves from Štrbinci (III.a.2.,3.): their cross-like plans testify almost indisputably to the Christian affiliation of the deceased, but there is no single hint of Christianity contained in the otherwise abundant grave-goods. These burials were accurately dated to later than AD 313; their overall aspect was then probably less the result of avoiding publicity, and was more a spontaneous and deliberate sticking to pagan burial practices, based on mixed religious feelings.

The spa of Aquae Iasae is an outstanding example of variously manifested religious syncretism. A Christian basilica was built there not later than the 2nd half of the 4th century, yet to no detriment to pagan monuments, such as an inscription to Sol or a statue of Minerva; at the time the basilica was adapted, the former was placed (or replaced) in the porch of the capitolium, while the latter remained in one of the temples of the Capitolium complex. Moreover, the possibility cannot be discarded that the Christian basilica was put to use in the period when the cult of the Capitolium Triad was still flourishing (cf. I.b.). Such a tolerant cosmopolitan atmosphere can hardly be envisaged at Siscia or Cibalae or Mursa - all of them experiencing Christian martyrdoms in the 4th century.

b. Arianism and relationship between Romans and Barbarians

Arianism marked outstandingly the religious history of Pannonia throughout the 4th century, and has been also sufficiently studied by scholars (Thomas E B 1980a: 200-204; Jarak 1994: 172 ff.). Contrary to gnosis, the Arian creed is, in terms of doctrine, clearly distinguishable from orthodox Christianity. Despite such favourable conditions, establishing Arian characteristics on the material evidence is both painstaking and dubious; on the whole there appear to be no peculiar Arian elements in any form of monumental or applied arts and crafts of the period (Testini 1958: 531; Demugeot 1965; Pillinger 1989: 85; Tóth 1994: 244; Christie 1995: 304). Attempts at differentiating orthodox from Arian forms of basic Christian devices, such as the cross and the chi-rho, remain precarious in spite of the dogmatic justification (Arians denying the divinity of Christ) for this procedure. As for dogma, the lack of crosses, chi-rhos (particularly those accompanied by an alpha and omega) and symbols of the Trinity is on the whole expected with Arians, based on their denial of the Holy Trinity. Alternatively, thus marked Christian objects are at times automatically ascribed to the orthodox, if on insufficiently substantiated grounds (Cabrol 1924: 6, 17; Engemann 1976; Giordani 1978; Bratož 1996: 327-328). Such a line of reasoning is not completely wrong, but should not be taken as a hard and fast rule either. Good cases in point are examples of the numismatic iconography, most persuasive of which are those relating to Constantine the Great and his son Constantius II. While the father was Christianized by an Arian bishop and the son was a zealous Arian, both had chi-rhos applied to their coinage (Sutherland - Litt - Carson 1981: 36, passim; see also VIII.2.). The same is true of Arian Gothic kings (Arslan 1994: 260, Tav. 25-26); curiously enough, in the art of prevalently Arian Germanic peoples in the 5th and 6th centuries, the cross was often employed, accompanied at times even by the alfa and omega (Arrhenius 1986; Arbeiter 1994; Bierbrauer 1994). On balance, the Arians' general negligence of Christian symbolism might possibly have had some impact on the distribution of material evidence in northern Croatia (cf. Thomas E B 1980: 113-114). In other words, the high ratio of the material from Siscia to all other sites can possibly be viewed in the light of the see of Siscia sticking consistently to Christian orthodoxy (Jarak 1994: 176). This suggestion seems to be backed also by meagre finds from the two Arian bishoprics, Mursa and Cibalae. With this in mind, the *basilica martyrum* at Mursa could tentatively be perceived as the reflection of the well-known Arian zeal for the cult of martyrs (Thomas E B 1987: 287-288). Likewise, some grounds exist for bringing the surprising lack of small finds with Christian signs at Ludbreg and Varaždinske Toplice in relation to the putative Arian presence at the former site, and, by implication, also at the latter (Šašel 1992: 746-747; Migotti 1994: 195); these questions need further investigation.

Of all the Barbarian peoples recorded in the territory of Pannonia in the 4th/7th centuries, the Goths and the Longobards had the most conspicuous role; when Christianized, both peoples adhered, with some negligible exceptions, to the Arian creed (Thompson 1963; Menghin 1985: 143; Pavan 1991493 ff.; Giustechi Conti 1994: 146; Christie 1995: 307-310). The relationship between the Roman Christians and the barbarian Arians in Pannonia was therefore a complex issue comprising religious, ethnic and cultural components and amounting apparently to yet another form of spiritual syncretism. When, however, its attributes are tentatively traced in the archaeological evidence, the results are quite meagre. Artistically, a Romano-barbarian syncretism can be recognized in peculiar stylizations of the cross and its replacement by the swastika/meander (V.a.14.) and the duplex knot (V.b.7.), or in an amalgamation of the cross with the masque (V.b.1.). It would in this regard be very revealing to clarify also the attribution of the ambiguous finds from Daruvar (II.2.,3.).

For two reasons, the issue of the relationship between the orthodox Christianity of the Romans and the Arian Christianity of the Barbarians has not been pursued in this study to a large measure. First, the study has on the whole focussed upon a different topic, and second, the given issue is very complex and needs much more disposable data than currently at disposal for southern Pannonia. Scholars find it hard to address this specific problem even in circumstances when broader relationships between the Romans and the barbarians are somewhat better explored (Salamon - Barkóczi 1971: 71; Vágó - Bóna 1976: 168-174; Thomas 1987; Schulze-Dörrlamm 1991: 334-354).

c. Western and eastern influences

As a religious teaching originating in the East, the Arian creed naturally became more widespread in eastern Pannonian regions. Throughout the Roman period these were in any event influenced from the eastern more than western sections of the Empire (Thomas E B 1955: 269; Šašel 1992b: 744; Jarak 1994: 176-177; Bratož 1996: 303). 'Eastern' or 'western' features in the material are nevertheless hardly traceable at this stage. It would be worthwile to investigate this question in the light of the documentary sources, claiming for southern Pannonia the position in the sphere of influences of both the sees of Aquileia and Sirmium (Map 3) (Testini 1958: 522; Bratož 1986: 103-104, 137-141; Pavan 1991: 476 ff.; Jarak 1994: 157-172); this would amount to establishing the measure to which the archaeological data supports the general historical outline. In the face of justifiable claims for *Pannonia* as an area of variegated and mixed influences, it was a western province first politically and then linguistically and culturally throughout the Roman period; it is Aquileia that is generally held to have played the most important role in effecting these circumstances (Menis 1973: 291-293; Mócsy 1974: 258; Bilkei 1979: 37; Thomas E B 1980a: 193-194; Pavan 1991: 477; Weiler 1996).

Seeking to establish oriental or other features in early Christian artistic material is hazardous in itself, particularly in regard to southern Pannonia, the subject of relatively little archaeological investigation. This issue is therefore best approach by means of onomastic data, compiled from both the epigraphic and literary sources; they should either bolster or invalidate statements from the source literature of

Pannonia as generally a western province.

The names from the Croatian section of southern Pannonia (all given in Latin script) recorded in a) literary sources and b) epigraphic material, are the following:

a):
Amantius, Constantinus, Constantius, Eusebius, Joannes, Marcus, Pollio, Quirinus and Valens.

b):
I: Felicissima (III.b.2.); Flavius Maurus (III.c.2.); Marcellianus (III.b.1.); Martoria (III.c.1.); Sacmeneunus (III.b.2.); Severilla (III.b.1.); Venatorinus (III.c.1.); Victorinus (III.b.2.).
I(?): Diogenes (VI.b.3.); Gaianus (VI.b.3.).
II: Eusebius (V.e.7.); Lucerinus (III.c.4.); Paulinus (III.c.4.).
III: Gaudentius (III.c.9.); Finctor (IX.2.); Qvintianus (VII.2.); Sarion (V.e.11.); Teofila (I.b.1.).

Note: Eusebius is a tentative rading of the contraction evsebi as inscribed on a ring, and could have been intended for a verb, and not a name in the first place.

Of the total of 18 (17 if Eusebius is omitted) names, only 4 (3) are Greek - Eusebius (twice?), Diogenes, Sarion and Teofila. Diogenes and Sarion are the sole instances of names rendered in Greek, while both Eusebius and Teofila were transliterated in Latin and Latinized in terms of form (Teofila instead of Theofila and Eusebius instead of Eusebios). Symptomatically Greek names are mostly dated to the 3rd century. An inscription from the 4th century, giving the names of father and son, has only the former in Greek (that of father Diogenes), while the latter is Latin (Gaianus, the son). All these facts point to Greek names being typical of the 3rd century and only sporadically the 4th, a feature otherwise relevant universally (Kajanto 1963: 57-59). Names of two Siscian bishops, Joannes and Marcus, are oriental only as regards their ultimate origin; they are otherwise universally spread throughout the Christian world and therefore irrelevant in terms of cultural influences. The given onomastic data would then seem to support a hypothesis, advanced by a number of scholars, of direct oriental sources for south-Pannonian early Christianity (Mócsy 1974: 323; Barton 1975: 24 ff.; Šašel 1992c: 790). The theory is, however, likely to be contested on grounds that oriental names spread in the west like something in the nature of a fashion and failing to indicate the origin in and of themselves (Kempt - Reusch 1965: 37; Mócsy 1965: 221); Christians bearing oriental names in south Pannonia have been occasionally suspected to be of the Aquileian origin (Fitz 1980: 168; Gáspár 1995: 117). It is also worth mentioning in this context that the single Greek name attributable without reservation to a Christian was that of the Cibalitan bishop Eusebius. On the other hand, Diogenes - recorded in a most probably Christian description - need not himself have necessarily been a Christian, as transpires from the phrasing of the text.

To sum up, there are no sufficient data in the onomastic material from northern Croatia to support the otherwise historically acceptable fact of the oriental origins of early Christianity of the whole of southern Pannonia. In other words, the hypothesis of the see of Sirmium exerting its

influences in southern Pannonia in the earlier period, with Aquileia assuming this role from the 5th century onwards (Menis 1973: 291-293; Bratož 1983: 268-269; Barton 1975: 11-18; Jarak 1994: 157), is not finally attested by the onomastic material; the early occurrence of two Greek names is not supportive enough. Also unattested remains the fact that within the whole of southern Pannonia its eastern sections were somewhat more Greek-oriented in terms of language (Tóthe 1977: 115; Fitz 1980: 164; Šašel 1992b: 744). On the other hand, Pannonia's western linguistic appurtenance is fully supported by the given evidence, which also fits well with the total of the epigraphic material, inscribed in Latin. Yet another onomastic fact, irrespective of the issue of eastern-western influences, transpires from the repertoire of the names. Apparently in Pannonia, like other areas, neutral or even blatantly pagan names were in use with Christians up to the mid 4th century or even in the 5th (Harnack 1915: 407-415; Kaufmann 1917: 35; Kajanto 1965: 58-59; Mócsy 1965: 221).

5. Social status of Christians

Considering the insufficient quantity of the relevant archaeological material, hardly more than a few observations can at this stage be attempted on the issue of the position of Christians in the social scale. Most telling in this regard should in principle be grave finds. However, exemplarily - excavated and thoroughly studied - late Roman/early Christian cemeteries in northern Croatia are lacking. A brief survey of the funerary evidence (III.a.b.c.) gives the impression that the majority of the Christians of the area were more or less well-off people. This clearly is a distorted picture, based on the insufficient data, and leaving unrevealed the funeral practices of people too poor to provide either for sarcophagi and inscribed stone slabs or abundant grave goods.

A small-scale rescue excavation on the site of Štrbinci has revealed three early Christian graves, quite luxury in terms of grave goods (III.a.1.-3.). Two of them (III.a.2.,3.) were excavated at a small distance from each other; the nearby surface was not touched, leaving unknown a broader context for finds. The third grave (III.a.1.), some two hundred metres from the other, was excavated in conjunction with some ten surrounding plain skeletal burials provided with poor grave goods. It can reasonably be supposed that these too were Christian, furnishing a more realistic picture of the overall social fabric of Christian communities in the area. This single isolated example of an excavated (if only partly) Christian cemetery proves that with more such sites the picture of the social status of south-Pannonian Christians will emerge to be different to what it appears to be at this stage.

***

The early Roman records of Pannonia were as a rule produced in exaggeratedly dismal terms, picturing both its people and the country itself as hostile and harsh, as indeed it must have been in the perception of spoiled Mediterranean lords and men of letters. Later sources were occasionally more favourable, if only in a measure, but were also contradictory. Above all they were imbued with catastrophic reports on the Barbarian conquerors devastating the land materially and spiritually (Mócsy 1962: 535-582; Oliva

1962: 13-22; Barkóczi 1980; Pavan 1991: 490 ff.; Christie 1995: 303); remarks on Pannonia as a prosperous and rich province were only sporadic. Whatever the case, during the late Roman period Pannonia was a most important area politically if not otherwise (Mócsy 1974: 342-351; Lengyel - Radan 1980: 17; Soproni 1980b: 219; Pavan 1991: 434-480; Šašel 1992a; Lippold 1996: 19); it follows therefore that the archaeological study of Pannonia has been confronted by a task of reconciling contradictory written sources. By the time investigation based on excavation made considerable advances, a misinterpretation of the archaeological evidence, that by the beginning of the 5th century Pannonia was more or less abandoned and bare of its Romanized inhabitants (contrary: Šašel 1992a: 761) - had already been added to the contradictory historical evidence. Archaeological investigation into the early Christian material evidence is therefore of the utmost importance for the clarification of the issues of the late Roman history of Pannonia. This is particularly true of its southern section, which, although provided with more favourable living conditions in late antiquity in comparison to northern Pannonia, is as yet far less researched (Mócsy 1974: 332; ARP, passim). Moreover, southern Pannonia was earlier and to a grater degree urbanized (Fitz 1980: 169; Póczy 1980a: 240; Thomas E B 1980a: 193-194), providing thereby the most favourable background for the spreading of Christianity.

The primary aim of this study has been to provide evidence against the previously accepted view of southern Pannonia as unexpectedly poor in early Christian finds. The finds compiled and discussed are still far from abundant and are mostly bare of their contexts. Of the total of 120 categorized entries (section I included) only 47 may be declared unquestionably Christian and a further 47 as probably so, while to the remaining 26 Christian attributes were attached only hypothetically. They are, on the other hand, variegated and curious in many aspects, and some of them are unique or even spectacular. It is these attributes that justifies the hope of finding much more early Christian material, particularly building remains by means of planned systematic excavations. Finds like those from Veliki Bastaji (III.b.4.; III.c.3.), for instance, would not spring up from a barren land, neither is northern Croatia 'an early Christian archaeological desert', as I named it metaphorically in the hope of compiling proof to the contrary. Although full of tantalizing might-have-beens and despite its raising more questions than answering them, I hope this study provides a useful foundation for future work.

Abbreviations

AA	Antichità Altoadriatiche, Udine
AanH	Acta Antiqua Academiae Scientiarum Hungaricae, Budapest
AArH	Acta Archaeologica Academiae Scientiarum Hungaricae, Budapest
ACIAC	Atti del Congresso Internazionale di Archeologia Cristiana
AÉ	Archaeologia Értesítő, Budapest
AI	Archaeologia Iugoslavica, Beograd, Ljubljana
AIJ	Hoffiler V - Saria B, Antike Inschriften aus Jugoslawien, Heft I. *Noricum* und *Pannonia* Superior, Zagreb 1938
AJ	The Antiquaries Journal, Oxford
AP	Arheološki pregled, Beograd/Ljubljana
AR	Alba Regia, Székesfehérvár
ARP	Lengyel A - Radan G T B, The Archaeology of Roman Pannonia, Budapest 1980
Atlante I	Anselmino L *et al.*, Atlante delle forme ceramiche, I. Ceramica fine romana nel bacino mediterràneo (medio e tardo imperio), Enciclopedia dell'arte antica, classica e orientale, Roma 1981
AV	Arheološki vestnik, Ljubljana
BAR	British Archaeological Reports, Oxford
BJ	Bonner Jahrbücher, Köln
Boreas	Boreas, Münster
BRGK	Bericht der Römisch-Germanischen Kommission, Mainz am Rhein
BV	Bayerische Vorgeschichtsblätter, München
CA	Cahiers archéologiques, Paris
Carinthia I	Carinthia. Zeitschrift für geschichtliche Landeskunde von Kärnten, Klagenfurt
CIL	Corpus inscriptionum Latinorum, Berlin
Dacia	Dacia, Revue d'archéologie et d'histoire ancienne, Bucarest
DACL	Dictionnaire d'Archéologie chrétienne et de Liturgie, Paris
DAG	Dissertationes archaeologicae Gandenses, Brugge
DOP	Dumbarton Oaks Papers, Cambridge/Mass.
EC	Enciclopedia Cattolica, Roma
FA	Folia archaeologica, Budapest
Gallia	Gallia. Fouilles et monuments archéologiques en France métropolitaine, Paris
GDV	Germanische Denkmäler der Völkerwanderungszeit, Stuttgart,Berlin
I Goti	Catalogue of Exhibition, Milano 1994
HAM	Hortus artium medievalium, Zagreb - Motovun
JAC	Jahrbuch für Antike und Christentum, Münster
JPMÉ	Janus Pannonius Múzeum Évkönyve, Pécs
JRGZM	Jahrbuch des Römisch-Germanischen Zentralmuseums Mainz, Mainz
Katalog	From the Invincible Sun to the Sun of Justice. Early Christianity in Continental Croatia (Catalogue of Exhibition), Zagreb 1994
MAI	Mitteilungen des Archäologischen Instituts der Ungarischen Akademie der Wissenschaften, Budapest
Mullus	JAC, Ergänzungsband 1, 1964
OA	Opuscula archaeologica, Zagreb
OHAD	Obavijesti Hrvatskog arheološkog društva, Zagreb
OZ	Osječki zbornik, Osijek
PBSR	Papers of the British School at Rome, London
PIAZ	Prilozi Instituta za arheologiju u Zagrebu, Zagreb
RAC	Rivista di archeologia cristiana, Roma
RAChr	Reallexikon für Antike und Christentum, Stuttgart
RE	Pauly A F - Wisowa G, Realencyclopädie der classischen Altertumswissenschaft, Stuttgart
RIC	Roman Imperial Coinage, London
SA	Studia Aegyptiaca, Budapest
SALONA I	Duval N - Marin E - Metzger C (eds.), Salona I. Catalogue de la sculpture architecturale paléochrétienne de Salone, Rome - Split 1994
Situla	Situla. Dissertationes Musei nationalis Labacensis, Ljubljana
SJ	Saalburg Jahrbuch. Bericht des Saalburgmuseums, Frankfurt/Berlin
SP	Starohrvatska prosvjeta, Split
Spätantike	Spätantike und frühes Christentum. Catalogue of Exhibition, Frankfurt am Mein 1983

TZ	Trierer Zeitschrift, Trier
VAHD	Vjesnik za arheologiju i historiju dalmatinsku, Split
VAMZ	Vjesnik Arheološkog muzeja u Zagrebu, Zagreb
VHAD	Vjesnik Hrvatskog arheološkog društva, Zagreb
VKAG	Veröffentlichungen der Kroatischen archäologischen Gesellschaft, Zagreb
VMPK	Vjesnik Muzeja Požeške kotline, Slavonska Požega

Museum abbreviations

AMZ	Arheološki muzej u Zagrebu
GMB	Gradski muzej Bjelovar
GMV	Gradski muzej Vinkovci
MĐĐ	Muzej Đakovštine, Đakovo
MGK	Muzej grada Koprivnice
MMČ	Muzej Međimurja, Čakovec
MPK	Muzej Požeške kotline, Požega
MPS	Muzej Prigorja, Sesvete
MS	Muzej Sisak
MSO	Muzej Slavonije, Osijek
ZMO	Zavičajni muzej, Ozalj
ZMVT	Zavičajni muzej, Varaždinske Toplice

Bibliography

Alföldi A, 1942, Eine lateinische Inschrift aus Siebenbürgen, *AÉ* 3 (1-2), 255-258

Alföldi G, 1958, Collegium-organisationen in Intercisa, *AAnH* 6 (1-2), 177-198

Alföldi G, 1960, Pannoniciani augures, *AAnH* 8 (1-2), 145-164

Alföldi G, 1965, *Bevölkerung und Gesellschaft der römischen Provinz Dalmatien*, Budapest

Alföldi G, 1969, *Die Personennamen in der römischen Provinz Dalmatia*, Heidelberg

Alföldi M R, 1964, Die Sol Comes-Münze von Jahre 325, in: *Mullus*, 10-16

Altmann A, 1931, Das früheste Vorkommen der Juden in Deutschland: Juden im römischen Trier, *TZ* 6 (2-3), 104-125

Anamali S, 1971, Një varrezë e mesjetës së hershme në Bukel të Mirditës (Une necropole haute-médiévale à Bukel të Mirditës), *Iliria* 1, 209-224, Tiranë

Arbeiter A, 1994, Aspetti dell'arte in Spagna, in: *I Goti*, 328-335

Arrhenius B, 1986, Einige christliche Paraphrasen aus dem 6. Jahrhundert, in: Roth 1986, 129-151

Arslan E A, 1994, La monete dei Goti in Italia, in: *I Goti*, 252-265

Arthur P *et al.*, 1996, Masseria Quattro Macine - a deserted medieval village and its territory in southern Apulia: an interim report on field survey excavation and document analysis, *PBSR* 64, 181-237

Bagatti B, 1958, Note sul contenuto dottrinale dei musaici di Aquileia, *RAC* 34 (1-4), 119-135

Bagatti B, 1964, Lucerne fittili di Palestina dei secoli VII-VIII, *RAC* 40 (3-4), 253-269

Bálint Cs, 1985, Zur Frage der byzantinischen Beziehungen im Fundmaterial Ungarns, *MAI* 14, 209-223

Barb A A, 1953, Diva matrix. A faked gnostic intaglio in the possession P. P. Rubens and the iconography of a symbol, *Journal of Warburg*, 16, 193-238, London

Barb A A, 1963, The Survival of Magic Arts, in: Momigliano 1963, 100-125

Barb A A, 1964, Krippe, Tisch und Grab. Ein Versuch zur Formsymbolik von Altar und Patene, in: Mullus, 17-27

Bargebuhr F P, 1991, *The Paintings of the "New" Catacomb of the Via Latina and the Struggle of Christianity against Paganism*, Heidelberg

Barkóczi L, 1965, New data on the history of Late Roman Brigetio, *AAnH* 13 (1-2), 215-257

Barkóczi L, 1973, Beiträge zur Steinbearbeitung in Pannonien am Ende des 3. und zu Beginn des 4. Jahrhunderts, *FA* 24, 67-112

Barkóczi L, 1980, History of Pannonia, in: *ARP*, 85-124

Barkóczi L - Mócsy A, 1972, *Die römischen Inschriften Ungarns* I, Amsterdam

Barkóczi L - Salamon Á, 1971, Remarks on the 6th Century History of "Pannonia", *AArH* 23 (1-4), 139-153

Barnea J, 1977, *Les monuments paléochrétiennes de Roumanie*, Roma

Barnish J B, 1987, Pigs, Plebeians and Potentes: Rome's economic Hinterland, c. 350-600 A. D., *PBSR* 55, 157-185

Barton P, 1975, *Die Frühzeit des Christentums in Österreich und Südostmitteleuropa bis 788*, Wien - Köln - Graz

Bassier C - Darmon J-P - Tainturier J-L, 1981, La grande mosaïque de Migenne (Gonne), *Gallia* 39 (1), 123-148

Bastien P, 1988, *Perpetuitas imperii* et le monnayage de Valentinien I, *Situla* 26, 159-163

Behrens G, 1950, Römische Fibeln mit Inschrift, *Reinecke Festschrift*, Mainz

Benea D - Şchiopu A - Vlassa N, 1974, Un mormînt gnostic de la Dierna; Interpretarea plăcuţei de aur de Dierna (Ein gnostisches Grab in Dierna), *Acta Musei Napocensis* 11, 115-141, Cluj

Bermond Montanari G (ed.), 1983, Ravenna e il porto di Classe, *Fonti e studi* 7, Ravenna

Berti F, 1983, Lucerne, in: Bermond Montanari 1983, 147-154

Beyer H W, 1925, *Der syrische Kirchenbau*, Berlin

Bielefeld D, 1993, Zum Klinensarkophag von S. Lorenzo, in: Koch G 1993, 91-96

Bierbraurer V, 1992, Kreuzfibeln in der mittelalpinen romanischen Frauentracht des 5.-7. Jahrhunderts, in: Trentino und Südtirol, Archivio per l' Alto Adige. *Rivista di studi alpini* 86, 1-26

Bierbrauer V, 1994, Archeologia degli Ostrogoti in Italia, in: *I Goti*, 170-177

Bilkei I, 1979, Die griechischen Inschriften des römischen Ungarns, *AR* 17, 23-48

Bíró T M, 1987, Bone-carvings from Brigetio in the collection of the Hungarian National Museum, *AArH* 39 (3-4), 153-192

Bíró-Sey K, 1980, Currency, in: *ARP*, 337-348

Bogaert R, 1976, s. v. Geld, *RAChr* 9, 797-907

Böhme A, 1972, Die Fibeln der Kastelle Saalburg und Zugmantel, *SJ* 29, 5-112

Böhme H W, 1986, Bemerkungen zum spätrömischen Militärstil, in: Roth 1986, 25-49

Bojović D, 1983, *Rimske fibule Singidunuma* (Die römischen Fibeln von Singidunum), Beograd

Βοκοτοπουλος Π Λ, 1980, Ανασκαφή τοῦ καθολικοῦ τῆς μονης Παντανάσσης Φιλιππιάδος, Πρακτικα (1977), 149-153, Ην Αθηναις

Bóná I, 1963, Beiträge zur Archäologie und Geschichte der Quaden, *AArH* 15 (1-4), 239-307

Bónis É, 1980, Pottery, in: *ARP*, 357-383

Bovini G, 1974, *Le antichità cristiane della fascia costiera istriana da Parenzo a Pola*, Bologna

Brandenburg H, 1983, Die Darstellungen maritimen Lebens, in: *Spätantike*, 249-256

Bratož R, 1983, Cerkvenopolitični in kulturnozgodovinski odnosi med Sirmijem in Akvilejo (Die kirchenpolitischen und kulturhistorischen Beziehungen zwischen Sirmium und Aquileia), *Zgodovinski časopis* 37, 259-272, Ljubljana

Bratož R, 1986, *Krščanstvo v Ogleju in na vzhodnem vplivnem območju oglejske cerkve od začetkov do nastopa verske svobode* (Christianity in Aquileia and the Eastern influential Area of the Aquileian Church from its Beginnings to the Introduction of Religious Freedom), Ljubljana

Bratož R, 1996, Christianisierung des Nordadria- und Westbalkanraumes im 4. Jahrhundert, *Situla* 34, 299-362

Bratož R - Šašel-Kos M (eds.), 1992, *Jaroslav Šašel: Opera selecta*, Situla 30

Brenk B, 1994, Zum Baukonzept von Hagios Demetrios in Thessaloniki, *Boreas* 17, 27-38

Briesenick B, 1964, Typologie und Chronologie der südwest-gallischen Sarkophage, *JRGZM* 9 (1962), 76-182

Brøndsted J, 1928, La basilique des cinq martyrs à Kapljuč, in: *Recherches à Salone*, Copenhague

Brunšmid J, 1902, Colonia Aurelia Cibalae, *VHAD* 6, 117-166

Brunšmid J, 1909, Kameni spomenici hrvatskog narodnog muzeja u Zagrebu, *VHAD* 10 (1908-1909), 149-222

Brunšmid J, 1911, Kameni spomenici hrvatskog narodnog muzeja u Zagrebu, *VHAD* 11 (1910-1911), 61-144

Buhagiar M, 1986, *Late Roman and Byzantine Catacombs and Related Burial Places in the Maltese Islands*, BAR, Int. Ser. 302

Bulat M, 1987, Nalazi terra sigillate na donjogradskom pristaništu u Osijeku 1961. godine (Terra sigillata Findings of 1961 in the Warf of Donji grad in the Osijek City), *OZ* 18-19, 37-76

Bulat M, 1989, Rimski zlatni nakit u Muzeju Slavonije (Römischer Goldschmuck im Museum Slawoniens), *OZ* 20, 279-297

Bulat M, 1989a, *Mursa - Osijek u rimsko doba* (Mursa - Osijek in Roman Era), Osijek

Bulat M, 1989b, Novi podaci za baziliku mučenika u Mursi (New Data on the Martyrs Basilica in Mursa), *Lychnid* 7 (A Collection of Articles), 195-202, Ohrid

Bullinger H, 1969, Spätantike Gürtelbeschläge - Typen, Herstellung, Tragweise und Datierung, *DAG* 12

Buora M, 1992, Note on the diffusion of swastika fibulae with horse-head decorations in the Late Roman Period, *AV* 43, 105-108

Burger A Sz, 1966, The Late Roman Cemetery at Ságvár, *AArH* 18 (1-4), 99-234

Burger A Sz, 1987, The Roman Villa at Kővágószőlős near Pécs (Sopianae) *JPMÉ* 30-31 (1985-1986), 65-226

Burkowsky Z, 1996, Nekropole antičke Siscije (Die Necropolen der antiken Siscia), *PIAZ* 10 (1993), 69-79

Buršić-Matijašić K, 1985, Antički kapiteli iz Pule i okolice (Roman kapitals from Pula and surroundings), *Histria archaeologica* 15-16 (1984-1985), 45-84

Buzov M, 1996, Segestika i Siscija - topografija i povijesni razvoj (Segestika und Siscia - Topographie und geschichtliche Entwicklung), *PIAZ* 10 (1993), 47-68

Cabrol F, 1920, s. v. Deo gratias, *DACL* 4 (1), 649-652

Cabrol F, 1924, s. v. *AΩ*, *DACL* 1 (1), 2-25

Cabrol F, 1924a, s. v. Acclamations, *DACL* 1 (1), 240-265

Cambi N, 1975, La figure du Christ sur les monuments paléochrétiens de Dalmatie, *Disputationes Salonitanae* (197O), Split, 51-68

Cambi N, 1993, New Attic Sarcophagi from Dalmatia, in: Koch G 1993, 75-87

Cambi N, 1994, *The Good Sheperd Sarcophagus and its Group*, Split

Cavada E, 1994, Trento in età gota, in: *I Goti*, 224-231

Centuries of Natural Science in Croatia: Theory and Application, Catalogue of the Exhibition, Zagreb 1996

Chevalier P, 1996, *Salona II - Ecclesiae Dalmatiae. L'architecture paléochrétienne de la province romaine de Dalmatie (IVe-VIIe s.)*, Rome/Split

Christie N, 1995, The Survival of Roman Settlement along the Middle Danube: Pannonia from the fourth to the tenth Century A. D., *AR* 25 (1994), 303-319

Ciglenečki S, 1987, *Hohenbefestigungen aus der Zeit vom 3. bis 6. Jh. Im Ostalpenraum*, Dela Slovenske akademije znanosti in umetnosti 31, Ljubljana

Claude D, 1969, *Die byzantinische Stadt im 6. Jh.*, München

Clover F M, 1986, Felix Karthago, *DOP* 40, 1-16

Corby Finney P, 1978, Gnosticism and the Origins of Early Christian Art, *ACIAC* 9 (1), 391-405, Roma

Corby Finney P, 1987, Images on finger rings and Early Christian art, *DOP* 41, 181-186

Coscarella A, 1983, Lucerne di "tipo mediterraneo" o "africano", in: Bermond Montanari 1983, 155-165

Craveri M, 1969, *I vangeli apocrifi*, Torino

Cumont F, 1944, *Lux perpetua*, Paris

Cumont F, 1959, *Die orientalischen religionen im römischen heidentum*, Stuttgart

Cüppers H (ed.), 1983, *La civilisation romaine de la Moselle à la Sarre, (Catalogue of the Exhibition)*, Mainz

Čučković L, 1992, Ozalj - zaštitna arheološka iskopavanja 1992. godine, (Archaeological rescue Excavations in 1992), *OHAD* 24 (3), 49-51

Čučković L, 1994, *Ozalj od neolita do Frankopana*, Ozalj

Daniélou J, 1966, *Études d'exégèse judeo-chrétienne*, Paris

Daniélou J, 1969, Christianity as a Jewish sect, in: Toynbee 1969, 261-282

Dannheimer H - Kriss-Rettenbeck L, 1964, Die Eininger Eisenkreuze, ihre Deutung und Datierung, *BV* 29, 192-205

Degmedžić I, 1979, XI novela cara Justinijana II. Bassianae - Požega, *VMPK* 2-3, 93-102

Deichmann F W, 1970, Martirerbasilika, Martyrion, Memoria und Altargrab, *Mitteilungen des Deutschen Archaeologischen Instituts* (Roemische Abteilung) 77, 144-169

Delehaye H, 1907, Saints de Chypre, *Analecta Bollandiana* 26, 161-274, Bruxelles

Delehaye H, 1912, *Origines du culte des martyrs*, Bruxelles

Demandt A, 1986, Der Kelch von Ardabur und Anthusa, *DOP* 40, 113-117

Demandt A, 1989, *Die spätantike. Römische Geschichte von Diokletian bis Justinian 284-565. n. Chr.*, München

Demo Ž, 1986, The Roman Period. Notes from the History of Archaeological Research in Northwestern Croatia, in: *40 Jahre archäologischer Untersuchungen auf dem Gebiet des nordwestlichen Croatien, (Catalogue of Exhibition)*, 37-53, Koprivnica

Demugeot E, 1965, Y eut-il une forme arienne de l'art paléochrétien, *ACIAC* 6, 491-519, Roma

Diehl Ch, 1969, *Justinien et la civilisation byzantine au VIe siècle*, 2 vols., Paris

Dimitrijević S, 1979, Archäologische Topographie und Auswahl archäologischer Funde vom Vinkovcer Boden, in: *Corolla memoriae Iosepho Brunšmid dicata*, VKAG, 201-268, Vinkovci

Din E, 1957, s. v. Delphin, *RAChr* 3, 667-682

Dinkler E, 1962, Kreuzzeichen und Kreuz, *JAC* 5, 93-109

Dinkler E, 1964, Bemerkungen zum Kreuz als *TPOITAION,* in: Mullus, 71-78

van Doorselaer A, 1967, *Les nécropoles d'époque romaine en Gaule septentrionale*, DAG 10

Dorigo W, 1966, *Pittura tardoromana*, Milano

Dölger F J, 1958, Beiträge zur Geschichte des Kreuzzeichens I, *JAC* 1, 5-19

Dölger F J, 1959, Op. cit. II, *JAC* 2, 15-29

Dölger F J, 1960, Op. cit. III, *JAC* 3, 5-16

Dölger F J, 1963, Op. cit. VI, *JAC* 6, 7-34

Dölger F J, 1964, Op. cit. VII, *JAC* 7, 5-38

Dölger F J, 1966, Op. cit. VIII, *JAC* 8-9 (1965-1966), 7-52

Dölger F J, 1967, Op. cit. IX, *JAC* 10, 7-29

Dumaine H, 1920, s. v. Dimanche, *DACL* 4 (1), 858-994

Dumaine H, 1925, s. v. Bains, *DACL* 2 (1), 111-117

Dupont-Sommer A, Une hymne syriaque sur la cathédrale d'Édesse, *CA* 2, 29-39

Duval N, 1974, L'architecture chrétienne de l'Afrique du nord dans ses rapports avec le nord de l'Adriatique, *AA* 5, 353-368

Egger R, 1963, *YTIEA,* in: *Römische Antike und frühes Christentum II,* 170-171, Klagenfurt

Eizenhöfer L, 1960, Die Siegelbildforschläge des Clemens von Alexandrien und die älteste christliche Literatur, *JAC* 3, 51-69

Eliade M, 1952, *Images et symboles, Essais sur le symbolisme magico-religieux*, Paris

Eliade M, 1987, s. v. Eternity, in: *Encyclopedia of Religion* 5, 167-171, New York-London

Ellmers D, 1974, Eine byzantinische Mariendarstellung als Vorbild für Goldbrakteaten, *JRGZM* 18 (1971), 233-237

Engemann J, 1969, s. v. Fisch, Fischer, Fischgang, *RAChr* 7, 959-1097

Engemann J, 1972, Anmerkungen zu spätantiken Geräten des Alltagsleben mit christlichen Bildern, Symbolen und Inschriften, *JAC* 15, 154-172

Engemann J, 1975, Zur Verbreitung magischer Übelabwehr in der nichtchristlichen und christlichen Spätantike, *JAC* 18, 22-48

Engemann J, 1976, Zu den Dreifaltigkeitdarstellungen des frühchristlichen Kunst, *JAC* 19, 157-172

Engemann J, 1983, Die bukolischen Darstellungen, in: *Spätantike*, 257-259

Faber A, 1973, Građa za topografiju antičkog Siska (Materialien zur Topographie der antiken Stadt Siscia), *VAMZ* 6-7, 133-162

Fasola U M, 1961, La regione delle cattedre nel Cimitero Maggiore, *RAC* 37 (3-4), 237-267

Ferrua A, 1949, s. v. Agnello, *EC* 1, 459-464

Ferrua A, 1958, Scoperta di una nuova regione della catacomba di Commodilla (II), *RAC* 34 (1-4), 5-56

Ferrua A, 1963, Un picolo ipogeo sull'Appia antica, *RAC* 39 (3-4), 175-187

Février P A, 1977, À propos du repas funéraire: Cult et sociabilité, *CA* 26, 29-45

Février P A, 1978, La culte des morts dans les communautés chrétiennes durant le IIIe siècle, *ACIAC* 9 (1), 211-274, Roma

Fiedler U, 1992, *Studien zu Gräberfeldern des 6. bis 9. Jahrhunderts an der Unteren Donau*, Teil 1, Bonn

Fisković I. 1995, Apport des reconstructions d'églises de l'antiquité tardive dans la formation du premier art roman sur le littoral croate, *HAM* 1, 14-27

Fitz J, 1980, The Way of Life, in: *ARP*, 161-175

Fitz J, 1980a, Economic Life, in: *ARP*, 323-335

Fitz J, 1980b, Population, in: *ARP*, 141-159

Fıratlı N, (ed.) 1990, La sculpture byzantine figurée au Musée archéologique d'Istanbul, in: *Catalogue revue et présenté par C. Metzger, A. Pralong et J. P. Sodini,* Paris

Forstner D, 1982, *Die Welt der christlichen Symbole*, Innsbruck

Frend W H C, 1964, A Note on the Influence of Greek Immigrants on the Spread of Christianity in the West, in: Mullus, 125-129

Furtwängler A, 1900, *Die antiken Gemmen. Geschichte der Steinschneidekunst im klassischen Altertum*, Leipzig/Berlin

Fülep F, 1984, *Sopianae. The History of Pécs during the Roman Era and the Problem of the Continuity of the Late Roman Population*, Budapest

Gabler D, 1968, Scratched Inscriptions on Terra Sigillata in Pannonia, *AAnH* 16, 297-306

Gagé J G, 1969, Graeco-Roman Society and Culture, in: Toynbee 1969, 147-170

Gamzigrad, 1983, *Gamzigrad - kasnoantički carski dvorac (Gamzigrad - an Imperial Palace of the Late Classical Times),* Catalogue of the Exhibition, Beograd 1983

Garraffo S. 1981, Su alcuni rinvenimenti monetari nell'area cimiteriale della ex Vigna Cassia a Siracusa, *RAC* 57 (1-2), 283-324

Garrucci R, 1873, *Storia della arte cristiana nei primi otto secoli della Chiesa* II, Prato

Garrucci R. 1877, Op. cit. IV

Garrucci R, 1879, Op. cit. V

Garrucci R, 1880, Op. cit. VI

Gáspár D, 1986, *Römische Kästchen aus Pannonien*, MAI 15, vols 1-2

Gáspár D, 1995, Urchristliche Forschung in Pannonien seit der Tätigkeit István Járdányi Paulovics, *Acta classica Universitatis scientiarum Debreceniensis* 30 (1994), 111-120

Giordani R, 1978, Probabili echi della crisi ariana in alcune figurazioni paleocristiane, *RAC* 54 (3-4), 229-263

Giustechi Conti P M, 1994, Gli Ostrogoti all'Italia, in: *I Goti*, 138-153

Goethert K, 1993, Die verzierten Spätantiken Tonlampen des Rheinischen Landesmuseums Trier, *TZ* 56, 135-248

Gorenc M - Vikić B, 1979, Das fünfundzwanzigjahrige Jubiläum der Untersuchungen der antiken Lokalität Aquae Iasae (Varaždinske Toplice), *AI* 16 (1975), 32-50

Gorenc M - Vikić B, 1986, Antičko nasljeđe ludbreškog kraja (The Classical Heritage of the Ludbreg Region), in: *Ludbreg*, 59-71, Ludbreg

Gough M, 1973, *The Origins of Christian Art*, London

Grabar A, 1968, *Christian Iconography. A Study of its Origins*, Princeton

Grant R M, 1969, Gnosticism, Marcion, Origen, in: Toynbee 1969, 317-330

Grassl H, 1996, Der Südostalpenraum in der Militärgeographie des 4./5.Jahrhunderts, *Situla* 34, 177-184

Graziani Abbiani M, 1969, *Lucerne fittili paleocristiane nell'Italia settentrionale*, Bologna

Gregl Z, 1993, Antičko nalazište Repišće kod Jastrebarskog (Die römerzeitliche Fundstelle Repišće bei Jastrebarsko), *VAMZ* 24-25 (1991-1992), 145-150

Gregl Z, 1994, Kasnoantička nekropola Štrbinci kod Đakova - istraživanja 1993. g. (Late Roman Cemetery Štrbinci, Đakovo Vicinity), *OA* 18, 181-190, Zagreb

Guarducci M, 1969, Il fenomeno orientale del simbolismo alfabetico e i suoi sviluppi nel mondo cristiano d'Occidente, in: *Atti del Convegno sul tema: tardo antico e alto medioevo*, Academia nazionale dei lincei 105 (1967), 467-481, Roma

Guiraud H, 1989, Bagues et anneaux à l'époque romaine en Gaule, *Gallia* 46, 173-211

Haberl J, 1958, Lebensbaum und Vase auf antiken Denkmälern Österreichs, *Jahreshefte des Österreichischen Archäologischen Institutes in Wien* 43 (1956-1958), 222-247, Wien

Halsberghe G H, 1972, *The cult of Sol Invictus*, Leiden

Harhoiu R, 1994, La Romania all'epoca degli Ostrogoti, in: *I Goti*, 154-159

Harmatta J, 1970, The last Century of Pannonia, *AAnH* 18 (3-4), 361-369

von Harnack A, 1915, *Die Mission und Ausbreitung des Christentums in der ersten drei Jahrhunderten*, Leipzig

Hayes J W, 1972, *Late Roman Pottery*, London

von Heintze H, 1983, Sol invictus, in: *Spätantike*, 145-146

Henkel F, 1913, *Die römische Fingerringe der Rheinlande und der benachbarten Gebiete*, Berlin

Hermann A, 1967, Das erste Bad Heilands und des Helden in spätantiker Kunst und Legende, *JAC* 10, 61-81

Hicke W, 1985, Frühchristliches Burgenland - eine Zusammenfassung archäologischer Quellen vom Anfang des 4. bis zum Anfang des 6. Jahrhunderts n. Chr., *Burgenländische Heimatblätter* 47 (4), 145-185

Higgins J G, 1987, *The Early Christian Cross Slabs, Pillar Stones and Related Monuments of County Galway*, Part 1, BAR, Int. Ser. 375

Hopfner Th, 1928, s. v. Mageia, *RE* 14 (1), 301-393

Hubert J, 1964, Note sur la date des dalles de marbre sculpté de Limans (Basses-Alpes), *CA* 14, 85-94

Huskinson J, 1974, Some Pagan Mythological Figures and Their Significance in Early Christian Art, *PBSR* 42, 68-97

Iskra Janošić I, 1984, Arheološka istraživanja na području općine Vinkovci (Archäologische Forschungen im Gebiet der Gemeinde Vinkovci), *VKAG* 9, 143-151

Jarak M, 1994, The History of Early Christian Communities in continental Croatia, in: *Katalog*, 155-179

Jeločnik A, 1973, The Čentur Hoard: Folles of Maxentius and of the Tetrarchy, *Situla* 12

Johns C M - Potter T W, 1985, The Canterbury Late Roman Treasure, *AJ* 65 (2), 312-352

Johnson P, 1982, A History of Christianity, Harmondsworth

Jones A H M, 1963, The Social Background of the Struggle between Paganism and Christianity, in: Momigliano 1963, 17-37

Kádár Z, 1969, Lineamenti dell'arte della Pannonia nell'epoca dell'antichità tarda e paleocristiana, *Corsi di cultura sull'arte ravennate e bizantina* 15, 179-201

Kaiser-Minn H, 1983, Die Entwicklung der frühchristlichen Sarkophagplastik bis zum Ende des 4. Jahrhunderts, in: *Spätantike*, 318-338

Kajanto I, 1963, *Onomastic Studies in the early Christian Inscriptions of Rome and Carthage*, Acta Instituti Romani Finlandiae, Vol. II:1, Helsinki

Kajanto I, 1965, *The Latin Cognomina*, Commentationes Humanorum Litterarum 36 (1-4), Helsinki

Kajanto I, 1967, *Supernomina. A Study in Latin Epigraphy*, Helsinki

Kákosy L, 1989, Survivals of Ancient Egypt Religion. Other Domains of Culture. Egyptian Influence on Gnosticism and Hermetism, *SE* 12, 263-287

Kantorowicz E, 1964, Constantinus Strator, in: Mullus, 181-189

Kaufmann C M, 1913, *Handbuch der christlichen Archäologie*, Paderborn

Kaufmann C M, 1917, *Handbuch der altchristlichen Epigraphik*, Freiburg

Kaufmann-Bühler D, 1962, s. v. *Eusebeia*, *RAChr* 6, 985-1052

Kautsch R, 1936, *Kapitellstudien. Beiträge zu einer Geschichte der Spätantike Kapittels im Osten* vom vierte bis ins siebente Jahrhundert, Berlin/Leipzig

Kempt K - Reusch W, 1965, *Frühchristliche Zeugnisse im Einzugsgebiet von Rhein und Mosel*, Trier

Khatchatrian A, 1962, *Les baptistères paléochrétienns*, Paris

Kirsch J P, 1924, s. v. Anchre, *DACL* 1 (2), 1999-2031

Kiss A, 1960, Balatonkörnyéki római épülettagozatok (Membres d'architecture romains de la région du Balaton, *AÉ* 87 (2), 210-221

Kiss A, 1994, Archeologia degli Ostrogoti in Pannonia, in: *I Goti*, 164-167

Klaić N, 1986, Ecclesia seu monasterium sancti Michaelis de Rudina, *VMPK* 4-5, 33-59

Klauser T, 1958, Studien zur Entstehungsgeschichte der christlichen Kunst I, *JAC* 1, 20-51

Klauser T, 1959, Op. cit. II, *JAC* 2, 115-145

Klauser T, 1964, Op. cit. VII, *JAC* 7, 67-76

Klein-Pfeuffer M, 1993, *Merowingzeitliche Fibeln und Anhänger aus Pressblech,* Marburger Studien zur Vor- und Frühgeschichte, Band 14, Marburg

Knific T - Sagadin M (eds.), 1991, *Carta sine litteris. The Archaeology of the first Centuries of Christianity in Slovenia,* (Catalogue of the Exhibition), Ljubljana

Koch G (ed.), 1993, *Grabeskunst der römischen Kaiserzeit*, Mainz

Koch G - Sichtermann H, 1982, *Römische Sarkophage*, München

Koepp L, 1958, Die Konsekrationsmünzen Kaiser Konstantins und ihre religionspolitische Bedeutung, *JAC* 1, 94-104

Kondić V - Popović V, 1977, *Caričin Grad. Site fortifié dans l'Illyricum byzantin,* Catalogue of the Exhibition, Beograd

Koščević R, 1979, Die Werkstätte kräftig profilierter Fibeln in Siscia, *AI* 16 (1975) 51-61

Koščević R, 1991, *Antička bronca iz Siska. Umjetničko-obrtna metalna proizvodnja iz razdoblja rimskog carstva (Roman Bronze from Sisak. Metal Art and Craft Production from the first to fourth Centuries AD),* Zagreb

Koščević R - Makjanić R, 1995, *Siscia - Pannonia Superior,* BAR, Int. Ser. 621

Krautheimer R, 1963, *Early Christian and Byzantine Architecture,* Harmondsworth

Kubinyi M K, 1948, Zaubertext auf Silberplättchen, *AÉ* 7-9 (1946-1948), 277-278

Kukuljević I, 1891, *Natpisi sredovječni i novovjeki u Hrvatskoj i Slavoniji, Zagreb*

Kurz R, 1960, Metodische Bemerkungen zum Studium der Kollegien im Donaugebiet, *AAnH* 8 (1-2), 133-144

Kühnel B, 1994, Crosslike Compositions and Crosses. The Limits of Neutrality in Early Christian Art, *Boreas* 17, 159-169

Kyll N, 1966, Heidnische Weihe- und Votivagben aus der Römerzeit des Trierer Landes, *TZ* 29, 5-113

Lányi V, 1972, Die spätantiken Gräberfelder von Pannonien, *AArH* 24 (1-3), 53-212

Lassus J, 1935, *Inventaire archéologique de la région au nord-est de Hama,* Tome 1, Damas

Leclercq H, 1920, s. v. *Depositio, depositus, DACL* 4 (1), 668-673

Leclercq H, 1921, s. v. *Dominus, DACL* 4 (2), 1386-1387

Leclercq H, 1922, s. v. Funérailles, *DACL* 5 (2), 2705-2715

Leclercq H, 1924, s. v. Abrasax, *DACL* 1 (1), 127-155

Leclercq H, 1924a, s. v. Anneaux, *DACL* 1 (2), 2174-2223

Leclercq H, 1924b, s. v. Gemmes, *DACL* 6 (1), 794-864

Leclercq H, 1924c, s. v. Gammadia, *DACL* 6 (1), 610-613

Leclercq H, 1924d, s. v. Gabata, *DACL* 6 (1), 3-10

Leclercq H, 1924e, s. v. *Ad bestias, DACL* 1 (1), 449-462

Leclercq H, 1924f, s. v. Astres, *DACL* 1 (2), 3005-3033

Leclercq H, 1924g, s. v. Amulettes, *DACL* 1 (2), 1784-1860

Leclercq H, 1924h, s. v. Agneau, *DACL* 1 (1), 877-905

Leclercq H, 1925, s. v. Baptistère, *DACL* 2 (1), 382-469

Leclercq H, 1925a, s. v. Basilidiens, *DACL* 2 (1), 514-525

Leclercq H, 1925b, s. v. Bretagne (Grande-). Archéologie, *DACL* 2 (1), 1158-1229

Leclercq H, 1925c, s. v. Benitier, *DACL* 2 (1), 758-771

Leclercq H, 1925d, s. v. *Benedictus, DACL* 2 (1), 741-745

Leclercq H, 1925e, s. v. Bracelets, *DACL* 2 (1), 1118-1121

Leclercq H, 1926, s. v. Iconographie, *DACL* 7 (1), 11-13

Leclercq H, 1926a, s. v. *Innocens, DACL* 7 (1), 602-607

Leclercq H, 1927, s. v. *IXΘΥΣ, DACL* 7 (2), 1990-2086

Leclercq H, 1931, s. v. Magie, *DACL* 10 (1), 1067-1114

Leclercq H, 1931a, s. v. Maléfice, *DACL* 10 (1), 1288-1292

Leclercq H, 1932, s. v. Mercure, *DACL* 10 (2), 456-458

Leclercq H, 1932a, s. v. Martyr, *DACL* 10 (2), 2359-2512

Leclercq H, 1936, s. v. Ophites, *DACL* 12 (2), 2157-2160

Leclercq H, 1936a, s. v. Noms propres, *DACL* 12 (2), 1481-1553

Leclercq H, 1937, s. v. Palme, palmier, *DACL* 13 (1), 947-961

Leclercq H, 1937a, s. v. Paon, *DACL* 13 (1), 1075-1097

Leclercq H, 1938, s. v. Peigne, *DACL* 13 (2), 2932-2959

Leclercq H, 1939, s. v. *PIE ZESES, DACL* 14 (1), 1024-1031

Leclercq H, 1939a, s. v. Plomb, *DACL* 14 (1), 1191-1222

Leclercq H, 1948, s. v. Chrisme, *DACL* 3 (1), 1481-1534

Leclercq H, 1948a, Citations bibliques dans l'épigraphie latine, *DACL* 3 (2), 1756-1779

Leclercq H, 1948b, s. v. Cheval, *DACL* 3 (1), 1286-1305

Leclercq H, 1948c, s. v. Clefs. Clefs de saint Pierre, *DACL* 3 (2), 1859-1867

Leclercq H, 1948d, s. v. Résurrection de la chair, *DACL* 14 (2), 2393-2398

Leclercq H, 1950, s. v. Salomon, *DACL* 15 (1), 588-602

Leclercq H, 1953, s. v. Thrason (cimétière de), *DACL* 15 (2), 2276-2283

Leclercq H, 1953a, s. v. Spes in Deo, *DACL* 15 (2), 1636-1637

Leclercq H, 1953b, s. v. Swastika, *DACL* 15 (2), 1752-1775

Lengyel A - Radan G T B, 1980, Introduction, in: *ARP*, 17-31

Leoni B, 1950, s. v. La croce nell'archeologia, *EC* 4, 963-970

Lippold A, 1996, Westillyricum und Nordostitalien in der Zeit zwischen 364 und 455 unter besonderer Berücksichtigung Theodosius I, *Situla* 34, 17-28

Lohmayer E, 1950, *AΩ, RAC* 1, 1-4

Lowrie W, 1974, *Art in the early Church*, New York

Lucchesi-Palli E, 1990, Geometrische und florale Ornamente in den Wandmaleraien von Bawit, *Boreas* 13, 113-133

Lucchesi-Palli E, 1994, Untersuchungen zum Inhalt der Bullae und anderer Amulettkapseln in Antike, Spätantike und Mittelalter, *Boreas* 17, 171-177

Lyon-Caen C - Hoff V, 1986, *Catalogue des lampes en terre cuite grecques et chrétiennes*, Musée du Louvre, Paris

Ljubić Š, 1876, Inscriptiones quae Zagabriae in Museo nationali asservantur, *Rad Jugoslavenske akademije znanosti i umjetnosti* 34 and 35, 5-74, Zagreb

Macrea M, 1959, La culte de Sabazius en Dacie, *Dacia* 3, 325-339

Mainstone R J, 1988, *Hagia Sophia. Structure and Liturgy of Justinian's Great Church*, New York

Maioli M G, 1983, La ceramica fine da mensa (terra sigillata), in: Bermond Montanari 1983, 87-112

Marbach E, 1927, s. v. Sol, *RE* 3 A1, 901-913

Marshall F H 1907, *Catalogue of the Finger Rings Greek, Etruscan and Roman in the Departments of Antiquities - British Museum*, London

Marucchi O, 1903, *Guide des catacombes romaines. Éléments d'archéologie chrétienne*, Vol. 2, Paris/Rome

Marucchi O, 1906, *Notions generales. Éléments d'archéologie chrétienne*, Vol. 1, Paris/Rome

Marucchi O, 1933, *Le catacombe romane*, Roma

Marucchi O, 1974, *Christian Epigraphy*, Chicago

Mawer C F, 1995 *Evidence for Christianity in Roman Britain*, BAR, Brit. Ser. 243

van der Meer F - Mohrmann Ch, 1959, *Bildatlas der frühchristliche Welt*, Amsterdam

Menghin W, 1985, *Die Langobarden. Archäologie und Geschichte*, Stuttgart

Menis G C, 1973, Le giurisdizioni metropolitiche di Aquileia e di Milano nell' antichità, *AA* 4, 271-294

Menis G C 1976, La basilica paleocristiana nelle regioni delle Alpi orientali, *AA* 9, 375-420

Menzel H, 1969, *Antike Lampen im Römisch-Germanischen Zentralmuzeum zu Mainz*, Mainz

Migotti B, 1987, Antički kolegiji i srednjovjekovne bratovštine. Prilog proučavanju kontinuiteta dalmatinskih ranosrednjovjekovnih gradova (Les collèges antiques et les confréries médiévales. Contribution à l'étude de la continuité des villes dalmates du haut moyen âge, *SP* 16 (1986), 177-186

Migotti B, 1994, The archaeological Material of the Early Christian Period in continental Croatia, in: *Katalog*, 187-209

Migotti B, 1995, "Sol iustitae Christus est". (Origenes) Odrazi solarne kristologije na ranokršćanskoj gra|i iz sjeverne Hrvatske (Elements of solar Christology in the Early Christian Objects from north Croatia), *Diadora* 16-17 (1994-1995), 263-292

Migotti B, 1996, Ranokršćanski grobni nalazi iz Velikih Bastaja kod Daruvara (Early Christian Grave Finds from Veliki Bastaji near Daruvar), *VAMZ* 28-29 (1995-1996), 127-157

Migotti B, 1997, An Early Christian Fresco from Štrbinci near Đakovo, *HAM* 3, 213-223

Milojčić V, 1963, Zur Frage der Zeitstellung des Oratoriums von Mühlthal an der Isar und des Christentums in Bayern zwischen 500 und 700 nach Chr., *BV* 28 (1-2), 117-138

Milojčić V, 1968, Zur Frage des Christentums in Bayern zur Merowingerzeit, *JRGZM* 13 (1966), 231-264

Milojčić V, 1970, Zu den spätkaiserzeitlichen und merowingischen Silberlöffeln, *BRGK* 49 (1968), 109-148

Milošević A, 1981, Arheološki spomenici gornjeg i srednjeg toka rijeke Cetine, *Zbornik Cetinske krajine* 2, 1-135, Sinj

Minguzzi S, 1983, I mortai, in: Bermond Montanari 1983, 178-179

Mócsy A, 1962, s. v. Pannonia, *RE*, Supplementband 9, 516-577

Mócsy A, 1965, Zur Bevölkerung in der Spätantike, in: Alföldi G, 1965, 212-226

Mócsy A, 1968, s. v. *Municipium (Municipium Iasorum)*, *RE* Supplementband 11, 1003-1004

Mócsy A, 1974, *Pannonia and Upper Moesia*, London

Mócsy A – Szentléleky T, 1971, *Die römischen Steindenkmäler von Savaria*, Budapest

Momigliano A (ed.), 1963, *The Conflict between Paganism and Christianity in the fourth Century* (Essays edited by A M), Oxford

Moracchini-Mazel G, 1984, L'église à double abside Santa Maria della Chiapella à Rogliano (Haute Corse), *ACIAC* 10 (2), Città del Vaticano/Thessalonique, 347-353

Murray Ch S, 1981, *Rebirth and Afterlife. A study of the transmutation of some pagan imagery in early Christian funerary art*, BAR, Int. Ser.100

Nagy T, 1945, Az Aquincumi kereszténység egy eddig félreismert emléke (Un monument méconnu du christianisme d'Aquincum), *AÉ* 5-6 (1944-1945), 266-282

Nedved B, 1981, Nakit rimskog razdoblja, in: *Nakit na tlu sjeverne Dalmacije od prapovijesti do danas (Parures dans la Dalmatie du nord depuis la préhistoire jusqu'à nos jours)*, 151-180, Zadar

Nenadić V, 1987, Prilog proučavanju antičke Siscije (A contribution to the Study of Roman Siscia), *PIAZ* 3-4, 71-103

Neiman D, 1969, Eden, the Garden of God, *AAnH* 17 (1-2), 109-124

Nikolajević I, 1984, Necropoles et tombes chrétiennes en Illyricum oriental, *ACIAC* 10 (1), 519-535

Noll R, 1954, *Frühes Christentum in Österreich*, Wien

Oldenstein J, 1977, Zur Ausrüstung römischer Auxiliareinheiten, *BRGK* 57 (1976), 49-284

Oliva P, 1962, *Pannonia and the Onset of Crisis in the Roman Empire*, Praha

Ovadiah A, 1970, *Corpus of the byzantine Churches in the Holy Land*, Bonn

Painter K S, 1973, A Roman Christian Silver Treasure from Biddulph, Straffordshire, England, *RAC* 49 (1-4), 195-209

Pavan M, 1955, *La provincia romana della Pannonia Superior,* Roma

Pavan M, 1991, Romanesimo, cristianesimo e immigrazioni nei territori pannonici, in: Pavan M, *Dall'Adriatico al Danubio, Saggi e materiali universitari* 17, Padova, 473-526

Petrović P, 1975, *Paleografija rimskih natpisa u Gornjoj Meziji (Paléographie des inscriptions romaines en Mésie Supérieure),* Beograd

Philipp H, 1983, Magische Gemmen, in: *Spätantike,* 153-160

Pillinger R, 1989, Zur Interpretation der Symbolik des Bodenmosaiks von Teurnia, *Carinthia* I 179, 81-95

Pinterović D, 1965, Geme s terena Murse (Roman Gems from Mursa), *OZ* 9-10, 25-60

Pinterović D, 1978, *Mursa i njeno područje u antičko doba (Mursa und sein Raum in der Zeit der Antike),* Osijek

Pinterović D, 1980, "*Basilica Martyrum*" u Mursi ("*Basilica Martyrum*" in Mursa), in: *Gunjačin zbornik,* 59-66, Zagreb

Piva P, 1995, Basilica doppia: appunti sulla storiografia dell'ultimo decennio, *HAM* 1, 111-116

Plesničar-Gec Lj et al., 1983, *Old Christian Center in Emona,* Katalogi in monografije 21, Ljubljana

Póczy K, 1980, Pannonian cities, in: *ARP,* 239-274

Post P G J, 1984, The interpretation of cock-scenes: method and application, *ACIAC* 10 (2), 429-443

Provoost A, 1978, Il significato delle scene pastorali del terzo secolo, *ACIAC* 9 (1), 407-431

Provoost A, 1986, Das Zeugnis der Fresken und Grabplatten in der Katakombe S. Pietro e Marcellino im Vergleich mit dem Zeugnis der Lampen und Gläser aus Rom, *Boreas* 9, 152-172

Pröttel Ph M, 1988, Zur Chronologie der Zwiebelknopffibeln, *JRGZM* 35 (1), 347-371

Quacquarelli A, 1973, L'Ogdoade patristica e i suoi riflessi nella liturgia e nei monumenti, *RAC* 49, 211-269

Quacquarelli A, 1978, Per una revisione critica degli studi attuali sulla simbolica dei primi secoli cristiani, *ACIAC* 9 (2), 401-416, Roma

Rahner H, 1964, *Symbole der Kirche,* Salzburg

Raunig B, 1980, Dva kasnoantička groba iz okolice Đakova (Zwei spätantike Gräber aus Umgebung von Đakovo), *VAMZ* 12-13 (1979-1980), 151-167

Reinecke P, 1927, Römische und frümittelalterliche Denkmäler vom Weinberg bei Eining an der Donau, in: *Festschrift zur Feier des fünfundsiebzigjährigen Bestehens des Römisch-Germanischen Zentral-Museums zu Mainz,* 157-166, Mainz

Reinhard Seeliger H, 1985, Christliche Archäologie oder spätantike Kunsgeschichte? Aktuelle Grundlagenfragen aus der Sicht der Kirchengeschichte, *RAC* 61 (1-2), 167-187

Rigoir J - Rigoir Y - Meffre J F, 1973, Les dérivées des sigilées paléochrétiennes du groupe Atlantique, *Gallia* 31 (1), 207-263

Ripoll López G, 1994, Archeologia visigota in Hispania, in: *I Goti,* 301-311

Roncaioli C, 1981, S. Quirino di Siscia e la sua traslazione a Roma. Analisi e critica delle fonti, *Quaderni dell'Istituto di Lingua e Letteratura Latina* 2-3 (1980-1981), 215-249, Roma

Roth H (ed.), 1983, Zum Problem der Deutung frühmittelalterlicher Bildinhalte, in: *Akten des 1. Intern. Kolloquiums in Marburg a. d. Lahn* (1983), Marburg

Sage W, 1984, *Das Reihengräberfeld von Alterending in Oberbayern I,* GDV, Serie A, Berlin

Sági K, 1968, Darstellung des altchristlichen Kreuzes auf einem römischen Ziegel, *AAnH* 16, 391-400

Salama P, 1971, Une couronne solaire de l'empereur Julien, in: *Acta of the Fifth Epigraphic Congress (Cambridge 1967),* 279-286, Oxford

Salamon Á - Barkóczi L, 1971, Bestattungen von Csákvár aus dem Ende des 4. und dem Anfang des 5. Jahrhunderts, *AR* 11 (1970), 35-76

Salamon Á - Barkóczi L, 1982, Pannonien in nachvalentinianischer Zeit, in: *Severin zwischen Römerzeit und Völkerwanderung, Catalogue of the Exhibition,* Linz, 147-178

Salamon Á - Sós Á Cs, 1980, Pannonia - fifth to ninth centuries, in: *ARP,* 397-425

Salin É, 1950-1959, *La civilisation mérovingienne d'après les sépultures, les textes et le laboratoire, Paris: Premier partie: Les idées et les faits,* 1950 *Second partie: Les sépoultures,* 1952 *Quatrième partie: Les croyances,* 1959

Salway P, 1993, *The Oxford illustrated History of Roman Britain,* Oxford/New York

Sanquer R, 1997, Circonscription de Bretagne, *Gallia* 35 (2), 335-367

Sartori A, 1994, *Guida alla sezione epigrafica delle raccolte archeologiche di Milano,* Milano

Sauer E, 1996, *The End of Paganism in the North-Western Provinces of the Roman Empire. The example of the Mithras cult,* BAR, Int. Ser.634

Sauer J, 1958, s. v. Christus monogram, *Lexikon für Theologie und Kirche,* 2, 1117, Freiburg

Schmitz W, 1993, "Alles Unheil halte fern!" Zu einigen Gussformen für Amulette aus römischer Zeit, *BJ* 93, 45-68

Schretter S, 1993, Fibeln vom Hemmaberg: Ausgrabungen 1990-1992, *Carinthia* I 183, 187-201

Schulze-Dörrlamm M, 1990, *Die spätrömischen und frühmittelalterlichen Gräberfelder von Gondorf, Gem. Kobern-Gondorf, Kr. Mayen-Koblenz,* GDV, Serie B, Die fränkischen Altertümer des Rheinlandes, B. 14, Stuttgart

Sennhauser H R, 1984, Recherches récentes en Suisse. Édifices funéraires, cimetières et églises, *ACIAC* 10 (2), Città del Vaticano/Thessalonique, 1515-1530

Simoni K, 1988, Srebrna žlica iz Siska (Ein Silberlöffel aus Sisak), *VAMZ* 21, 79-86

Simoni K, 1989, Nalazi vremena seobe naroda u zbirkama Arheološkog muzeja u Zagrebu (Funde aus der Völkerwanderungszeit in den Sammlungen des

Archäologischen Museums in Zagreb), *VAMZ* 22, 107-134

Sokač-Štimac D, 1984, Prilog arheološkoj topografiji Požeške kotline u svjetlu iskopavanja 1980. godine (Beitrag zur archäologischen Topographie des Beckens von Požega aufgrund der Ausgrabungen im Jahr 1980), *VKAG* 9, 129-141

Sokač-Štimac D, 1987, Rudina - Mediaeval Monastery, *AP* 27 (1986), 150-151

Sokač-Štimac D, 1989, Rudina - Romanesque Church and Monastery, *AP* 28 (1987), 175-177

Sokol V, 1986, Das nordwestliche Kroatien in der Zeitperiode zwischen den Jahren 400-800 (die zeit der grossen Völkerwanderungen), in: *40 Jahre archäologischer Untersuchungen auf dem Gebiet des nordwestlichen Kroatien)*, Catalogue of Exhibition, 57-60, Koprivnica

Soproni S, 1980, Geography of Pannonia, in: *ARP*, 57-63

Soproni S, 1980a, Roads, in: *ARP*, 207-217

Soproni S, 1980b, Limes, in: *ARP*, 219-238

St P, 1926, Römischer Grabfund bei Niederkail, *TZ* 1 (1), 39-40

Stommel E, 1959, s. v. *Domus aeterna, RAChr* 4, 109-128

Stommel E, 1959a, Christliche Taufriten und antike Badesitten, JAC 1, 5-15

Stuiber A, 1964, *Depositio καταθεσις,* in: Mullus, 346-351

Stumpf P, 1950, s. v. Anker, *RAChr* 1, 440-443

Stutzinger D, 1983, Einleitung. Der Gnostizismus, in: *Spätantike*, 82-97

Sudnik I, 1993, Putositnice Martinskim krajem, in: *Pod Okićem – zavičajna knjiga župa Sv. Marije i Sv. Martina,* 493-501, Zagreb

Sutherland C H V - Litt D - Carson R A G, 1966, *RIC,* Vol. 7

Sutherland C H V - Litt D - Carson R A G, 1981, *RIC,* Vol. 8

Szabó Gj, 1934, Iz prošlosti Daruvara i okolice, *Narodna starina* 28 (1932), 79-97

Šarić I, 1981, Gradina, Novačka - rimska nekropola, *AP* 22, 78-80

Šašel J, 1992, Antiqui Barbari. Zur Besiedlungsgeschichte Ostnoricums und Pannoniens in 5. und 6. Jahrhundert nach den Schriftquellen, in: Bratož - Šašel-Kos 1992, 746-760

Šašel J, 1992a, Zur historischen Etnographie des Mittleren Donauraums, in: Bratož - Šašel-Kos 1992, 761-765

Šašel J, 1992b, Divinis nutibus actus. Due Postille per San Martino di Bracara, in: Bratož - Šašel-Kos 1992, 740-745

Šašel J, 1992c, Inscriptions on the Mosaic Floor in the Baptismal Chapel and Church Portico in Emona, in: Bratož - Šašel-Kos 1992, 783-794

Šeper M, Antikne geme-amuleti nazvane gnostičkim gemama (with Riassunto), *VHAD* 22-23 (1941-1942), 5-53

Ševčenko I, 1992, The Sion Treasure: The Evidence of the Inscriptions, in: Boyd S A - Mundell Mango M (eds.), *Ecclesiastical Silver Plate in Sixth-Century Byzantium,* 39-56, Washington

Terry A, 1986, The Opus Sectile in the Eufrasius Cathedral at Poreč, *DOP* 40, 147-164

Testini P, 1958, *Archeologia cristiana*, Roma

Thomas E B, 1955, Bruchstück einer frühchristlichen Marmortischplatte mit Reliefverzierung aus Csopak, *AAnH* 3, 261-282

Thomas E B, 1974, Martyres Pannoniae, *FA* 25, 131-146

Thomas E B, 1980, Savaria christiana, *Savaria* 9-10 (1975-1976), 105-160, Szombathely

Thomas E B, 1980a, Religion, in: *ARP*, 177-206

Thomas E B, 1980b, Villa settlements, in: *ARP*, 275-321

Thomas E B, 1987, Die Romanität Pannoniens im 5. und 6. Jahrhundert, in: *Germannen, Hunnen und Awaren. Schätze der Völkerwanderungszeit* (Catalogue of Exhibition), Nürnberg, 284-294

Thomas J P, 1987, *Private religion Foundations in the Byzantine Empire,* Dumbarton Oaks Studies 24, Washington

Thomas S, 1967 Die germanischen Scheibenfibeln der römischen Kaiserzeit im freien Germanien, Berliner *Jahrbuch für Vor- und Frühgeschichte* 7, 1-187, Berlin

Thompson E A, 1963, Christianity and the northern Barbarians, in: Momigliano1963, 56-78

Tóth E, 1972, Figürlich verzierte Locullus-Platte aus Savaria, *FA* 23, 59-67

Tóth E, 1977, La survivance de la population romaine en Pannonie, *AR* 15 107-120

Tóth E, 1979, Römische Gold- und Silbergegenstände mit Inschriften im Ungarischen Nationalmuseum. Goldringe, *FA* 30, 157-183

Tóth E, 1988, Az Álsóhetény 4. századi erod és temetö kutatása, 1981-1986. (Vorbericht über die Ausgrabungen der Festung und des Gräberfeldes von Álsóhetény 1981-1986 - Ergebnisse und umstrittene Fragen), *AÉ* 114-115 (1) (1987-1988), 22-61

Tóth E, 1989, Liturgical Brooch from Álsóhetény/Iovia/, *SA* 12, 385-393

Tóth E, 1994, Das Christentum in Pannonien bis zum 7. Jahrhundert nach den archäologischen Zeugnissen, in: Boshof E - Wolff H (eds.), *Das Christentum im bairischen Raum* von den Anfängen bis in 11. Jahrhundert, Köln-Weimar-Wien, 241-272

Tovornik V, 1986, Die frühmittelalterlichen Gräberfelder von Gusen und Auhof bei Perg in Oberösterreich. Teil 1: Gusen, *Archaeologia Austriaca* 69, 165-250, Wien

Toynbee A (ed.), 1969, The Crucible of Christianity, London

Toynbee J M C, The Religious Background of Some Sarcophagi of North Italy and Dalmatia, *JAC* 18, 5-18

Török L, 1974, Abdallah Nirqi 1964. Finds with Inscriptions, *AArH* 26 (3-4), 369-393

Török L, 1975, Abdallah Nirqi 1964. The Finds from the Excavation of the Hungarian Mission I, *AArH* 27 (1-2), 119-133

Török L, 1975a, Miscellanea Nubica I - Archäologisches zur nubischen Taufliturgie, *MAI* 4 (1973), 97-103

Turcan R, 1966, *Les sarcophagues romains à représentations dionysiaques,* Paris

Turchi N, 1949, s. v. Abraxas, *EC* 1, 128-130

Vaes J, 1989, *"Nova construere sed amplius vetusta servare"*: le réutilisation chrétienne d'édifices antiques (en Italie), *ACIAC* 11 (1), 1989, 299-319, Roma

Vágó E. B. - Bóna I, 1976, *Die Gräberfelder von Intercisa. Der spätrömische Südostfriedhof,* Budapest

Velmans T, 1969, Quelques versions rares du thème de la fontaine de vie dans l'art paléochrétien, *CA* 19, 29-43

Vikan G, 1984, Art, Medicine and Magic in Early Byzantium, *DOP* 38, 65-86

Vikić-Belančić B, 1971, Antičke svjetiljke u Arheološkom muzeju u Zagrebu (Antike Lampensammlung im Archäologischen Museum in Zagreb), *VAMZ* 5, 97-182

Vikić-Belančić B, 1978, Elementi ranog kršćanstva u sjevernoj Hrvatskoj (Les éléments du christianisme primitif en Croatie septentrionale), *AV* 29, 588-606

Vikić-Belančić B, 1984, Sustavno istraživanje u Ludbregu od 1968-1979 (Systematic Excavations at Ludbreg 1968-1979), *VAMZ* 16-17 (1983-1984), 119-166

Vikić-Belančić B - Gorenc M, 1970, Završna istraživanja antičkog kupališnog kompleksa u Varaždinskim Toplicama (Abgeschlossene Ausgrabungen des Antiken Badekomplexes in Varaždinske Toplice - Aquae Iasae), *VAMZ* 4, 121-157

Vikić B - Gorenc M, 1984, Arheološko-urbanistička problematika Ludbrega (La problématique archéologique et d'urbanisme de Ludbreg), *VAMZ* 14, 85-95

Vinski Z, 1955, Zlatni prsten nađen u Samoboru i nakit arhitektonskog tipa u VI i VII stoljeću (La bague en or de Samobor et le type architectural de l'orfévrerie aux VIe-VIIe siècles), *Tkalčićev zbornik* 1, 31-43, Zagreb

Vinski Z, 1958, O nalazima 6. i 7. stoljeća u Jugoslaviji s posebnim osvrtom na arheološku ostavštinu iz vremena prvog avarskog kaganata (Zu den Funden des 6. und 7. Jahrhunderts in Jugoslawien mit besonderer Berücksichtigung der archäologischen Hinterlassenschaft aus der Zeit des ersten awarischen Khaganates), *OA* 3, 13-67

Vinski Z, 1968, Krstoliki nakit epohe seobe naroda u Jugoslaviji (Kreuzförmiger Schmuck der Völkerwanderungszeit in Jugoslawien), *VAMZ* 3, 103-166

Vinski Z, 1971, Haut moyen-âge, in: *Époque préhistorique et protohistorique en Yougoslavie - Recherches et résultats, Publié à l'occasion du VIIIe Congrès de l'UISPP,* 375-397, Beograd

Vinski Z, 1974, Kasnoantički starosjedioci u salonitanskoj regiji prema arheološkoj ostavštini predslavenskog supstrata (Die altsässige Bevölkerung der Spätantike im salonitanischen Bereich gemäss der archäologischen Hinterlassenschaft des vorslawischen Susbstrats), *VAHD* 69 (1967), 5-86

Vinski Z, 1991, Razmatranja o iskopavanjima u Kninu na nalazištu Greblje (Betrachtungen zu den Grabungen in Knin, Fundstelle Greblje), *SP* 19 (1989), 1991, 5-73

Virc Z, 1969, Plandište - novi arheološki lokalitet (with Zusammenfassung), *Zbornik slavonskih muzeja* 1, 137-140, Županja

Voelkl L, 1951, s. v. Illuminazione nelle chiese antiche, *EC* 6, 1629-1632

Vogt J, 1957, s. v. Constantinus der Grosse, *RAChr* 3, 306-379

Volbach F W, 1958, *Frühchristliche Kunst,* München

Waltzing J P, 1948, s. v. *Collegia, DACL* 3 (2), 2107-2140

Ward-Perkins J B, 1994, *Roman Imperial Architecture,* New Haven/London

Watts D J, 1988, Circular Lead Tanks and their Significance for Romano-British Christianity, *AJ* 68 (2), 210-222

Weiler I, 1996, Zur Frage der Grenzziehung zwischen Ost- und Westteil des Römischen Reiches in der Spätantike, *Situla* 34, 123-143

Werner J, 1962, *Die Langobarden in Pannonien,* München

Wharton A J, 1992, The Baptistery of the Holy Sepulcher in Jerusalem and the Politics of Sacred Landscape, *DOP* 46, 313-325

Whitting P D, 1973, *Byzantine Coins,* New York

Winkelmann F, 1961, Konstantins Religionspolitik und ihre Motive im Urteil der literarischen Quellen des 4. und 5. Jahrhunderts, *AAnH* 9 (1-2), 239-256

Wolfram H, 1994, L'irruzione degli Unni e la nuova migrazione visigota, in: *I Goti,* 282-291

Wortmann D, 1968, Neue magische Texte, *BJ* 168, 56-111

Zellinger J, 1928, *Bad und Bäder in der Altchristlichen Kirche,* München